TRADING STOCK OPTIONS AND WARRANTS

3rd EDITION

Strategies for Generating a Regular Income on the Australian Stock Market

CHRIS TEMBY

Wrightbooks

Also by Chris Temby:

Technical Analysis for Trading Index Warrants

Money, Markets and Derivatives

(both published by and available from Wrightbooks)

First edition published in 1997. Second edition published in 1999.
This third edition published by Wrightbooks in 2001.

Wrightbooks Pty Ltd
PO Box 270
Elsternwick
Victoria 3185

Ph: (03) 9532 7082
Fax: (03) 9532 7084
Email: info@wrightbooks.com.au
Website: www.wrightbooks.com.au

National Library of Australia Cataloguing-in-Publication Data:

Temby, Chris.
Trading stock options and warrants: strategies for generating a regular income on the Australian stock market.
3rd ed.
Bibliography.
Includes index.
ISBN 1 876627 58 1.
1. Stock options - Australia. 2. Stock warrants - Australia. I. Title.
332.63228

Cover design by Rob Cowpe
Printed in Australia by Griffin Press
ISBN: 1 876627 58 1

DISCLAIMER

The material in this publication is of the nature of general comment only, and neither purports nor intends to be advice. Readers should not act on the basis of any matter in this publication without considering (and if appropriate, taking) professional advice with due regard to their own particular circumstances. The author and publisher expressly disclaim all and any liability to any person, whether a purchaser of this publication or not, in respect of anything and of the consequences of anything done or omitted to be done by any such person in reliance, whether whole or partial, upon the whole or any part of the contents of this publication.

ACKNOWLEDGMENTS

The extracts from the Call Options, Put Options and Call Warrants tables in *The Australian* are reproduced with kind permission.

Most of the charts are drawn by SuperCharts4 using data from Just Data, with the BHP call and put warrant charts drawn by Ezy Charts V3.

Thanks go to David Robinson of Salomon Smith Barney stockbrokers for general assistance, and to Jonathon Kur of Hogan & Partners stockbrokers for supplying option matrix numbers.

There is a tide in the affairs of men, which,
taken at the flood, leads on to fortune;
Omitted, all the voyage of their life is bound
in shallows and in miseries,
On such a full sea are we now afloat, and we
must take the current when it serves, or lose
our ventures.

Julius Caesar Act 4, Scene 3

CONTENTS

CONTENTS (Cont'd)

PREFACE to the Third Edition

THE FIRST EDITION of this book published in June 1997 was well received, and sold out within around 18 months, as did the second edition published in January 1999.

In preparing this third edition the overall thrust and content of the book remains the same, though some changes have been made to keep abreast of ongoing changes in the option and warrant markets. Option and price charts for Woodside are included, as the rise in world oil prices have focused attention on major oil stocks. The main change is a completely new Appendix II which covers the basic option strategies of buying options or writing options, and compares them with a selection of option bull and bear spread strategies. Numeric examples and pay-off diagrams are given for trading the popular options on the London FTSE 100 index.

The book's main merit lies in the principles discussed, along with the conclusions drawn from the illustrative examples, and not from the absolute values used in the examples. However, in preparing this third edition, the stock charts are extended to September 2000, and some of the analysis results are also extended to this date. The numerical examples using BHP are recalculated using the September 2000 price of around $21.00. Similarly, the option charts are redrawn to reflect the new stock prices and parameter changes at this time.

Chris Temby
Adelaide
October 2000
temby@senet.com.au

Chapter 1

INTRODUCTION

THIS BOOK DISCUSSES the use of *exchange traded options* and *equity warrants*, in conjunction with technical trading systems and money management procedures, to derive regular profits from the stock market. The stocks of particular interest are the heavyweight miners, the major banks and other blue chip stocks which go through regular price cycles.

The book is for people who are prepared to spend time analysing the market, and derive some pleasure from keeping themselves informed of the national and international events which drive the market.

My spur in writing was the dismal performance of the 'Capital Stable' superannuation funds in 1994—when investors learnt that 'capital stable' in a falling interest rate climate meant 'loss'.

This loss was of great concern to investors, particularly to retirees, who began to question the wisdom of leaving their nest-egg in a fund that was going backwards. Consequently, millions of dollars were withdrawn from the capital stable funds at that time and channelled into other investment avenues. The 'Balanced' funds became popular as they encompassed bonds, equities, properties and cash, and are less susceptible to changing interest rates. More recently, the early part of 1998 gave poor returns for many equity funds concentrating on local stock, though they recovered in the last quarter. 1999 was a good year for local and international share funds, but global markets were adversely affected by the sharp fall in the technology-based Nasdaq index in early 2000, which continued throughout the year.

For people wanting to manage their own investments, one simple and cost-effective approach is to buy some high-yielding industrial shares (possibly banks and property trusts), and put some cash into various length term deposits. The shares and term deposits can be proportioned such that the franked dividends from the shares offset the interest from the term deposits, and so help to minimise overall tax payable.

An alternative way to use funds committed to the stock market is to place these funds with a broker to earn interest, then use them as a deposit to trade options and warrants on the major stocks like News Corp, Telstra, AMP, BHP, RIO, WMC, Normandy, Woodside and the "Big Four" banks ANZ, Commonwealth, NAB and Westpac. Also available are options and warrants on the local and some overseas indices. Rather than being a risky exercise, an investor can set a realistic financial goal for the year, and with discipline can methodically work towards achieving a return above the market average.

History shows that the stock market can be an arena for generating wealth through long-term investment in appreciating stocks and through astute trading. Many investors and retirees hold shares or 'dabble' in shares, and so have some acquaintance with the stock market.

It is obvious that buying when the market is going up leads to making a profit, while buying or holding when the market falls results in a loss. It is less well known (or practised) that profits can be made in rising *and* falling markets by using options and warrants. Further, writing (selling) options is a safer strategy than taking (buying) options, as written options can be profitable when the market moves in our favour, sideways, or even slightly against us.

The market trends are always changing, as the players who make up the market respond to market news and perceptions of present and future profits and conditions. Successful stock-market investment is centred on knowing the market medium-term to long-term trend, and knowing when that trend is about to change, or has just changed.

Using a computer, charting and technical analysis software plus a stock price database, it is possible to have access to a host of technical indicators which help determine trends on individual stocks. The software allows us to back-test the indicators on the stock price data, and so choose a technical trading system to suit our particular needs.

We also need to develop a trading strategy which delivers profits, and comprises both a trading system and principles of market risk and money management. The trading system is a selection of chart analysis and technical indicators that give trading signals on the stocks, and we filter these signals to take only those with the highest probability of success. The market risk and money management principles limit losses in accordance with the size of our investment kitty.

Before writing options, brokers require a deposit to cover the variations in price in the underlying stock. The size of the deposit varies according to the uncertainty, or stability, in the overall market, and deposit sizes can range from full cover to as little as, say, $10,000. The numeric examples given later are based on trading a parcel of five BHP options, which equates to controlling about $100,000 worth of BHP shares trading around $20.00. For warrants, the parcel size is about $4,000. In either case, sufficient cash needs to be lodged with our broker to cover the trading. The broker lodges these funds with a merchant bank at overnight rates of about 5.0%, and then draws on the funds from time to time to meet our trading needs.

Some brokers require only $10,000 deposit to allow clients to write five BHP put or call options. Thus a trading kitty of, say, $15,000 allows us to employ a full strategy of both writing options and buying warrants. At other times when the full cash deposit on writing options is required, a $15,000 kitty would limit our trading to just buying warrants or buying options.

Charting and technical indicators form part of an extensive body of knowledge which assists in achieving success in the market. Rather than duplicate this work, only those indicators relevant to the method of trading we are concerned with in this book are discussed in detail. A list of useful references to other indicators is given in Chapter 18, for those who wish for or require further information. Also listed is a selection of software and database providers.

The Black-Scholes Option Pricing Model (BSOPM) is discussed, along with numerical examples of calculating the value of BHP put and call options, to help the reader become more familiar with the parameters that influence the pricing of options.

Chapter 2

PRELIMINARIES

EXCHANGE TRADED options (ETOs) and equity warrants (known throughout this book simply as options and warrants) are two of a collection of financial instruments known as derivatives, because they are derived from some other product. A BHP option is a form of buying or selling contract over BHP shares, and the price of the option is related to the price of the shares. Similarly, *index options* and *index warrants* are a form of option or warrant over particular local and overseas stock market indices, while futures are another form of derivatives.

One feature of the derivatives which makes them attractive to investors and traders is their gearing, whereby a percentage move in the underlying product (i.e. its share price or index points) translates to a greater percentage move in the derivative. A second feature of derivatives is that they make it possible to profit from both a rising or a falling market, provided the direction of the market trend is picked correctly. However, if the direction of the market is picked wrongly, these same two features will leave us with a loss, the size of which depends upon our risk and money management skills.

Many investors and traders[1] own stocks and so have some knowledge of the operations of particular companies, their field of activity, past performance and future prospects, composition of the board, etc. It need be only a small step from owning and trading stocks, to trading options or warrants on those or other stocks. Similarly, exchange traded index options are available on the stock market benchmark index, so rather than trade options on individual stocks, it is possible to trade options on the overall market.

[1] Rather than write "investors and traders" each time, the single term "traders" will be used, as it is normally associated with people who deal in options.

On 3 April 2000 the Australian Stock Exchange (ASX) changed the way in which the various indices were calculated. Prior to 3 April 2000 the index options were calculated on the All Ordinaries Index. The situation at the time of writing in early 2001 is that index options are available on the new S&P/ASX 200 Index, and for brevity are referred to in the financial press as SPI index options.

Another way of trading the overall market is to trade on the Sydney Futures Exchange (SFE). Contracts available include futures and options on the old All Ordinaries Index and the new S&P/ASX 200 Index. (The SFE calls these contracts the SPI and the SPI 200 respectively, with its SPI due to terminate in September 2001.) SFE futures contracts are also available on bank bills and bonds, and a few of the blue chip stocks. Thus the SFE and the ASX provide some overlap in their derivative products.

There is a perception amongst the public that futures are dangerous. Clangers of the 1990s in the billion-dollar class were the Nick Leeson (of Barings Bank) and Yasuo Hamanaka (of Sumitomo Corp) incidents—the latter of which sparked the copper price slump, and both of which were the result of massive futures losses. This perception of danger in trading the futures markets is reinforced by many a burnt small trader.

In reality, the options market in Australia is a well-regulated and active market. Many books on investment have chapters devoted to options. Some of these books are very mathematical and beyond the scope of the lay reader.

However, some informative books which are available from major bookstores are *Understanding Options Trading in Australia* by Christopher Tate, *Speculating on the Australian Sharemarket* by William Harper, *Equity Options* by Hugh Denning and *Sensible Share Investing* by Austin Donnelly. The Australian Stock Exchange also offers introductory and advanced courses on trading options. (Chapter 18 lists comprehensive references grouped into topics. When a specific reference is mentioned, the author's name will be given.)

Christopher Tate's book is very readable and presents the basic options terminology, then moves to strategies for trading in Australian put and call options. Tate also discusses useful defensive actions to protect a winning options trade, and ways of converting a losing trade into a neutral or a profit transaction. In *Trading Stock Options and Warrants* it is assumed that the reader has a general knowledge of options and has possibly bought options from time to time. If this is not the case, then Tate's book is recommended to grasp the fundamentals of options.

Trading Stock Options and Warrants moves on to apply option theory in a practical way and formulates option strategies aimed at achieving an annual rate of return above the market average with manageable risk. Illustrative examples are given using five BHP options covering about $100,000 of BHP stock. Option price charts are given for News Corp, Telstra, AMP, BHP, RIO, WMC, Normandy, Woodside, ANZ, CBA, NAB and Westpac, to help the reader to develop trading strategies in these stocks.

Options terminology and the general behaviour of put and call options are treated briefly, but the reader needing a better understanding of these topics is referred to the above books by Tate, Harper, Denning or Donnelly.

OPTION STOCKS

At October 2000 options were traded in some 55 stocks (herein called "option stocks") which cover the major sectors of the stock market, along with options on the SPI. The stocks are listed in Table 2.1 below, along with their stock-market code, and will subsequently be referred to by this code.

Table 2.1 Option Stocks

Company	Code	Company	Code
Australian Gas Light	AGL	Lihir Gold	LHG
Amcor	AMC	Lend Lease Corp	LLC
AMP	AMP	LookSmart	LOK
Australia & NZ Banking Group	ANZ	Mayne Nicholas Limited	MAY
AXA Asia Pacific Holdings	AXA	Macquarie Bank	MBL
The Broken Hill Pty Company	BHP	Mount Isa Mines	MIM
Brambles Industries	BIL	National Australia Bank	NAB
Boral	BOR	Newcrest	NCM
Commonwealth Bank	CBA	News Corp	NCP
Coca-Cola Amatil	CCL	News Corp Preferred	NCPPD
Coles Myer	CML	Normandy	NDY
Computershare	CPU	NRMA Insurance Group	NRM
CSR	CSR	Origin Energy	ORG
Cable & Wireless Optus	CWO	Orica	ORI
David Jones	DJS	Oil Search	OSH
Davnet	DVT	Pasminco	PAS
ERG	ERG	Publishing & Broadcasting	PBL
Foster's Brewing	FBG	Pacific Dunlop	PDP
Fairfax (John)	FXJ	Paperlinx	PPX
Goodman Fielder	GMF	Qantas Airways	QAN

Table 2.1 (Cont'd)

Company	Code	Company	Code
QBE Insurance	QBE	Telstra Corp	TLS
QCT Resources	QRL	TAB Queensland	TQL
Rio Tinto	RIO	Westpac Banking Corp	WBC
Seven Network	SEV	WMC	WMC
St George Bank	SGB	Woolworths	WOW
Southcorp Holdings	SRP	Woodside	WPL
Santos	STO	Westfield Holdings	WSF
NSW Tab	TAB		
Tabcorp Holdings	TAH	Exchange Traded Index Option Share Price Index	XPI
Ten Network	TEN		

The sharemarket tables in *Shares* magazine give a market summary of option statistics. Using the October 2000 edition, which gives August 2000 information, Table 2.2 below lists some details of the most popular option stocks.

Table 2.2 Option Open Positions and Contracts Exercised

Stock	Price Move in September (%)	Open Positions		No. of Contracts Exercised	
		Call	Put	Call	Put
AMP	2.7	10,666	5,442	1,697	5
ANZ	1.6	13,182	5,183	3,336	150
BHP	4.7	29,087	20,398	3,687	203
CBA	-0.4	25,250	14,397	5,354	7
CWO	-7.6	21,743	16,223	700	2,608
MIM	6.5	41,936	17,078	4,342	665
NAB	2.6	13,411	14,258	1,944	841
NCP	8.3	23,052	11,688	12,158	1,656
NDY	2.0	24,038	39,531	13,179	9,654
QAN	-0.5	21,814	23,563	4,550	438
RIO	4.1	14,021	14,456	1,598	142
TLS	-11.5	26,387	29,157	630	1,523
WMC	6.9	48,782	22,592	9,879	254
WPL	12.2	18,737	6,473	405	10

The number of options open on a stock vary month by month, but the stocks listed in Table 2.2 usually show high levels of option trading.

OPTION DEFINITIONS

Call Options

A call option gives the taker (buyer) the right, but not the obligation, to purchase a parcel of shares at the strike price at any time during the life of the option.

Conversely, the writer (seller) of a call option is obliged to deliver the shares covered by the option at the strike price at any time during the life of the option, if the purchaser so asks.

A writer may sell call options against shares already owned, which is described as "covered call writing". Alternatively, when the call option is written without owning the stock it is described as "naked call option writing", and must be covered with cash or share deposits and margin calls as required (see the section on 'Option Transaction Costs' later in the chapter).

The option taker can make a profit from a rise in the price of the stock and hence of the option price. The option writer makes a profit if the share price falls or moves sideways, as the option value falls or expires worthless.

Put Options

A put option gives the taker (buyer) the right, but not the obligation, to sell a parcel of shares at the strike price at any time during the life of the option.

Conversely, the writer (seller) of a put option is obliged to purchase the shares covered by the option at the strike price at any time during the life of the option, if the purchaser so asks.

Writing a put option is a "naked" transaction and must be covered with cash deposits and margin calls as required.

The option taker can make a profit from a fall in the price of the stock and hence a rise in the option price. The option writer makes a profit if the share price rises or moves sideways, as the option value falls or expires worthless.

Expiry Months

Options series generally expire on the last Thursday of each month, though there are some exceptions. The option expiry dates for 2001 are listed in Table 2.3 below.

Each year the ASX produces an Option Expiration Calendar which lists useful information about option stocks, additional to the expiry dates. The expiry months for some popular stocks are:

ANZ, CBA, NAB, WBC, MIM	January/ April/ July/ October
NCP, NDY	February/ May/ August/ November
AMP, BHP, RIO, WMC, WPL, TLS	March/ June/ September/ December

Some stocks also have a spot expiry month, but these series are not as popular as the major expiry series. Trading in the spot month begins midway through the previous month, i.e. February BHP options begin trading in mid-January and have a maximum of six weeks to expiry.

Table 2.3 Option Expiry Dates 2001

Product	Month	Day	Date
Exchange traded options	January	Thursday	25
	February	Thursday	22
	March	Thursday	29
	April	Thursday	26
	May	Thursday	24
	June	Thursday	28
	July	Thursday	26
	August	Thursday	30
	September	Thursday	27
	October	Thursday	25
	November	Thursday	29
	December	Thursday	20
Index options	March	Friday	30
	June	Friday	29
	September	Friday	28
	December	Monday	31

Strike Price Increments and Notation

The option strike price is usually set in the following bands:

Stocks priced:	**up to $1.00**	at 10¢ intervals
	$1.00 to $5.00	at 20¢ or 25¢ intervals
	$5.00 to $10.00	at 25¢ or 50¢ intervals
	$10.00 to $30.00	at 50¢ or $1.00 intervals
	above $30.00	at $1.00 intervals

In this book the option strike price is written without the preceding $ sign, so a December $10.00 option is written as Dec 10.00.

At-the-money, In-the-money, Out-of-the-money

The first column in Table 2.4 below shows a series of call options on a stock selling at $20.00. The option with the strike price of 20.00 is called "at-the-money", the option with a strike price of 20.50 or above is called "out-of-the-money", while the option with the strike price of 19.50 or below is called "in-the-money".

The right-hand column in Table 2.4 shows a series of put options on a stock selling at $20.00. The option with the strike price of 20.00 is called "at-the-money", the option with a strike price of 19.50 or below is called "out-of-the-money", while the option with the strike price of 20.50 or above is called "in-the-money".

Table 2.4 Put and Call Options for Stock Selling at $20.00

Call Options	Option Strike Price ($)	Put Options
2nd out-of-the-money	21.00	2nd in-the-money
1st out-of-the-money	20.50	1st in-the-money
At-the-money	20.00	At-the-money
1st in-the-money	19.50	1st out-of-the-money
2nd in-the-money	19.00	2nd out-of-the-money

Contract Size

One option contract covers 1,000 shares. However, when a stock makes a new issue or a bonus issue, the number of shares in the original option contract changes, and so too does the strike price. When BHP made a 1-for-10 bonus issue in May 1995, a pre-bonus option with strike price of 19.00 became 17.27 strike price and covered 1,100 post-bonus shares.

Option Quotations

Options are quoted daily in *The Australian* and *The Australian Financial Review*, but not generally in the local newspapers. The segment listed in Figure 2.1 below is from *The Australian* on Thursday 21 September 2000 and the column headings are the stock name and expiry month, strike price, buyer quote, seller quote, last sale price, number of options traded that day, and the total number of options open. *The Australian Financial Review* also lists the delta and annual percentage return. (The annual percentage return is discussed later in this chapter, and delta is discussed in Chapter 4.)

Call Options

Stock	Strike Price	Buyer	Seller	Last Sale	T.O. 000	Open Int
Up to 4:52pm Wednesday September 20th 2000						
A.G.L. Last Sale Price $11.00						
2000						
Sep	7.50	3.41	3.61	1.72		10
Sep	8.00	2.91	3.11	1.71		67
Sep	8.50	2.42	2.60	2.52		110
Sep	9.00	1.92	2.10	2.02		211
Sep	9.50	1.43	1.59	1.39	5	1043
Sep	10.00	.94	1.08	.81	3	296
Sep	10.50	.46	.58	.25	104	500
Sep	11.00	.12	.18	.14	30	354
Sep	11.50		.04	.15		260
Sep	12.00		.01	.05½		12
Dec	9.50	1.43	1.59	1.34	23	49
Dec	10.00	.99	1.13	.95	10	222
Dec	10.50	.66	.80	.70	9	258
Dec	11.00	.44	.53	.44	116	295
Dec	11.50	.24	.33	.23	8	170
2001						
Mar	10.50	.96	1.10	.87	3	41
Mar	11.50	.51	.63	.47	10	1
Amcor Last Sale Price $5.126						
2000						
Nov	5.00	.27	.36	.77		19
Nov	5.25	.15	.22	.22		327
Nov	5.50	.07	.13	.07		2262
Nov	5.75	.02	.08	.08		1802
Nov	6.00		.04	.05½		311
Nov	6.25		.02	.02		365
2001						
Feb	5.25	.30	.31	.31	50	5
AMP Last Sale Price $16.96						
2000						
Sep	14.00	2.89	3.07	3.59		341
Sep	14.50	2.40	2.56	3.09		382
Sep	15.00	1.90	2.06	2.60		1366
Sep	15.50	1.41	1.55	2.09		942
Sep	16.00	.93	1.05	1.60		1350
Sep	16.50	.48	.58	.39		825
Sep	17.00	.16	.22	.16	10	1005
Sep	17.50	.04	.08	.06	50	2507
Sep	18.00		.02	.02	1	2376
Sep	18.50		.01	.02		1522
Sep	19.00		.01	.01½		667
Oct	17.00	.32	.40	.38	24	22
Oct	18.00	.06	.12	.10½	25	240
Nov	17.00	.50	.60	.51	8	30
Nov	17.50	.30	.38	.32	3	20
Nov	18.00	.18	.24	.18	1	35
Dec	17.50	.44	.54	.43	5	1074
Dec	20.00	.02	.08	.06	10	193
ANZ Last Sale Price $12.85						
2000						
Sep	11.50	1.30	1.44		2	17
Sep	12.00	.81	.93	1.36	11	129
Sep	12.50	.34½	.40½	.35	1	1073
Sep	13.00	.06	.10	.08	20	935
Sep	13.50		.02	.01½		715
Sep	14.00		.01	.01		155
Oct	12.50	.52	.58	.58	10	2285
Oct	13.00	.25	.28½	.29	5	2579
Oct	13.50	.10	.12	.10	15	1259
Nov	12.50	.57	.67		11	20
2001						
Jan	11.50	1.39	1.53	1.75	2	203

Put Options

Stock	Strike Price	Buyer	Seller	Last Sale	T.O. 000	Open Int
Up to 4:52pm Wednesday September 20th 2000						
A.G.L. Last Sale Price $11.00						
2000						
Dec	10.50	.30	.39	.40	4	15
2001						
Mar	9.00	.08	.14	.12	1	22
Amcor Last Sale Price $5.126						
2000						
2001						
Feb	5.25	.30	.38	.32	20	14
AMP Last Sale Price $16.96						
2000						
Sep	17.00	.18	.24	.20½	35	1043
Sep	17.50	.52	.62	.73	10	988
Sep	18.00	.98	1.10	1.23	1	199
Oct	16.50	.26	.32	.31	3	66
Oct	17.00	.49	.59	.65	5	249
Nov	16.50	.36	.46	.42	2	5
Nov	18.00	1.28	1.42	.85	1	5
Dec	16.00	.28	.36	.33	2	1253
Dec	16.50	.44	.55	.59	5	328
ANZ Last Sale Price $12.85						
2000						
Sep	13.00	.18	.23½	.27½	4	752
Sep	13.50	.60	.66	.62	10	176
Oct	12.00	.02	.06	.07	3	247
Oct	12.50	.12½	.16	.15	203	722
Oct	13.00	.31	.36½	.33	15	438
Oct	13.50	.64	.71	.64	5	191
Nov	12.50	.28	.36	.30	10	95
AXA Asia Last Sale Price $2.66						
2000						
Sep	2.50		.01	.02		260
Oct	2.20	.00½	.05	.01		995
Oct	2.40		.02	.05		623
Oct	2.60	.04	.08	.06		113
Oct	2.80	.14	.20	.13		69
BHP Last Sale Price $20.97½						
2000						
Sep	20.00	.05	.06	.05	11	741
Sep	20.50	.08	.13	.18	52	316
Sep	21.00	.26	.34	.38	10	128
Oct	19.50	.09	.14	.16	25	211
Oct	20.00	.25	.33	.30½	41	391
Oct	20.50	.32	.40	.43	21	269
Oct	21.00	.54	.64	.68	10	94
Oct	21.50	.81	.93	1.02	50	63
Nov	20.50	.49	.59	.64	3	22
Dec	16.50		.04	.07	30	1074
Dec	18.00	.06	.11	.21	10	895
Dec	20.00	.43	.53	.72	1	331
2001						
Mar	16.00	.04	.08	.14	2	63
Mar	18.00	.24	.32	.40	2	707
Jun	20.00	1.02	1.14	1.25	2	157
Brambles Last Sale Price $47.13						
2000						
Sep	45.00	.04	.10	.10	8	103
Sep	47.00	.63	.77	.70	14	381
Sep	48.00	1.32	1.48	1.47	28	138
Sep	49.00	2.20	2.38	2.18	28	136
Sep	50.00	3.16	3.36	3.27	50	131
Sep	51.00	4.16	4.36	2.75	3	117
Dec	38.00		.06	.08	5	
Dec	44.00	.61	.73	.76	10	500
Dec	45.00	.91	1.05	1.07	4	550

Figure 2.1 Option Quotes

Trading Options

In October 1997 options trading changed from open outcry to screen-based trading. This change was brought about by the ASX introducing the automated options trading system known as Derivatives Trading Facility, which is a customised version of the Swedish CLICK system. All options traded are subject to the rules and regulations of the OCH, which also guarantees the performance of the options and is the options registrar.

OPTION TRANSACTION COSTS

Brokerage on Options

Stockbrokers charge differing amounts of brokerage for handling options. Some brokers charge on a percentage basis while others charge a fixed fee. Indicative minimum brokerage fees are:

To open or close an option trade: around $50

To exercise an option contract involving buying or selling shares: around $60

These fees are inclusive of GST, and increase as order sizes increase.

Additional to the brokerage fee, the OCH charges $1.12 per option for both opening and closing the trade, and 55¢ per option for exercising (both prices inclusive of GST). Most States charge stamp duty on share transactions and this is incurred when shares are bought or sold in exercising options. Stamp duty and OCH charges are not included in the numerical examples later.

Deposits and Margin Calls

Before we purchase put or call options or warrants, the full amount of the purchase price must be held by the broker, but there are no margin calls or further deposits required.

To write call or put options a deposit is required. Some brokers require full cover, which means that if we want to write, say, five BHP call options, then we need to deposit with the broker either 5,000 BHP shares, or cash to the value of 5,000 BHP shares. (If we are exercised we have to deliver the 5,000 shares either from our own account, or through buying them in the market and on-selling them to the option exerciser.) Similarly, to write five BHP put options we need to deposit cash with the broker to cover the purchase price of 5,000 BHP shares.

At times of high volatility and uncertainty, as occurred after the October 1997 mini-crash, brokers may demand full cover for clients writing options, or may even stop taking this type of order. During normal market times, brokers relax the rules to allow options to be written on a much reduced deposit, though individual brokers make their own rules. For example, at October 2000 the discount broker TD Waterhouse required a 20% cash deposit for writing put options but 100% cash or shares deposit for writing call options. Some other brokers required cash deposits of, say, three times the option value plus a further $10,000, i.e. a deposit of $20,000 would allow five BHP put or call options to be written, if each option was priced below $600. It is customary for deposits on writing options to be in the form of cash, or part-cash and part-shares.

The value of our written options fluctuates each day, and the debit or credit passes between the OCH and our broker to keep our account square with the OCH. The Derivatives Division of the ASX has issued a booklet entitled *Margins* which explains how to calculate the value of margin calls. Very briefly, the margin is calculated taking into account the market value of the option, and the effect that the largest likely intra-day change in the value of the underlying security would have upon the value of the option.

Before opening an options trading account it is necessary to shop around to find a broker whose deposit requirements match what we are prepared to allocate to this exercise, and whose scale of fees is also acceptable.

The monthly magazines *Personal Investor* and *Shares* carry ads by cut-price and Internet brokers, along with a full list of Australian stockbrokers.

PRICING THE OPTION

The factors that influence the price of an option are:

1. Stock price, or price of the underlying financial instrument.
2. Option strike (or exercise) price.
3. Time to expiry.
4. Risk-free interest rate for the same length of time as the option expiry.
5. Volatility of the stock.
6. Underlying mood of the market.

The price of an option comprises the intrinsic value plus the time premium. Suppose the BHP share price is $20.35 and the 20.00 call option is 75¢. The intrinsic value is 35¢ (share price – strike price) and the remaining 40¢ of option price is the time premium.

Similarly, suppose the BHP share price is $20.35 and the 20.50 put option is 60¢. The intrinsic value is 15¢ (strike price – share price), and the remaining 45¢ of option price is the time premium.

At-the-money and out-of-the-money put and call options have a time premium but no intrinsic value.

The time premium is a wasting asset. For both put and call options, as the time to expiry shortens, the time premium falls linearly until about the last four weeks when it begins to fall more steeply. This behaviour is discussed further in Chapter 4.

The current "risk-free" interest rate (e.g. the 90-day bill rate) has a minor effect upon the option price, with higher/lower interest rates producing slightly higher/lower option prices.

The volatility of a stock has a considerable effect upon the option price. NCP has a higher volatility than BHP, which is higher than NAB. Higher volatility leads to a higher time premium in the option price.

The market mood also affects the option price. For a fixed stock price and strike price, a particular call option will command a slightly higher price in a buoyant market than in a flat market.

Chapter 4 discusses in detail the Black-Scholes Option Pricing Model (BSOPM) which is typical of the mathematical models used in determining the fair price of an option. We will use this model to confirm the price of various options and to quantify the effect of the parameters listed above.

Annual Percentage Return

The annual percentage return is a measure of the return available to the writer of an option if the option is held to expiry.

$$\text{Annual \% return} = 100 \times \frac{\text{time premium}}{\text{stock price}} \times \frac{365}{\text{days to expiry}} \ \%$$

Suppose the stock price is $18.20 and a call option with a strike price of $18.00 and time to expiry of 65 days is selling for 72¢. The time premium is 72 – (1820 – 1800) = 52. Then:

$$\text{Annual \% return} = 100 \times \frac{52}{1820} \times \frac{365}{65} = 16.0\%$$

At-the-money options have the highest time component so these options give the highest annual percentage return values.

Option Value at Expiry

At expiry, the value of an option comprises only the intrinsic value. For a call option this is the stock price minus the strike price, and for a put option is the strike price minus the stock price.

A call option will expire worthless if the stock price is less than the option strike price at the date of expiry. The writer of this call option pockets the money from the sale of the call option.

A put option will expire worthless if the stock price is higher than the option strike price at the date of expiry. The writer of the put option pockets the money from the sale of the put option.

A put or call option which expires in-the-money may be sold for the residual value of the option.

Exchange traded options are American-style, which means that they can be exercised at any time up to the expiry date. Thus options can be bought, sold or converted to shares at any time before their expiry date. Options that are allowed to run to the expiry date are either exercised or expire worthless. The profit/loss situation for options at expiry depends on whether the stock has risen, fallen or moved sideways as listed in the table below.

Stock Price at Expiry	Buy Call	Write Call	Buy Put	Write Put
Up	Profit	Loss	Loss	Profit
Steady	Loss	Profit	Loss	Profit
Down	Loss	Profit	Profit	Loss

EXERCISE OF OPTIONS

An option can be exercised at any time prior to expiry by informing our broker of our intention. The exercise is transacted after the close of business on that day. Thus, if we exercise a bought call option the purchase of the shares is booked on that day, and the shares should be available to us on day T+3 (three business days after the transaction day). Theoretically we can on-sell the shares the same day that we exercise, but this needs to be discussed with our broker, so as not to fall foul of the T+3 rules on delivery of shares.

Similarly, if we exercise a bought put option, then the sale of the shares is booked that day, and we must deliver the shares to the seller of the option by day T+3.

When the OCH receives a request from a buyer to exercise an option, it selects at random an option from the pool of written options to match that request. Whenever a written option becomes in-the-money there is a chance of it being exercised.

Our strategy is to write options. If we are exercised, the following morning the broker rings to give us the news. It is then too late to close the option, and we must either deliver the shares or take up the shares, depending on whether we wrote calls or puts.

REGISTERED TRADERS

Registered Traders (RTs) are a necessary part of the options trading mechanism. The role of the RTs is to make a market in a particular stock's options, by always standing in the market with a buying and a selling quote, and with a minimum number of contracts on offer. Consequently, RTs are sometimes called "market makers" and sometimes something less polite. RTs are professional traders often employed by broking houses whose aim is to make a profit for themselves while also "making a market".

For actively-traded option stocks like BHP or NAB, the market will comprise many private traders as well as the RTs, which results in close bid/ask quotes, as supply and demand is satisfied. However, for less actively-traded option stocks the only people standing in the market may be RTs, who set a wider bid/ask spread in order to maximise their profit and so cover their risk.

A further problem with less actively-traded option stocks is that the RTs' bid/ask quotes have a mirage-like quality and move further away as we close in on them. To minimise these RT problems, it is safest to restrict our options trading to only the actively-traded option stocks and the active series within those stocks. The active series are the at-the-money, first out-of-the money and first in-the-money options.

EXCHANGE TRADED INDEX OPTIONS

Exchange traded index options are options over the S&P/ASX 200 Index, and are called SPI index options. These options which trade on the ASX are *not* the same as the index options which trade on the SFE, and are also called SPI options.

The specifications for the SPI options trading on the ASX are:

Contract Name:	ASX Share Price Index Option
Underlying Index:	S&P/ASX 200 Index
Index Multiplier:	$10; each index point is equal to $10
Exercise Style:	European, i.e. exercisable only on the last trading day
Exercise Intervals:	25 index points
Type:	Call and put options
Contract Months:	March, June, September, December
Last Trading and Expiry Day:	At 4.15 p.m. on the last business day of the contract month
Settlement:	Cash, settled at the closing quotation of the SPI on the last trading day

These SPI options offer a method of trading the broad market, though at the time of writing turnover is not large, so there may be problems in closing a trade at a satisfactory price.

EQUITY WARRANTS

These warrants are available on a range of Australian stocks, and their numbers are continually increasing. Equity warrants are offered by merchant banks and large finance houses, and when initially offered have expiry times as long as two years. The warrant may be European or American-style, the difference being that European-style warrants can only be exercised on the expiry date, while American-style warrants can be exercised at any time up to the expiry date.

For the trader or investor, the warrant can be likened to a long-term put or call option, and offers leveraged gains in a falling or rising market (and losses if we pick the trend wrongly). Warrants are covered more fully in Chapter 11, where the available warrants are listed.

ENDOWMENT, INSTALMENT & CAPITAL PLUS WARRANTS

Another form of warrant available on the ASX is the endowment warrant. Endowment warrants are a much longer-term investment tool, and were initially issued in 1996 with a ten-year term. Their performance is dependent upon the underlying share paying an increasing rate of dividend over the ten years, and the dividend stream effectively purchasing the shares over the ten years.

Instalment warrants, as the name implies, are paid for in two instalments over a period of typically two years.

Capital Plus warrants cover a basket of shares and the purchaser is guaranteed a minimum capital return at the warrant expiry which is typically five years.

Endowment, instalment and Capital Plus warrants are intended for long-term investors, and possibly for inclusion in superannuation funds, so are not included in our trading strategy.

INDEX WARRANTS

Index warrants are a derivative product introduced to the ASX in January 1998. In essence, these warrants act as put and call options on the ASX benchmark index, and are now over the S&P/ASX 200 Index. These warrants can be used as a trading or investing tool to generate profits in both rising and falling markets. Alternatively, they can be used to provide insurance against a share portfolio in a falling market.

Index warrants are discussed fully in my second book, *Technical Analysis for Trading Index Warrants*.

Put and call warrants are also available on the American Nasdaq 100 and Standard & Poor's 500 indices, and the Japanese Nikkei 225. These index warrants trade on the Stock Exchange Automated Trading System (SEATS) just like stocks and equity warrants (see page 133).

Chapter 3

GOALS

THE TRADER SHOULD use technical indicators to monitor the medium-term trends in the option stocks, and enter only those trades which the indicators show have a high probability of success.

The strategy is to write put and call options, and buy long-term put and call warrants, while employing market risk and money management principles.

Conventional wisdom holds that blue chip Australian stocks will, on average, pay a dividend of 5% per annum and appreciate in value by 5% per annum, giving a gross gain of 10% per annum. Some years this is indeed true, but there are years when returns fall far short of the goal, or are negative.

The strategy of writing options allows us to use the stock market to generate a steady income, but without tying up funds in purchasing shares.

To start, we deposit our trading funds with a broker, who then transfers this money to an interest-bearing account earning about 5% per annum.

We use the funds as deposit for writing put and call options, with the intent that the options expire worthless, whereby the initial sale becomes our profit. We also use some of the funds to buy long-term put and call warrants, with the intention of selling them at a profit.

Our goal is to achieve a steady trading return above the market average on funds allocated to the stock market, with manageable risk.

Depending on market conditions and consequently broker deposit requirements, there may be times when our deposits are not sufficient to write put and call options. At these times we may still trade warrants, and possibly have one or two trades open at a time. Over a typical year there may be several warrant trading opportunities. If we choose only those with the most reliable technical signals, we can expect to achieve a satisfactory overall profit result.

Chapter 4

THE BLACK-SCHOLES OPTION PRICING MODEL

IN EARLY 1997 when the first edition of *Trading Stock Options and Warrants* was written, BHP was trading at around $18.00. The second edition of the book was written in late 1988 and at that time BHP was in the doldrums around $13.50. This third edition written in late 2000 finds BHP testing new highs around $21.00—such are the fortunes of the once "Big Australian", and underscore one of the reasons for trading options, rather than adopting a buy and hold strategy. In this chapter the numeric values have not been altered to reflect these price changes, other than adding some comments at its conclusion. Maintaining the $18.00 values for BHP highlights the fact that the market is always dynamic, and our aim is to understand the underlying market principles, irrespective of prices at any particular time.

To trade options confidently it is necessary to understand the mechanics of option pricing, and how options respond to market forces. There are a number of mathematical formulae used to calculate the fair price of an option. One popular formulation is that developed by Black and Scholes, and discussion is confined to this Black-Scholes Option Pricing Model (BSOPM).

The model is defined, and then used to calculate the price of a BHP call option and the price of a BHP put option. The way in which option prices are dependent upon strike prices, time to expiry, risk-free interest rates and the stock volatility is shown.

Lee, Finnerty and Worth define the BSOPM option price as a function of the parameters:

S current stock price (¢)

X option strike price (¢)

T time to expiry (years)

r risk-less interest rate for the same time duration as the option expiry

v volatility of the stock

The BSOPM assumes the option is held to expiry, and the stock pays no dividends during the life of the option.

Using these assumptions, the Put-Call Parity theorem states:

$$C = P + S - X e^{-rT}$$

where:

C = value of the call option

P = value of the put option

The Put-Call Parity theorem applies for a put and a call option with the same strike price and the same time to expiry.

For call options the BSOPM value is:

$$C = SN(d_1) - X e^{-rT}N(d_2)$$

For put options the BSOPM value is:

$$P = -SN(-d_1) + X e^{-rT}N(-d_2)$$

where:

$$d_1 = \frac{\ln\left(\frac{S}{X}\right) + \left(r + \frac{v^2}{2}\right)T}{v\sqrt{T}}$$

and:

$$d_2 = d_1 - v\sqrt{T}$$

Further:

N () is the cumulative normal distribution

e is the exponential = 2.718

ln is the natural logarithm

The volatility v is defined as the square root of the annualised variance v^2.

To calculate the annualised variance, firstly the arithemetic mean, m, of the daily compounded return is determined over, say, 30 days as:

$$m = \frac{1}{30}\sum_{t=2}^{30} \ln\left(\frac{P_t}{P_{t-1}}\right) = \frac{1}{30} \ln\left(\frac{P_{30}}{P_1}\right)$$

where:

P and P_{t-1} are share prices on day t and t – 1 respectively

$\frac{P_t}{P_{t-1}} = R_t$ the daily holding period return on the stock

The annualised variance v^2 is:

$$v^2 = 365 \times \frac{1}{30-1}\sum_{t=1}^{30}\left(\ln R_t - m\right)^2$$

Whence:

$$\text{volatility} = \sqrt{v^2} = v$$

By convention, volatility is expressed as a percentage. Thus, if the annualised variance = 0.09, then the volatility = 0.30 which equates to 30%.

HISTORIC, FUTURE AND IMPLIED VOLATILITY

The BSOPM uses five parameters to calculate the option price. The stock price, strike price, time to expiry and risk-free interest rate are readily known, but finding the correct value for volatility is less certain.

The volatility formula above uses past data for its calculation, so this is referred to as "historic volatility". A problem arises in that different data sample lengths result in different values for the historic volatility. A second problem is that a better estimate of the option price would come from using the "future volatility", i.e. the stock volatility from now to the option expiry. Of course, we do not know if the volatility in the future will be the same as the volatility in the past.

To overcome this problem it is customary to use "implied volatility", which is the market's estimate of the future volatility, to calculate the option price. For this, we select a particular stock and a number of option series with different strike prices and expiry times. We then equate the BSOPM prices to the various market option prices, and solve iteratively to obtain the volatility values. These volatility values should be close to one another, and the average becomes the implied volatility being used by the market. This implied volatility can be used to calculate other option series prices for that stock, which will be close to the market value. These volatility concepts are illustrated in the example below.

EXAMPLE OF CALCULATING BHP CALL AND PUT OPTION PRICES

The BSOPM formula is used to calculate the value of a BHP call option and a BHP put option. Input data is BHP price $17.97, strike price 18.00, time to expiry 56 days, risk-less rate 6.0%, and the implied volatility is estimated as 21%. The BSOPM call option value C is calculated using:

S	1797¢
X	1800¢
T	time to maturity = 56 days = 0.1534 years
r	6.0% = 0.06
v	21% = 0.21 and v^2 = 0.0441

Then:

$$d_1 = \frac{\ln\left(\frac{1797}{1800}\right) + \left(0.06 + \frac{0.0441}{2}\right) \times 0.1534}{0.21\sqrt{0.1534}}$$

$$= \frac{-0.00167 + 0.01259}{0.08225}$$

$$= 0.1328$$

and:

$$d_2 = 0.1328 - 0.0823$$

$$= 0.0505$$

Whence:

$$N(d_1) = 0.553$$

$$N(d_2) = 0.520$$

$$e^{-0.06 \times 0.1534} = 0.991$$

The BSOPM call option price C is:

$$C = 1797 \times 0.553 - 1800 \times 0.991 \times 0.520$$
$$= 66¢$$

Similarly, the BHP put option price P is calculated as:

$-d_1 = -0.1328$ $\quad N(-d_1) = 0.447$

$-d_2 = -0.0505$ $\quad N(-d_2) = 0.480$

Whence:

$$P = -1797 \times 0.447 + 1800 \times 0.991 \times 0.480$$
$$= 53¢$$

We may check these option values using the above Put-Call Parity theorem that states:

$$C = P + S - X\,e^{-rT}$$

Whence:

$$C = 53 + 1797 - 1800 \times e^{-0.06 \times 0.1534}$$
$$= 53 + 1797 - 1784$$
$$= 66¢$$

PUT OPTION PRICE vs CALL OPTION PRICE

The BSOPM gives different formulations for put and call options.

For at-the-money options, $S = X$, so the Put-Call Parity theorem term $S - Xe^{-rT}$ becomes $S\,(1 - e^{-rT})$ and is always > 0. Thus, for at-the-money strike price options in the same time series, the Put-Call Parity theorem requires the value of the call option to be higher than the value of the put option.

Normally this relationship holds, but as the time approaches a dividend payment, the call option may fall in value while the put option may increase in value. When the stock goes ex-dividend its price falls, and the option prices anticipate this change.

We can verify the accuracy (and usefulness) of the BSOPM by comparing a set of BHP actual option prices with calculated values from the model.

On 29.1.97 BHP closed at $17.97, which was up 10¢ from the previous close, i.e. a fairly steady day. At that time the active option strike prices were 17.50, 18.00 and 18.50.

Table 4.1 below lists the option market prices in cents for put and call at-the-money and 1st out-of-the-money options on 29.1.97. The at-the-money call option values were inputted to the BSOPM and the implied volatility being used by the market was found to be 21%. Using this value for volatility and a risk-free rate of 6.0%, all the BSOPM values were calculated and are listed in bold type in the table.

Table 4.1 illustrates a number of option principles when no dividends are payable during the life of the option:

1. The market value of at-the-money call options is higher than that of the corresponding at-the-money put options (18.00 series).
2. The market value of 1st out-of-the-money call options (18.50 series) is higher than that of the corresponding 1st out-of-the-money put options (17.50 series).
3. The implied volatility was determined by matching the BSOPM at-the-money call option values to the market values. Using this value of volatility in the BSOPM for other option series gives values very close to the market option prices.
4. The BSOPM is a valid representation of market option prices.

Table 4.1 Comparison Between Market and BSOPM Option Prices

Option Series	Type	Expiry Month February	March
18.00 call	Market	45	65
	BSOPM	**46**	**66**
18.00 put	Market	42	53
	BSOPM	**40**	**52**
18.50 call	Market	24	41
	BSOPM	**25**	**43**
17.50 put	Market	21	32
	BSOPM	**20**	**32**

Note: This particular time span was chosen because there were no dividend payments between 29.1.97 and the end of March, which would skew the option prices.

OPTION SENSITIVITY TO INPUT PARAMETERS

The Greeks

The Greek symbols delta, gamma, theta, vega and rho are used to define the sensitivity of the option price to changes in the model input parameters.

Sensitivity to Stock Price (Delta)

Delta = change in option price for a +1 point change in stock price

Call options have a positive delta between 0 and 1, while put options have a negative delta between 0 and -1. An at-the-money call option has a delta of about 0.7 (and a put option about -0.7). Out-of-the-money options have a delta between 0 and about 0.7, while in-the-money options have a delta between about 0.7 and 1.

Suppose BHP is at $18.00 and a particular series call option is 51¢. If BHP moves up to $18.10 and the option moves to 58¢, then the option delta is $\frac{7}{10} = 0.7$.

Figure 4.1 below shows the put and call option prices calculated from the BSOPM as the price of BHP moves from being out-of-the-money to being in-the-money.

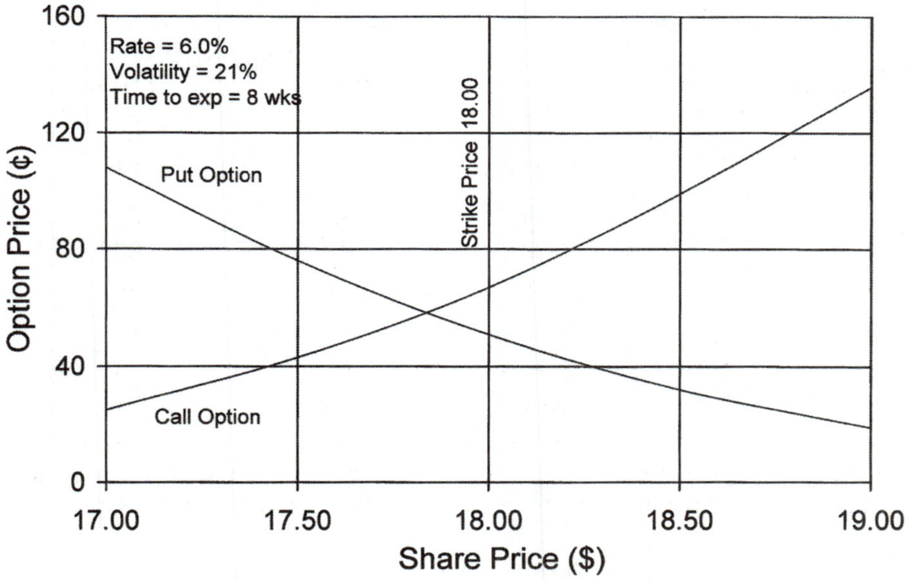

Figure 4.1 Option Price vs Share Price

The option is an 18.00 series call with r = 6.0%, volatility = 21% and eight weeks to expiry. For the call option, a share price move from $17.50 to $18.00 gives a smaller change in the option price than a share price move from $18.00 to $18.50, i.e. the call option delta rises as the share price moves from being out-of-the-money to being in-the-money.

Change in Delta Value (Gamma)

Gamma is a measure of this change in the value of delta as the stock price varies, and:

> Gamma = change in delta for a 1 point change in stock price

Sensitivity to Time to Expiry (Theta)

> Theta = amount option price declines due to passage of one day (all other factors remaining the same)

Figure 4.2 below shows the calculated put and call option prices for an 18.00 at-the-money BHP call as a function of time to expiry.

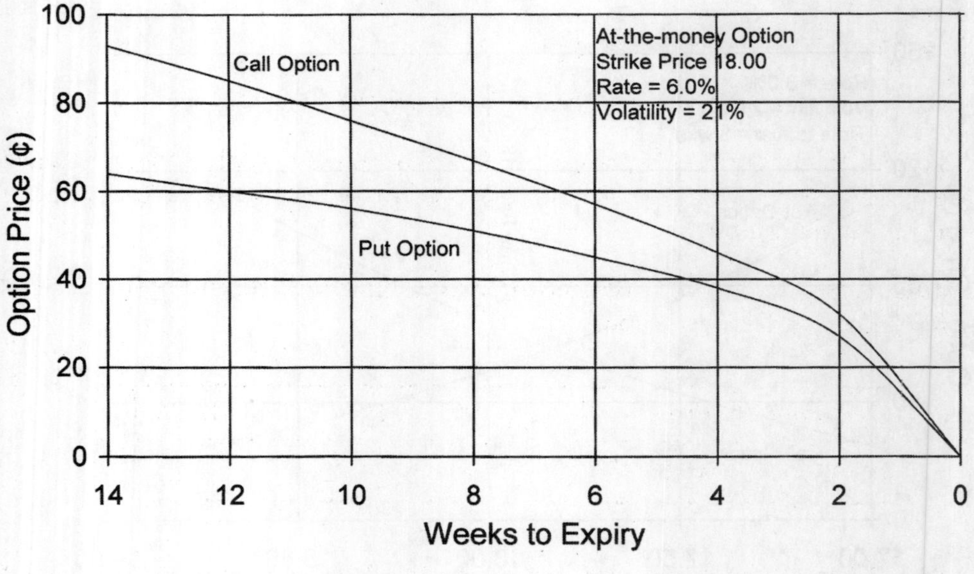

Figure 4.2 Option Price vs Time to Expiry

The option price falls linearly with time until about four weeks to expiry, after which it falls more quickly. In practice, during the last few weeks of trading, out-of-the-money options develop an inertia, and small rises in the stock price have little effect in raising the call option price, while small falls in the stock price have little effect in raising the put option price.

Sensitivity to Risk-free Interest Rate (Rho)

Rho = change in option price for a 1% change in interest rates

The risk-free interest rate is the rate that an investor could earn on money placed in a term deposit for the same length of time as the option has to expiry.

Option prices are not particularly sensitive to changes in the risk-free interest rate. Consider a call option with strike price = 18.50, stock price = \$18.00, time to expiry = eight weeks and volatility = 21%. The corresponding option prices for a range of interest rates r are shown below.

r (%)	5	6	7	8	9
Option Price (¢)	43	45	46	47	48

Sensitivity to Volatility (Vega)

Vega = change in the option price for a 1% change in stock volatility

The stock volatility is defined in the BSOPM discussed previously. It was noted that the value of the historic volatility is not constant, but is dependent on the number of data used in its calculation.

The volatility was calculated for BHP using daily data up to the end of January 1997, and the following values were obtained.

Number of Days	25	50	75	100
Historic Volatility (%)	19	23	24	25

On 29.1.97 BHP closed at \$17.97 and the March 18.50 call option was 41¢. Using the BSOPM with r = 6.0%, the theoretical option prices obtained for the listed volatility values are shown overleaf.

Volatility (%)	19	20	21	23	25
Price (¢)	38	41	43	48	54

This list shows that the option price is very sensitive to the volatility. The market value of 41¢ is obtained when the volatility is 20, i.e. the market is using an implied volatility of 20% for this option.

Sensitivity to Market Mood

The market mood has an effect on the option price, and in a rising market a call option will have a higher time component than in a flat market. This increase in option price is to be expected as the market is factoring in an increase in the future volatility of the stock.

Sensitivity to Strike Price

Figure 4.3 below gives BSOPM prices for various BHP put and call options having different strike prices, but the same time to expiry, and shows the gradual fall in the option price moving from in-the-money to out-of-the-money cases.

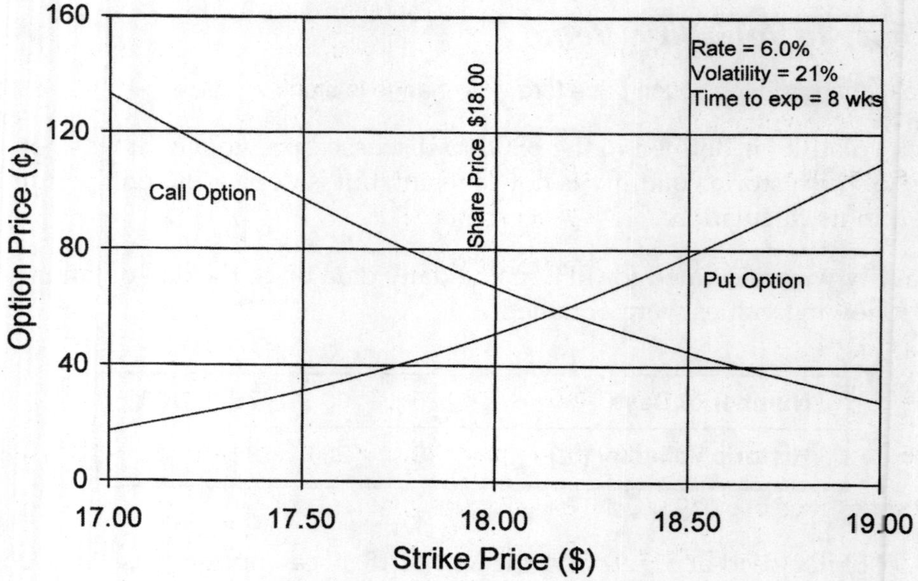

Figure 4.3 Option Price vs Strike Price

Option Prices for Differently-Priced Stocks

If two stocks have the same volatility then their at-the-money option prices with the same time to expiry will be proportional to the stock prices.

Suppose BHP is at $18.00 and RIO is at $19.00, and the market is using the same implied volatility for both stocks, then if an at-the-money BHP call option is 67¢, the RIO at-the-money call option with the same time to expiry should be about $67 \times \frac{19}{18} = 71$¢.

OPTIONS BEHAVIOUR ON FAST SHARE PRICE MOVES

The heavyweight resource shares often move quickly in response to sharp fluctuations in metal prices, and to perceived and actual profit results.

For example, in June 1996 the price of copper fell some 25% due to the Sumitomo Corp futures debacle, and the BHP share price fell from around $19.00 to around $17.00 in the space of five weeks. July saw the fall continue to $16.00 but then rally to $17.50 in August. Come September and the AGM and the market was reassessing BHP's bottom line profit due to the continuing low price of copper—and BHP fell again, below $16.00. September is a month when major BHP option series expire, so these moves in excess of $1.00 late in the month of September caused some options to double or treble in the space of a few days.

When these large stock price changes occur, it is useful to know which of the options presents the best trading profits. Table 4.2 overleaf lists BSOPM call option values in cents for the following conditions:

BHP share price of: $17.00 with 8 weeks to expiry
$18.00 with 7 weeks to expiry
$19.00 with 6 weeks to expiry

Rate = 6.0%

Volatility = 21%

Strike price 17.50, 18.00 and 18.50

Also listed are the BSOPM put option values for the same conditions but with:

BHP share price of: $19.00 with 8 weeks to expiry
$18.00 with 7 weeks to expiry
$17.00 with 6 weeks to expiry

The Move (%) column in the table is the change in option price reading from left to right across a row. Thus an option price change from 41¢ to 92¢ is a move of 124%, and from 92¢ to 169¢ is 84%.

Table 4.2 Call and Put Option Prices on Fast Share Moves

Share Price ($)	17.00	18.00	19.00	Move (%)	
Weeks to Expiry	8	7	6		
17.50 call option	41	92	169	124	84
18.00 call option	25	63	127	152	102
17.50 call option	14	40	90	186	125
Share Price ($)	**19.00**	**18.00**	**17.00**	**Move (%)**	
Weeks to Expiry	**8**	**7**	**6**		
18.50 put option	33	75	150	127	100
18.00 put option	19	48	105	153	119
17.50 put option	10	28	70	180	150

Considering the 18.00 call option, a share price rise from $17.00 to $18.00 gives an option price rise of 152%, while a share price rise from $18.00 to $19.00 gives an option price rise of 102%.

Similarly, for the 18.00 put option, a share price fall from $19.00 to $18.00 gives an option price rise of 153%, while a share price fall from $18.00 to $17.00 gives an option price rise of 119%.

For the call options, when the share price is $17.00 the 18.00 call option is 2nd out-of-the-money, and when the share price is $18.00 the same option is at-the-money.

These values demonstrate the general rule for put and call options in a fast-moving market:

> 2nd out-of-the-money options give a greater percentage gain than 1st out-of-the-money options, which give a greater percentage gain than at-the-money options (all other factors being equal).

The data from Table 4.2 is plotted in Figure 4.4 opposite using a semi-log scale.

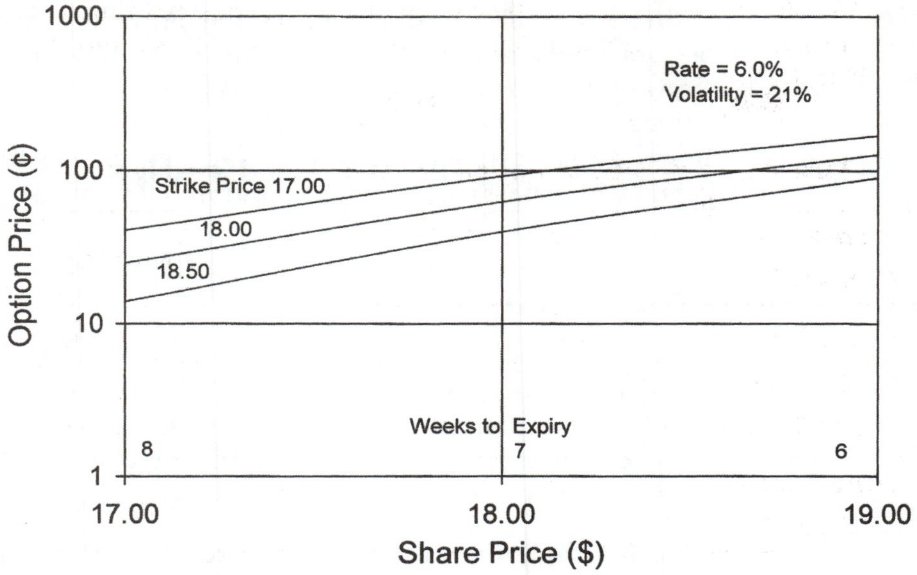

(a) Call Options

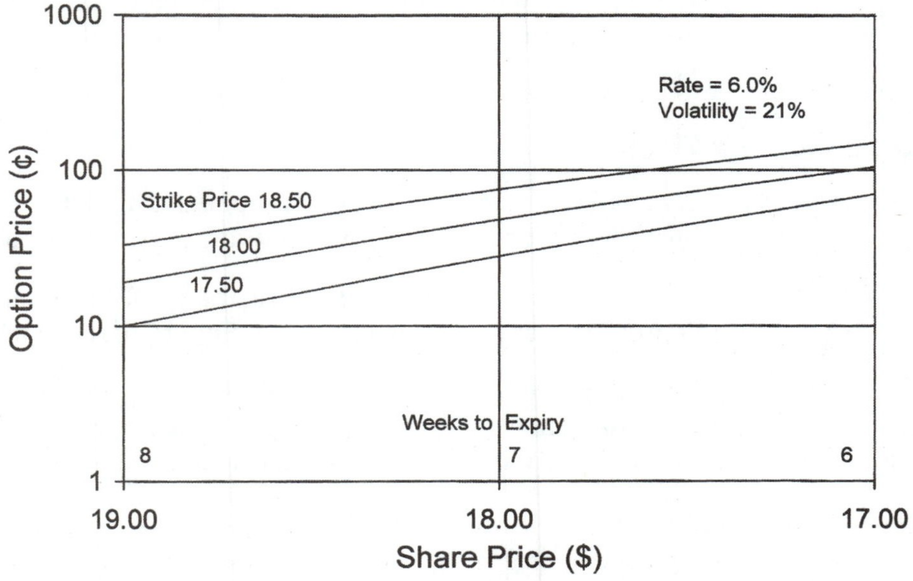

(b) Put Options

Figure 4.4 Option Price Behaviour on Fast Share Moves

An inspection of the data in the financial press shows that the most popular option series at any time are the 1st in-the-money, at-the-money and 1st out-of-the-money series. Thus, if we are buying options for a fast price move, it is preferable to purchase 1st out-of-the-money options, then if the market moves our way the options may become 1st in-the-money, and we can sell them to a ready supply of buyers. (Conversely, if the market moves against us, we may lose our initial purchase price.)

NOTE ON CHANGING VOLATILITY

The option charts in this chapter are based on a BHP share price around $18.00, risk-less rate 6% and volatility 21%, which were the prevailing values in January 1997. At the time of writing the third edition, September 2000, it is of interest to note that the values for BHP are a share price around $21.00, risk-less rate 5.0% and volatility around 25% after being as high as 45% during the October 1997 mini-crash.

The discerning reader who has digested this chapter will realise that changes in volatility can be a cause for concern. If volatility increases, while all the other parameters remain the same, then the value of both the put and call options will increase. This works against us if we have written options at a lower volatility. Conversely, if after we write options the volatility falls, then the value of the options will also fall thereby hastening our profit.

OPTIONS SOFTWARE

Options software is readily available from a number of suppliers. This software may be a single program, or it may be a part of a much larger charting and analysis package.

All the option charts in this book have been calculated using the BSOPM contained in the QuickOptions module from the larger Omega Research SuperCharts4 package.

Figure 4.5 opposite is a sample printout from the program showing the input data and the corresponding output data. If we input the option price the program calculates the volatility, while if we input the volatility the program calculates the option price.

Details of software suppliers are given in Chapter 18.

The ASX website www.asx.com.au states at the time of writing that an option pricing model will be available soon for downloading.

Interested readers can build their own BSOPM using an Excel spreadsheet. The various components of the formula given on page 22 can be calculated, where:

N(d) the normal distribution is equated as the Excel function NORMSDIST(d)

ln(S/X) the natural logarithm is equated as the Excel function LN(S/X)

	<A>
Asset Sym	BHP
Option Sym	
Model	Equity
Rate	6.0
Dividend	0.00
Calc Date	01/01/97
Exp Date	02/26/97
Strike	1800.0000
Underlying	1797.0000
Option Type	Long Call
Option Price	65.7249
Volatility	21.0000
Delta	0.5541
Gamma	0.0028
Theta	-0.6767
Vega	2.7838
Days Left	56

Input data

Calculated data

Enter price,
calculate volatility,
OR
Enter volatility,
calculate price.

Figure 4.5 Sample Printout of Option Software Calculation

Chapter 5

OPTION PRICE PLOTS

IN THIS CHAPTER, call option price plots are given for the major option stocks News Corp, Telstra, AMP, BHP, RIO, WMC, Normandy, Woodside, ANZ, CBA, NAB and Westpac. A put option price plot is also given for BHP.

The plots are calculated using price data from the latter part of September 2000. It is necessary to select values for implied volatility for each of the stocks, and ways of making this selection are discussed in Chapter 4. Further, most stockbrokers have software which gives immediate access to the volatility values being used by the RTs. The approach taken in this chapter is to select a day at the end of September 2000 with reasonably steady prices, and get from a stockbroker the RT list of implied volatilities being used by the RTs for the required stocks. Then using the BSOPM and a risk-free rate of 5.0%, the implied volatilities are checked against the at-the-money and 1st out-of-the-money call options prices for series with about four to eight weeks to expiry (and taking into account any dividends during that time). If there are discrepancies between the RT and BSOPM values of implied volatility for a stock, preference is given to the BSOPM value.

The Australian Financial Review prints a list of the option prices each day, along with the RT closing buyer and seller quotes, plus the volatility used that produces these buyer and seller quotes.

Table 5.1 opposite lists the relevant data used in generating the option plots.

The table shows that NDY has the highest volatility at 45%, followed by NCP at 41%, while AMP and the banks have the lowest volatility in the 18% to 20% range. The remaining stocks have volatilities between 25% and 34%. It should be stressed that these implied volatilities are not fixed, but can and do change over a period of time.

In September 1996 the implied volatility for BHP was 16%, at January 1997 it was 21%, at October 1997 after the mini-crash it was 45%, at October 1998 it was 29%, and at the time of writing in September 2000 it was 25%. Similarly, at October 1988 the four banks had volatilities around 30%, while at September 2000 their volatilities were around 20%.

Table 5.1 Data for Generating Option Plots

Stock	Volatility (%)	At-the-money Price ($)	Strike Price Intervals (¢)	Strike Increment/ Stock Price (%)
NCP	41	24.50	50	2.0
TLS	25	6.00	25	4.2
AMP	18	17.00	50	2.9
BHP	25	21.00	50	2.4
RIO	30	25.50	50	2.0
WMC	34	7.50	25	3.3
NDY	45	1.00	10 & 25	10 & 25
WPL	29	14.00	50	3.4
ANZ	19	12.50	50	4.0
CBA	19	27.00	50	1.9
NAB	20	24.50	50	2.0
WBC	20	12.50	50	4.0

The last column in Table 5.1 lists the ratio of strike price increment to stock price expressed as a percentage. NCP has a ratio of $\frac{100 \times 0.50}{24.50} = 2.0\%$. TLS and NDY have the largest ratios, and in practice this means that their 2nd out-of-the money options are a long way from the stock price, resulting in small time premiums which are probably unprofitable. Thus, for these two stocks we are limited to writing 1st out-of-the-money options, and only when the option strike price is not a full increment away from the stock price (see Figures 5.4 and 5.8). NDY is unusual in that the strike price increments below $1.00 are 10¢, while the strike price increments above $1.00 are 25¢.

Figure 5.1 (overleaf) shows the call option plots for BHP, while Figure 5.2 (on page 39) plots BHP put options. The values from these two plots show that for the at-the-money and 1st out-of-the-money options, the value of the put is:

put option = approximately 0.80 x call option

Only call option plots are given for the remainder of the stocks, but the put option values can be approximated using the above relationship.

The plots shown are valid at September 2000, but obviously the stock prices will change with time. BHP is likely to be $25.00 some time in the future, but if we assume the volatility remains the same, the new option prices can be approximated from the given plots by using a scaling factor of $\frac{25.00}{21.00}$.

As an example of reading the option plots, Figure 5.1 shows the BHP option price as a function of weeks to expiry and strike price. The share price is held constant at $21.00. With eight weeks to expiry the at-the-money (21.00 strike price) call option is 90¢, and the 1st out-of-the-money (21.50 strike price) call option is 67¢. Similarly, using Figure 5.2, with eight weeks to expiry the at-the-money (21.00 strike price) put option is 74¢, and the 1st out-of-the-money (20.50 strike price) put option is 52¢.

Inspection of the charts shows that if the stock price remains fixed during the life of the option, then the option prices for in-the-money and out-of-the-money options fall fairly uniformly with time. However, the fall in at-the-money options accelerates during the final three to four weeks to expiry.

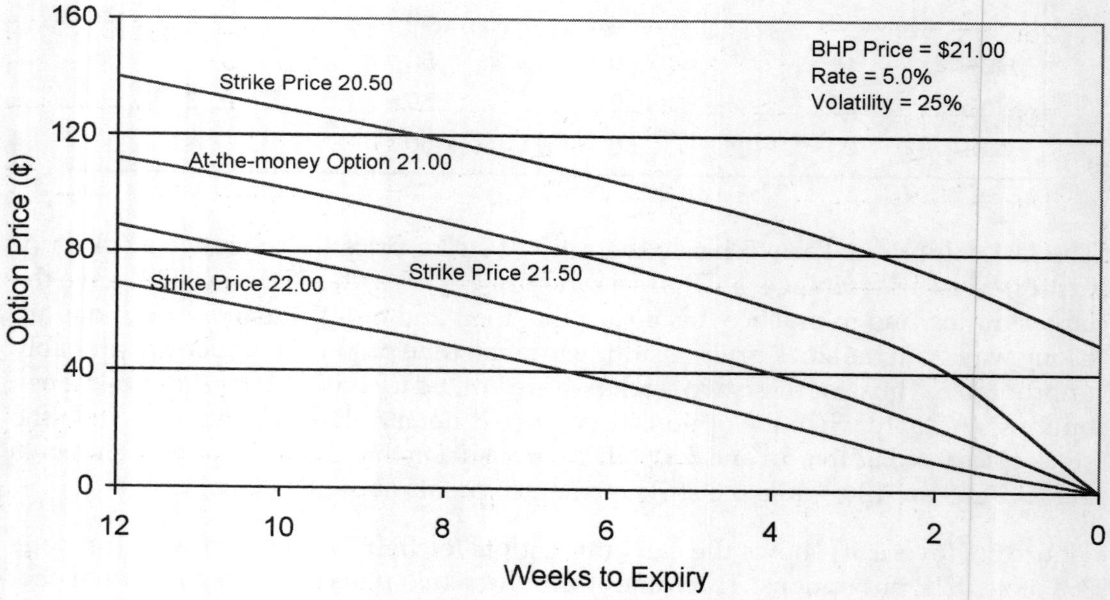

Figure 5.1 BHP Call Options vs Weeks to Expiry

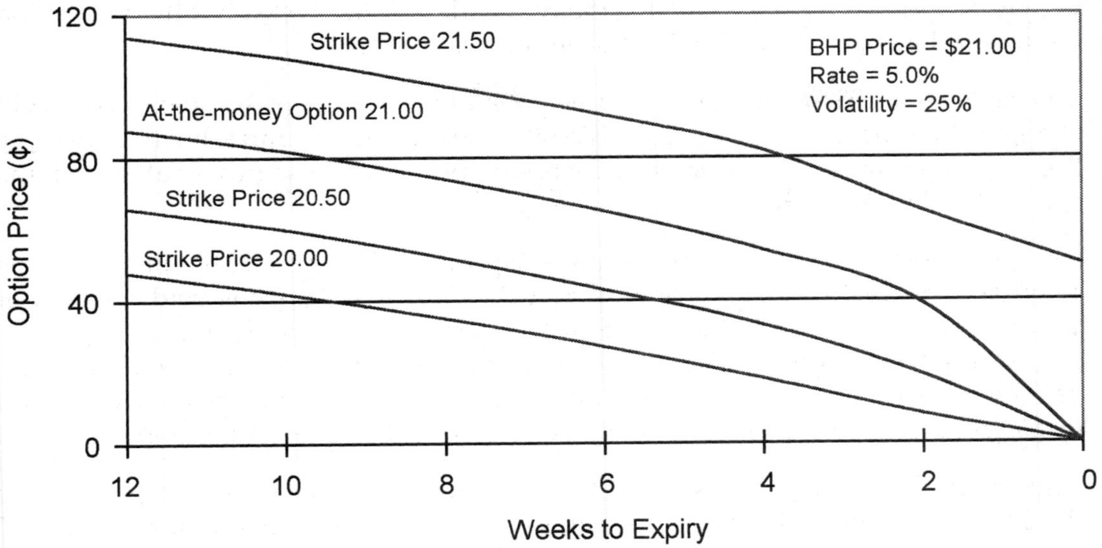

Figure 5.2 BHP Put Options vs Weeks to Expiry

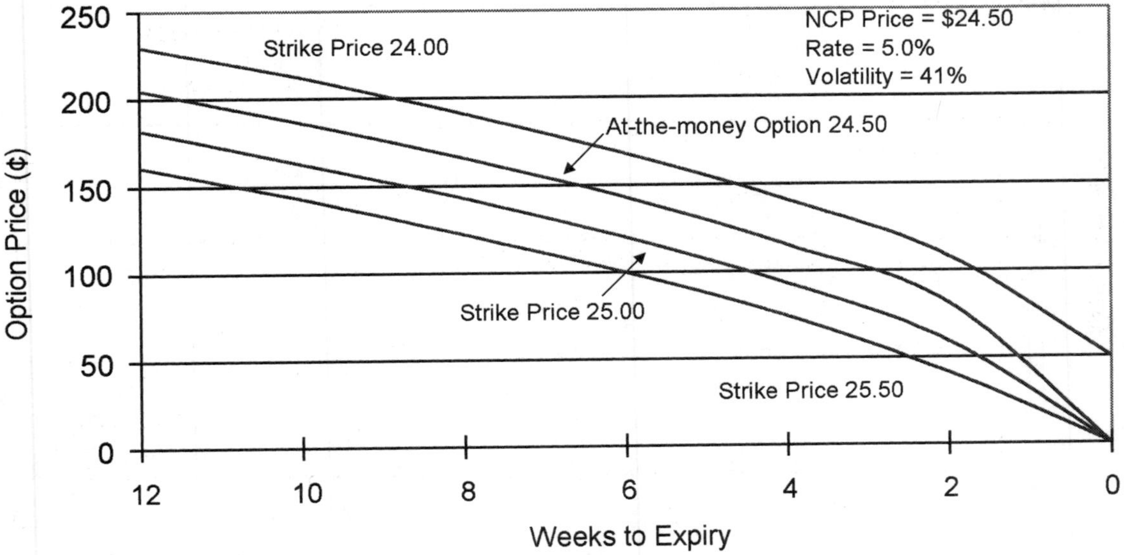

Figure 5.3 NCP Call Options vs Weeks to Expiry

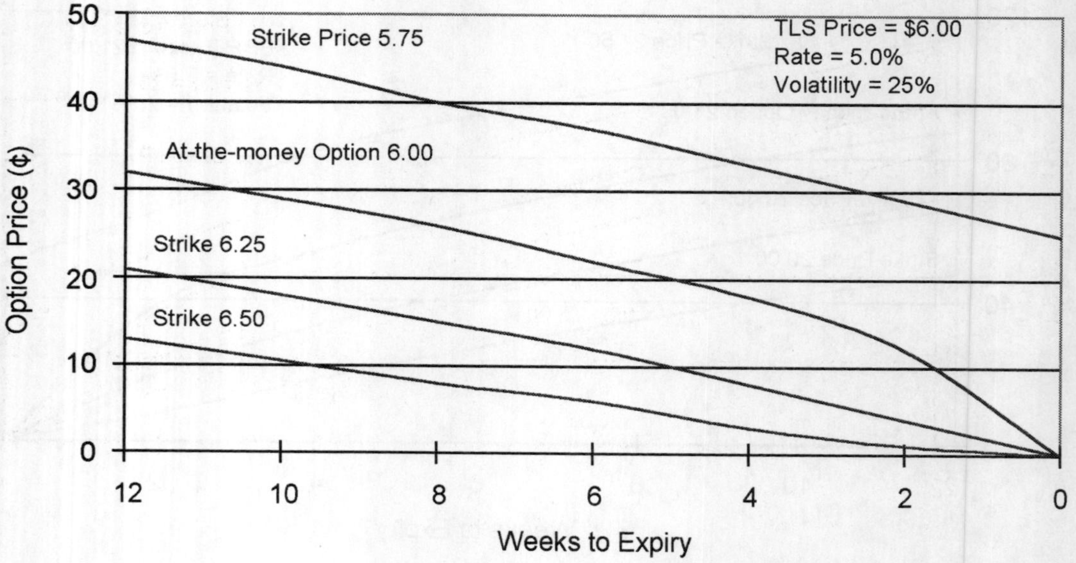

Figure 5.4 TLS Call Options vs Weeks to Expiry

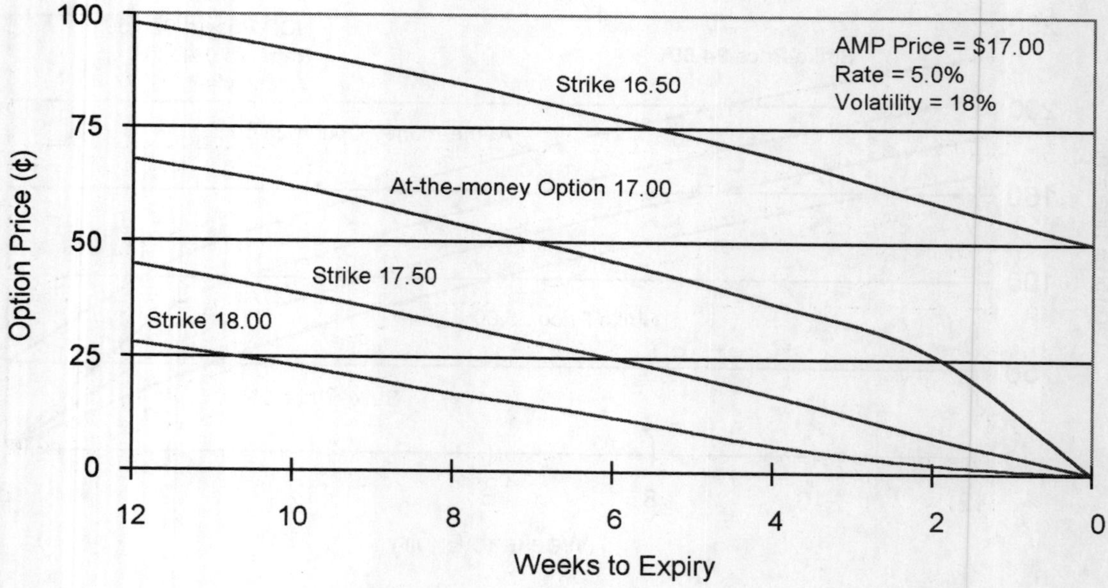

Figure 5.5 AMP Call Options vs Weeks to Expiry

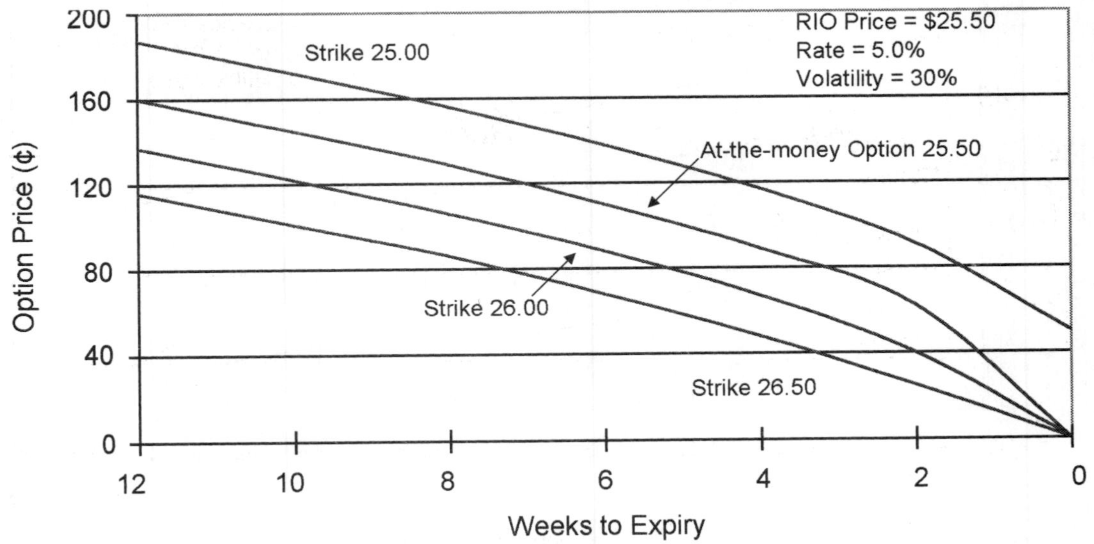

Figure 5.6 RIO Call Options vs Weeks to Expiry

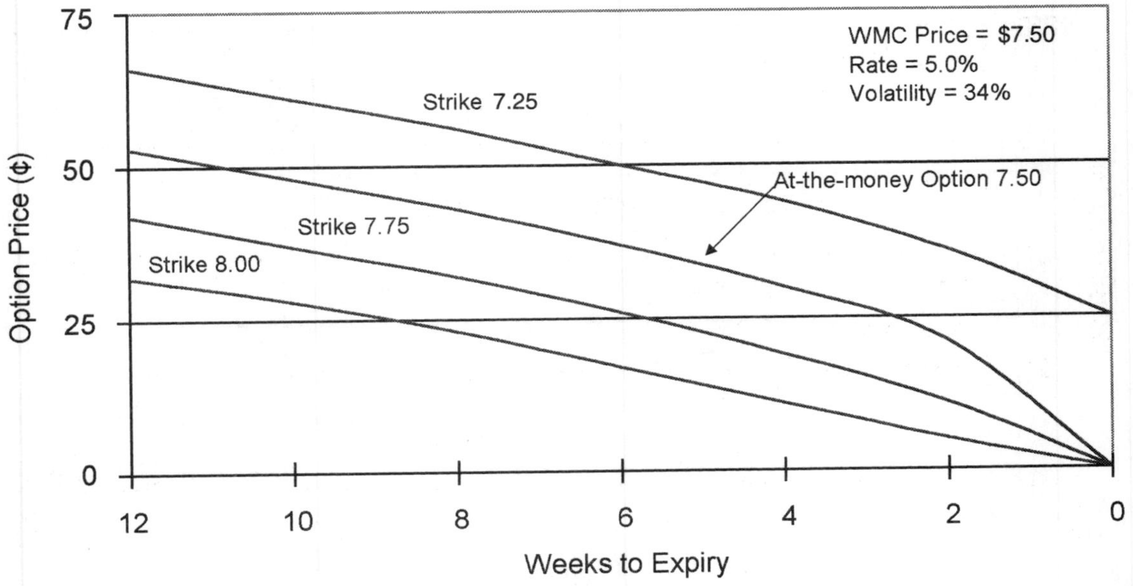

Figure 5.7 WMC Call Options vs Weeks to Expiry

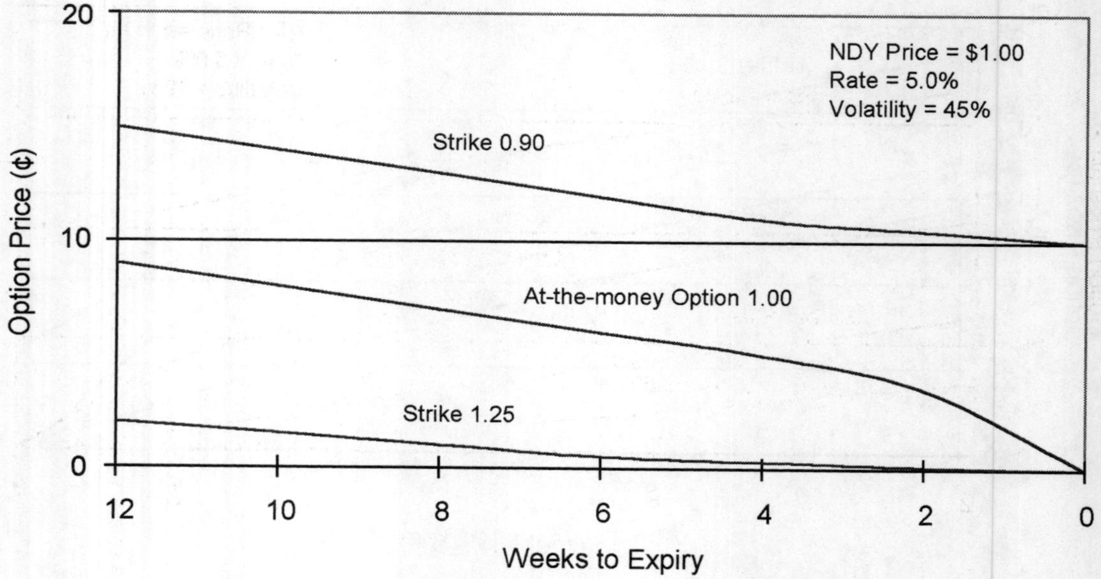

Figure 5.8 NDY Call Options vs Weeks to Expiry

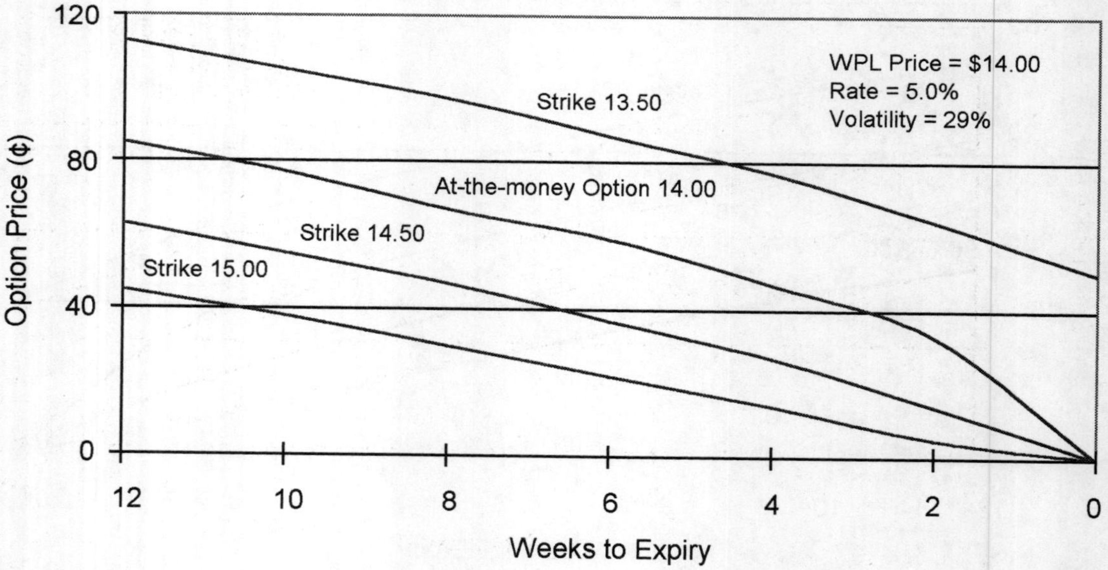

Figure 5.9 WPL Call Options vs Weeks to Expiry

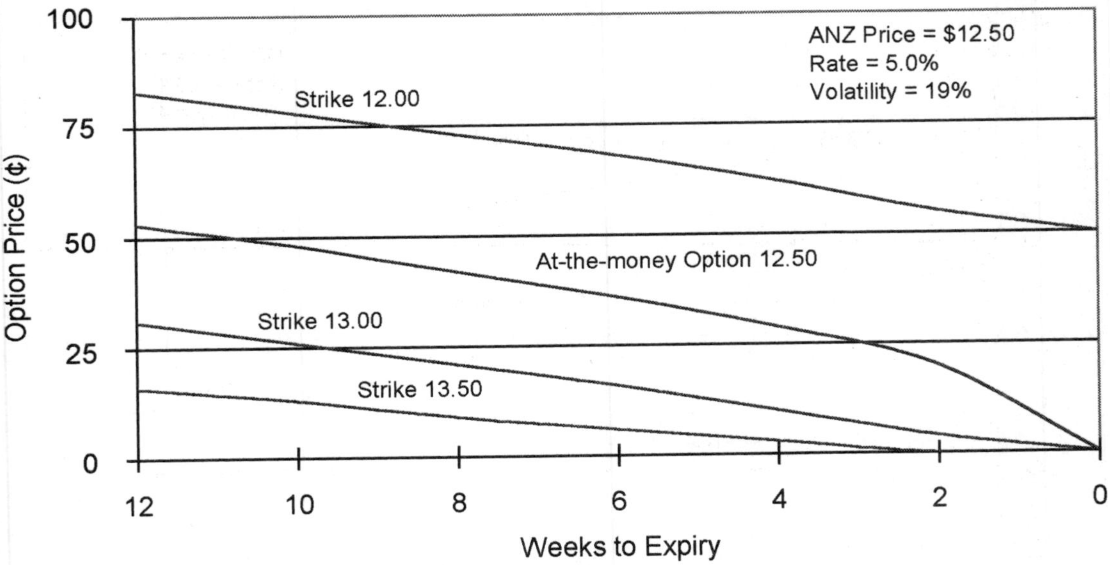

Figure 5.10 ANZ Call Options vs Weeks to Expiry

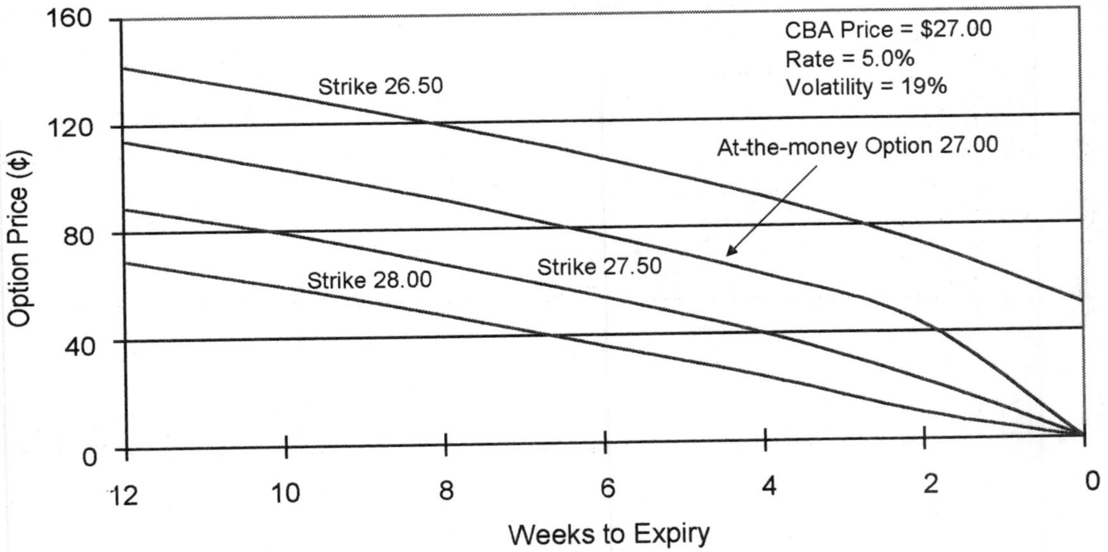

Figure 5.11 CBA Call Options vs Weeks to Expiry

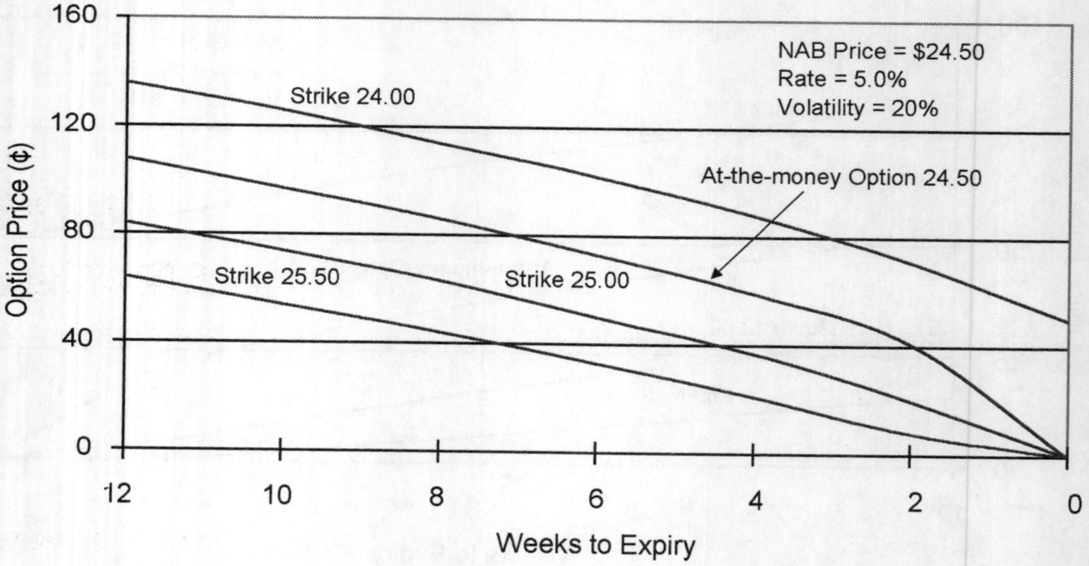

Figure 5.12 NAB Call Options vs Weeks to Expiry

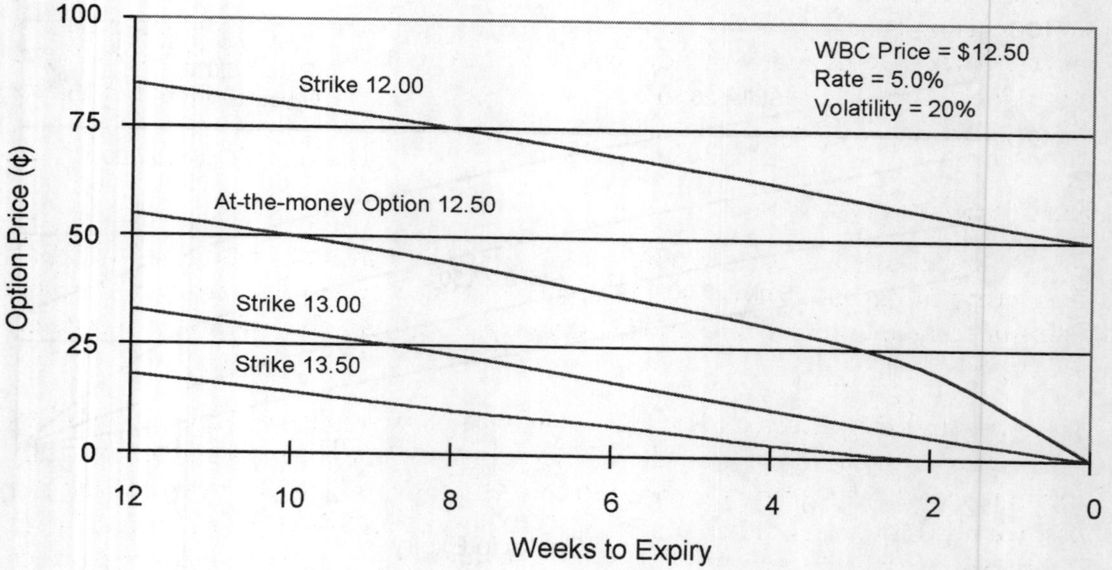

Figure 5.13 WBC Call Options vs Weeks to Expiry

Chapter 6

THE TRADING STRATEGY

IT IS NECESSARY to draw a distinction between a trading system and a trading strategy.

Trading System

Chapter 9 discusses some technical indicators used to determine stock trends, and some charting techniques commonly used to predict the direction and size of stock moves. After careful consideration and testing, a selection of these indicators and techniques is made. This selection is the trading system, which is used to determine the stock trends, and to choose those signals with a high probability of success.

Trading Strategy

Our trading strategy is based upon writing naked put and call options, and buying long-term put and call warrants. The choice of which option or warrant to trade is determined by market risk and money management principles, which are discussed in Chapter 14.

It is imperative that before writing put or call options, a defensive strategy be worked out, in case the market should turn sharply in the wrong direction and place the option in jeopardy of being exercised. If this strategy is to buy the options back at a loss, we need to do our sums in advance to know what loss is incurred in a 50¢ or $1.00 stock move against us. Alternatively, if we write puts, we may decide in advance that as the stock is so close to its bottom support levels, we will be happy to be exercised, and then write call options against the stock (see Chapter 7).

It is generally safest to write options that have six to ten weeks to expiry, as this allows the option to have a worthwhile time premium, but is short enough for current market conditions to prevail during the life of the option. Conversely, it is safest to choose warrants with more than, say, six months to expiry, but sometimes only shorter-term warrants will be available. If the market moves in our favour we quit the warrant at a profit, with little erosion of the time premium. Should the market move against us, there is time for the market to recover before the warrant expires.

For the trading system and strategy to be successful, the trades need to be profitable at least 70% of the time.

FALLING STOCK

When a stock is falling, the natural response is to buy put options. However, a safer strategy is to write call options.

The bought put option will only generate a profit if the stock falls sharply during the life of the option, while the written call option can return a profit if the market falls, moves sideways or slightly upwards (for out-of-the-money options).

Opening Strategy

When the trading system signals the start of a new downtrend:

1. Write out-of-the-money call options having expiry of six to ten weeks.

If we are confident that the stock is at the start of a major downtrend:

2. Buy put warrants with preferably about six months to expiry.

If we anticipate a short-term fast fall in the stock price:

3. Buy at-the-money or out-of-the-money put options. (This trade is really a gamble, and should only be taken for a specific reason such as discussed in Chapter 4.)

Defensive Strategy

1. If the stock rises the written call options may become in-the-money with the risk of being exercised.

Before this happens it is prudent to cancel our liability in the following ways:

a) If we feel that the stock direction has definitely turned from bearish to bullish, then buy back the call options and take a loss on the transaction.

b) If we feel that the stock has almost reached the top of a reversal correction after which the downtrend will continue, then wait for confirmation of either the reversal, or the beginning of a new uptrend, before quitting the option.

c) If we feel that the stock is in a downtrend and the up move is definitely only a correction, but the stock price rise brings the option to being in-the-money and at risk of being exercised, then the strategy is to roll the call option up. We do this by buying back the initial call options, and writing the same number (or more) of the next, higher, strike price call options. The loss from buying back the initial calls is offset by the credit from writing the new calls.

   This strategy will work once, but if the stock continues to rise it may be necessary to buy the second calls back, and so effectively take a double loss. A detailed numerical example of the rolling up defensive strategy is given in Chapter 7.

2. If the stock rises after buying put warrants they will lose value. It is prudent to only buy put warrants when the stock is in the upper half of a trend channel (or similar pattern) so there is a limited upside risk, and potential for a worthwhile price fall.

3. If the stock rises after buying at-the-money or out-of-the-money put options, they will expire worthless.

For items 2 and 3, we should quit the trades at a loss as soon as we are sure that the initial downtrend has run its course.

Figure 6.1 overleaf is a flow chart of the strategy to employ with a falling stock.

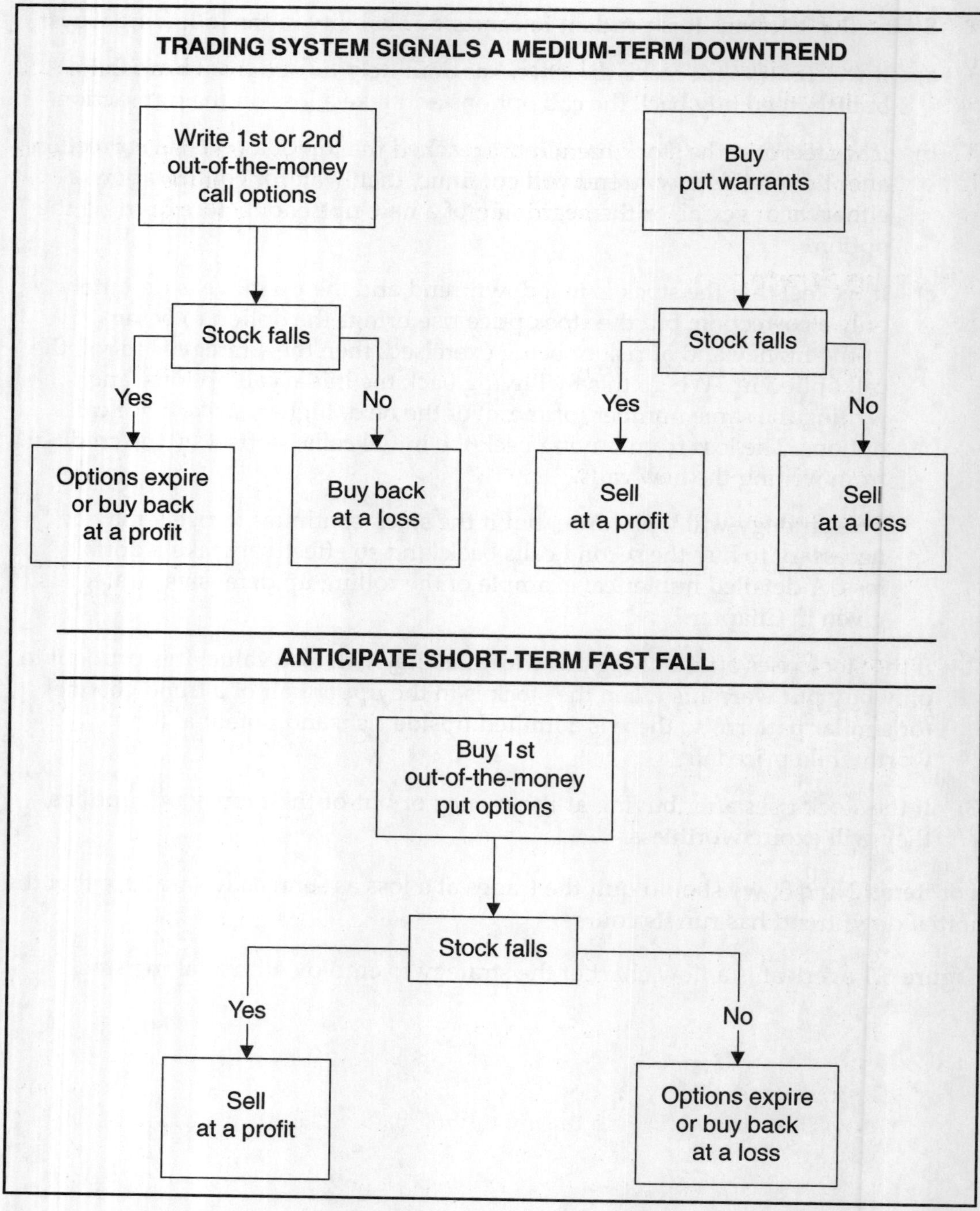

Figure 6.1 Trading Strategy and Outcomes for Falling Stock

RISING STOCK

When a stock is rising, the natural response is to buy call options. However, a safer strategy is to write put options.

The bought call option will only generate a profit if the stock rises sharply during the life of the option, while the written put option can return a profit if the market rises, moves sideways or slightly downwards (for out-of-the-money options).

Opening Strategy

When the trading system signals the start of an uptrend:

1. Write out-of-the-money put options having expiry of six to ten weeks.

If we are confident that the stock is at the start of a major uptrend:

2. Buy call warrants with preferably about six months to expiry.

If we anticipate a short-term fast rise in the stock price:

3. Buy at-the-money or out-of-the-money call options. (This trade is really a gamble and should only be taken for a specific reason, as discussed in Chapter 4.)

Defensive Strategy

1. If the stock falls the written put options may become in-the-money with the risk of being exercised. Before this happens it is prudent to cancel our liability in the following ways:
   a) If we feel that the stock direction has definitely turned from bullish to bearish, then buy back the put options and take a loss on the transaction.
   b) If we feel that the stock has almost reached the bottom of a reversal correction after which the uptrend will continue, then wait for confirmation of either the reversal, or the beginning of a new downtrend, before quitting the option.
   c) If we feel that the stock is in an uptrend and the down move is definitely only a correction, but the stock price fall brings the option to being in-the-money and at risk of being exercised, then the strategy is to roll the put option down. We do this by buying back the initial put options, and writing the same number (or more) of the next, lower, strike price put options. The loss from buying back the initial puts is offset by the credit from writing the new puts.

This strategy will work once, but if the stock continues to fall it may be necessary to buy the second puts back, and so effectively take a double loss.

A detailed numerical example of the rolling down defensive strategy is given in Chapter 7.

2. If the stock falls after buying call warrants they will lose value. It is prudent to only buy call warrants when the stock is in the lower half of a trend channel (or similar pattern) so there is limited downside risk, and potential for a worthwhile price rise.
3. If the stock falls after buying at-the-money or out-of-the-money call options, they will expire worthless.

For items 2 and 3, we should quit the trades at a loss as soon as we are sure that the initial uptrend has run its course.

Figure 6.2 opposite is a flow chart of the strategy to employ with a rising stock.

OTHER DEFENSIVE MEASURES

The major disadvantage in writing naked options is that should the market move strongly against us, we face a loss which grows while the market continues its unfavourable move. (We try to avoid this situation by prudently closing our trades as soon as the written options become in-the-money.) A variety of defensive strategies can be used to limit the loss if the stock price moves adversely. These strategies typically involve opening two option trades at the same time and are called "spreads". These spreads have descriptive names such as bull spreads, bear spreads, ratio spreads, calendar spreads, straddles, strangles and butterflies, etc. The advantage of spreads is that they limit the loss if the stock price moves badly against us, while the disadvantage is that they erode the available profit even when we pick the trend correctly.

Appendix II gives a comprehensive discussion of bull and bear spread strategies, and compares them to the basic strategies of writing or buying options as discussed to date. The spread strategies can work well provided the options involved are heavily traded, thereby allowing the spreads to be opened and closed at our discretion with close bid/ask quotes. For variety, and to extend the scope of the discussion, Appendix II gives numerical examples and pay-off diagrams for the very popular options on the London FTSE 100 index. All the examples given are calculated on the basis of the FTSE 100 trading at 6550 points, thereby allowing a practical comparison of the various strategies as the underlying index moves up and down.

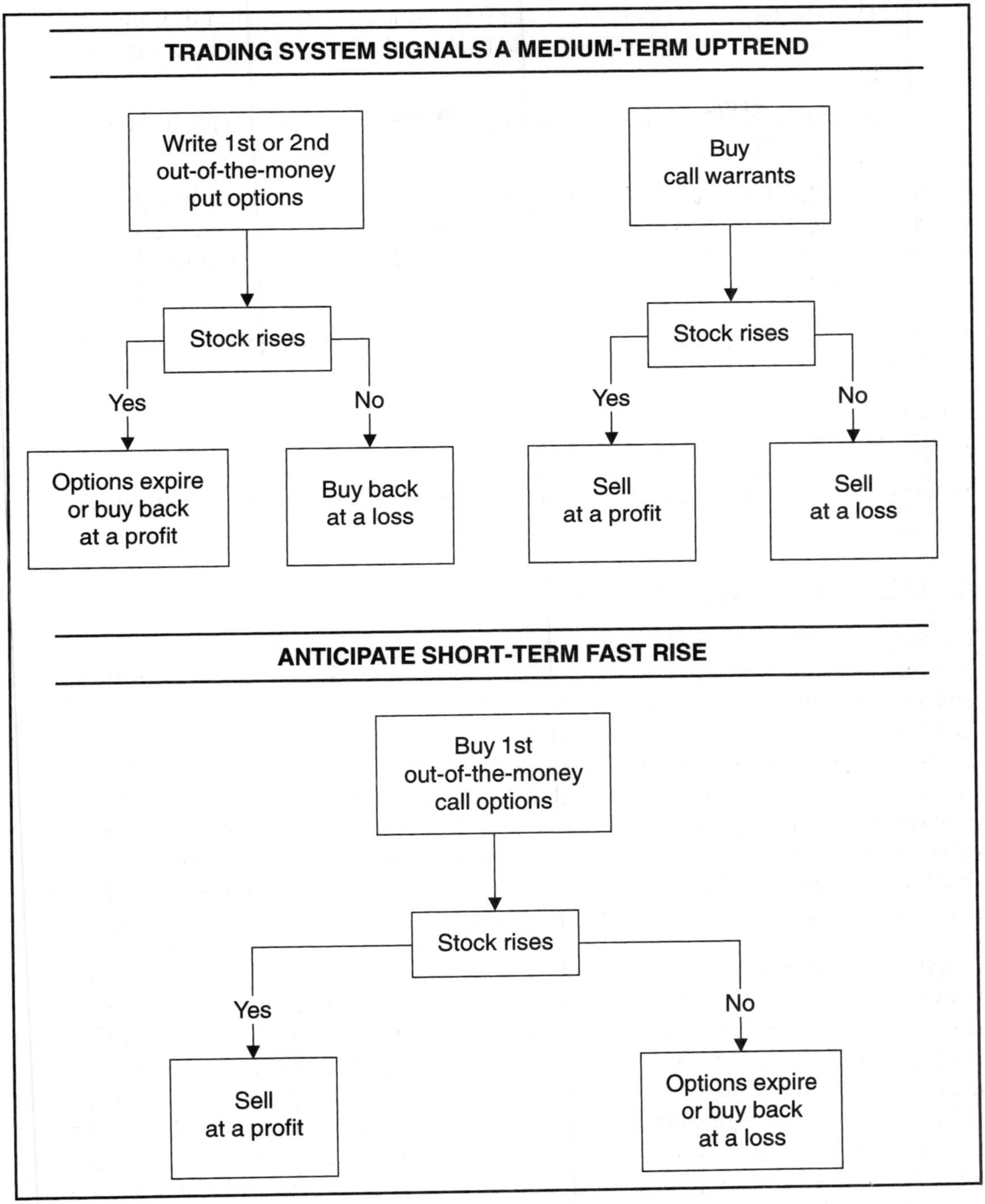

Figure 6.2 Trading Strategy and Outcomes for Rising Stock

Chapter 7

A PRACTICAL EXAMPLE: TRADING WITH BHP OPTIONS

THIS CHAPTER WORKS through several numerical examples, and shows the steps involved in trading BHP put and call options with various strike prices. We look at the cost of being exercised, and the credit/debit calculations in setting up defensive strategies with various times to expiry. All examples are based on BHP priced at $21.00 when the trade is opened. The initial trade is to write five options with eight weeks to expiry, and the defensive strategy is implemented two or four weeks later.

Writing five BHP options is equivalent to controlling about $105,000 of stock, and is the amount of money involved if the options are exercised.

To set up the defensive strategy of rolling the call options up or the put options down, we need a quick reference table of option prices versus share price. Table 7.1 opposite lists the call option prices with eight, six and four weeks to expiry with BHP prices of $21.00, $21.50 and $22.00, and option strike prices of 21.00, 21.50, 22.00 and 22.50. Once again, the option values are calculated using the BSOPM with BHP volatility of 25% and a risk-free rate of 5.0%.

The option prices move diagonally downwards through the table from left to right, i.e. BHP at $21.00 and strike price of 21.00 gives a similar option price as BHP at $21.50 and strike price at 21.50, etc. The first column of option prices are identical to those plotted in Figure 5.1.

Table 7.1 BHP Call Option Prices

BHP Price ($)	21.00	21.50	22.00
8 Weeks to Expiry			
21.00 call	90 (¢)	120 (¢)	154 (¢)
21.50 call	67	92	122
22.00 call	49	69	94
22.50 call	34	50	71
6 Weeks to Expiry			
21.00 call	77	107	142
21.50 call	54	79	109
22.00 call	37	56	81
22.50 call	24	39	58
4 Weeks to Expiry			
21.00 call	62	92	128
21.50 call	40	63	93
22.00 call	24	41	65
22.50 call	14	26	43

FALLING STOCK: WRITING NAKED CALL OPTIONS

We write call options if we expect the stock to fall.

Risk-Return for 2nd Out-of-the-money Option

With BHP trading at $21.00, write five BHP 22.00 call options with about eight weeks to expiry. Table 7.1 shows the option price is 49¢, so our credit is 5 x 490 = $2,450 less brokerage of $50 for a net of $2,400. If BHP is less than $22.00 at expiry the options expire worthless and we pocket the $2,400.

Defensive Strategy

The options are likely to be exercised if BHP rises above $22.00.

(In practice, this rise of $1.00, or 4.8%, may well signal a change in trend, and we would quit the downtrend trade and consider opening a new uptrend trade. However, we work through the calculations as an illustration of the costs involved in setting up the defensive strategy.)

If we are exercised, we have to buy the shares on the open market at the going price and deliver them at the strike price of $22.00. This incurs a loss as the market price will be greater than $22.00. We are insulated a little by the 49¢ credit received from selling the options.

The total exercise transaction consists of buying the 5,000 shares on the open market and then delivering them to the option exerciser. The related costs are:

	Credit $	Debit $
Option write net premium	2,400	
Share purchase brokerage (on $105,000)		100
Option exercise brokerage (on $105,000)		100
Net credit	2,200	

The net credit equates to 44¢ per share. Thus, an overall loss is incurred if we have to purchase the shares above $22.44 for delivery at $22.00. (In this, and subsequent calculations, we neglect stamp duty and OCH option charges.)

To alleviate this loss we could roll the option up by repurchasing the 22.00 options, and writing a new out-of-the-money option series. By rolling up we distance ourselves from the rising BHP price and avoid being exercised, provided BHP does not rise above the new option strike price.

Depending on the number of new options written, the loss can be converted to a smaller loss or to a credit situation.

Roll Up After Two Weeks

Suppose that two weeks after we write the options, BHP rises to $22.00. Table 7.1 shows that when BHP rises from $21.00 to $22.00, the 22.00 call option rises from the initial 49¢ to about 81¢, for a loss of 81 – 49 = 32¢. If we choose to write the new 1st out-of-the-money option, it now has a 22.50 strike price with value of 58¢. Thus, writing five new options converts the loss to a credit of 58 – 32 = 26¢ per option. The credit/debit calculation is shown at the top of the next page.

	Credit $	Debit $
Write 5 22.00 options 8-week expiry @ 49¢	2,450	
Brokerage		50
Buy 5 22.00 options 6-week expiry @ 81¢		4,050
Brokerage		50
Write 5 22.50 options 6-week expiry @ 58¢	2,900	
Brokerage		50
Total	5,350	4,200
Net credit	1,150	

Roll Up After Four Weeks

As a second example of rolling up, suppose that four weeks after we write the options BHP rises to $22.00. Table 7.1 shows that when BHP rises from $21.00 to $22.00, the 22.00 call option rises from its initial 49¢ to 65¢, for a loss of 65 – 49 = 16¢. If we roll up to the new 1st out-of-the-money option with 22.50 strike price the value is 43¢, so writing five new options converts the loss to a credit of 43 – 16 = 27¢ per option. The credit/debit calculation is:

	Credit $	Debit $
Write 5 22.00 options 8-week expiry @ 49¢	2,450	
Brokerage		50
Buy 5 22.00 options 4-week expiry @ 65¢		3,250
Brokerage		50
Write 5 22.50 options 4-week expiry @ 43¢	2,150	
Brokerage		50
Total	4,600	3,400
Net credit	1,200	

With only four weeks to expiry, it may be preferable to roll up and also roll out to the next time series. Suppose that four weeks after we write the options BHP rises to $22.00, and the 22.00 call option is 65¢ for a loss of 65 – 49 = 16¢. The new 1st out-of-the-money option is 22.50 strike price, and if we roll out to the next time series the time to expiry is about eight weeks. Table 7.1 shows this option is 71¢. Writing five new options, the credit/debit calculation is:

	Credit $	Debit $
Write 5 22.00 options 8-week expiry @ 49¢	2,450	
Brokerage		50
Buy 5 22.00 options 4-week expiry @ 65¢		3,250
Brokerage		50
Write 5 22.50 options 8-week expiry @ 71¢	3,550	
Brokerage		50
Total	6,000	3,400
Net credit	2,600	

Risk-Return for 1st Out-of-the-money Option

With BHP trading at $21.00, write five BHP 21.50 call options with about eight weeks to expiry. Table 7.1 shows the option price is 67¢, so our credit is 5 x 670 = $3,350 less brokerage of $50 for a net of $3,300. If BHP is less than $21.50 at expiry the options expire worthless and we pocket the $3,300.

Defensive Strategy

The options are likely to be exercised if BHP rises above $21.50. Taking into account the option credit of $3,300 and total exercise brokerage costs of $200, this equates to 62¢ per share. Consequently, a loss is incurred if we have to purchase the shares above $22.12 for delivery at $21.50.

To alleviate this loss we could roll the option up by repurchasing the 21.50 options, and writing the new 1st out-of-the-money series.

Roll Up After Two Weeks

Suppose two weeks after we write the options BHP rises to $21.50. Table 7.1 shows that when BHP rises from $21.00 to $21.50, the 21.50 call option rises from an initial 67¢ to 79¢, for a loss of 79 – 67 = 12¢. The 1st out-of-the-money option is now 22.00 strike price and has a value of 56¢, so writing five new options converts the loss to a credit of about 56 – 12 = 44¢ per option.

We may feel that the stock is undergoing a normal pull-back and will soon continue its downward trend. In this case, we may be prepared to increase our exposure by repurchasing the initial five options, and then writing, say, seven new options to convert the loss to approximately the original credit situation (but at the risk of increased losses if we have to cover this new position). The credit/debit calculation is:

	Credit $	Debit $
Write 5 21.50 options 8-week expiry @ 67¢	3,350	
Brokerage		50
Buy 5 21.50 options 6-week expiry @ 79¢		3,950
Brokerage		50
Write 7 22.00 options 6-week expiry @ 56¢	3,920	
Brokerage		50
Total	7,270	4,100
Net credit	3,170	

The reader can calculate the new number of options to write to maintain a neutral or credit trade, if needing to roll up with four weeks to expiry, and also the credit if rolling up and rolling out to eight weeks to expiry.

Risk-Return for At-the-money Option

With BHP trading at $21.00, write five BHP 21.00 call options with about eight weeks to expiry. Table 7.1 shows the option price is 90¢, so our credit is 5 x 900 = $4,500 less brokerage of $50 for a net of $4,450. If BHP is less than $21.00 at expiry the options expire worthless and we pocket the $4,450.

Defensive Strategy

The options are likely to be exercised if BHP rises above $21.00. Taking into account the option credit of $4,450 and total exercise brokerage costs of $200, this equates to 85¢ per share. Consequently, a loss is incurred if we have to purchase the shares above $21.85 for delivery at $21.00.

To alleviate this loss we could roll the option up by repurchasing the 21.00 options, and writing new at-the-money options.

Roll Up After Two Weeks

Suppose two weeks after we sold the options BHP rises to $21.50, and we think it prudent to raise the exercise price to 21.50. Table 7.1 shows that when BHP rises from $21.00 to $21.50, the 21.00 call option rises from an initial 90¢ to 107¢, for a loss of 107 – 90 = 17¢. The at-the-money option is now 21.50 strike price and has a value of 79¢, so writing five new options converts the loss situation to a credit of about 79 – 17 = 62¢ per option.

Again, we may think the stock is undergoing a normal pullback and will soon continue its downward trend. Thus we may be prepared to increase our exposure by repurchasing the initial five options, and then write seven new options to regain the initial credit (but at the risk of increased losses if we have to cover this new position). The credit/debit calculation is:

	Credit $	Debit $
Write 5 21.00 options 8-week expiry @ 90¢	4,500	
Brokerage		50
Buy 5 21.00 options 6-week expiry @ 107¢		5,350
Brokerage		50
Write 7 21.50 options 6-week expiry @ 79¢	5,530	
Brokerage		50
Total	10,030	5,500
Net credit	4,530	

If we are exercised the total exercise brokerage is $200, reducing the net credit to $4,330, which equates to 62¢ per share for the 7,000 shares. The rolling up exercise has raised the break-even point on exercise from $21.85 to $22.12, and maintains a profit in excess of the original $4,450 if not exercised.

Risk-Return for Writing Naked Call Options

We can summarise the risk-return for the above three option cases by listing the profit against the safety margin, shown in Table 7.2 opposite. The safety margin is the amount that BHP shares must rise for our initial call options to be exercised at a loss, taking into account brokerage on purchase of the shares and delivery to the exerciser of the options.

Table 7.2 Safety Margin and Profit for Written Call Options

	Safety Margin (¢)	Profit per Trade ($)
2nd out-of-the-money	145	2,400
1st out-of-the-money	112	3,300
At-the-money	85	4,450

The safety margin for the 2nd and 1st out-of-the-money cases comprises strike price leeway plus time premium, while the at-the-money safety margin comprises only time premium.

The values used in the illustrative examples above suggest the 2nd or 1st out-of-the-money call options give a satisfactory compromise between risk and reward. For these options to incur a loss, the share price must move more than 145¢ or 112¢ respectively against us during the eight weeks to expiry.

RISING STOCK: WRITING PUT OPTIONS

We write put options if we expect the stock to rise. Once again, assume that BHP is $21.00 when we write the put options. Table 7.3 overleaf gives the put option prices with eight, six and four weeks to expiry, and corresponds to the call option cases of Table 7.1.

The option prices move diagonally downwards through the table from left to right, i.e. BHP at $21.00 and strike price of 21.00 gives a similar option price as BHP at $20.50 and strike price at 20.50, etc. The first column of option prices are identical to those plotted in Figure 5.2.

Risk-Return for 2nd Out-of-the-money Option

With BHP trading at $21.00, write five BHP 20.00 put options with about eight weeks to expiry. Table 7.3 shows the put option price is 35¢, so our credit is 5 x 350 = $1,750 less brokerage of $50 for a net of $1,700. If BHP is above $20.00 at expiry the options expire worthless and we pocket the $1,700.

Table 7.3 BHP Put Option Prices

BHP Price ($)	21.00	20.50	20.00
		8 Weeks to Expiry	
21.00 put	74 (¢)	99 (¢)	129 (¢)
20.50 put	52	72	97
20.00 put	35	50	70
19.50 put	22	33	49
		6 Weeks to Expiry	
21.00 put	65	91	122
20.50 put	43	63	89
20.00 put	27	42	62
19.50 put	16	26	40
		4 Weeks to Expiry	
21.00 put	54	81	114
20.50 put	33	53	79
20.00 put	18	32	51
19.50 put	9	17	30

At this point we note that $1,700 is a relatively small return on the deposit held by the broker as collateral on the put options (depending on whether part or full cover is required). If we open this trade, we may not be inclined to roll the put options down if the share price moved against us, but may be more likely to buy the options back at a loss.

If we are exercised we have to accept the shares at the strike price of 20.00, and if we want to recoup our cash, then we sell the shares on the open market. This incurs brokerage costs of $200. The net credit equates to 30¢ per share, so an overall loss is incurred if we have to accept the shares at $20.00 and sell them below $19.70.

Risk-Return for 1st Out-of-the-money Option

With BHP trading at $21.00, write five BHP 20.50 put options with about eight weeks to expiry. Table 7.3 shows the option price is 52¢, so the credit is 5 x 520 = $2,600 less brokerage of $50 for a net of $2,550. If BHP is above $20.50 at expiry the options expire worthless and we pocket the $2,550.

Defensive Strategy

The options are likely to be exercised if BHP falls below $20.50.

If we are exercised we have to accept the shares at the strike price of $20.50, and then we may choose to sell them on the open market at the going price. This incurs a loss, as the market price will be less than $20.50. We are insulated a little by the 52¢ credit received from selling the options.

The total exercise transaction consists of accepting the 5,000 shares from the option exerciser, and then selling them on the open market. The related costs are:

	Credit $	Debit $
Option write net premium	2,550	
Share purchase brokerage		100
Option exercise brokerage		100
Net credit	2,350	

The net credit equates to 47¢ per share. Consequently, a loss is incurred if we have to take delivery of the shares at $20.50 and sell them below $20.03. To alleviate this loss we could roll the option down by repurchasing the 20.50 options, and writing new 1st out-of-the-money options.

Roll Down After Two Weeks

Suppose two weeks after we write the options BHP falls to $20.50. Table 7.3 shows that when BHP falls from $21.00 to $20.50, the 20.50 put option rises from an initial 52¢ to 63¢, for a loss of 63 – 52 = 11¢. If we choose to write the 1st out-of-the-money option it now has 20.00 strike price and a value of 42¢, so writing five new options converts the loss to a credit of 42 – 11 = 31¢ per option.

In the case of call options, it is possible to regain the initial credit by writing a larger number of options when we roll up. Similarly, for put options it is possible to regain the initial credit by writing a larger number of put options when we roll down. We may feel the stock is undergoing a normal pull-back and will soon continue its upward trend. In this case, we may be prepared to increase our exposure by repurchasing the initial five options, and then writing, say, seven new options to convert the loss to approximately the initial credit situation (but again at the risk of increased losses if we have to cover this new position). Thus the credit/debit calculation is:

	Credit $	Debit $
Write 5 20.50 options 8-week expiry @ 52¢	2,600	
Brokerage		50
Buy 5 20.50 options 6-week expiry @ 63¢		3,150
Brokerage		50
Write 7 20.00 options 6-week expiry @ 42¢	2,940	
Brokerage		50
Total	5,540	3,300
Net credit	2,240	

If we are exercised, the total exercise brokerage is $200, reducing the credit to $2,040, which equates to 29¢ per share for the 7,000 shares. The rolling down exercise lowers our break-even point on exercise from $20.03 to $19.71.

Roll Down After Four Weeks

As a second example of rolling down, suppose that four weeks after we write the options BHP falls to $20.50. Table 7.3 shows that when BHP falls from $21.00 to $20.50, the 20.50 put option will rise from an initial 52¢ to 53¢, for a loss of 53 – 52 = 1¢. If we choose the new 1st out-of-the-money option it now has 20.00 strike price and a value of 32¢, so writing five new options converts the loss to a credit of 32 – 1 = 31¢ per option.

With only four weeks to expiry, it may be preferable to roll down and also roll out to the next time series. Suppose that four weeks after we write the options, BHP falls to $20.50 and the 20.50 put option is 53¢, for a loss of 53 – 52 = 1¢. The new 1st out-of-the-money option is 20.00 strike price, and if we move out to the next time series the time to expiry is eight weeks. Table 7.3 shows this option is worth 50¢. If we write five new options the original loss is converted to a 50 – 1 = 49¢ credit per option.

Risk-Return for At-the-money Option

With BHP trading at $21.00, write five BHP 21.00 put options with about eight weeks to expiry. Table 7.3 shows the option price is 74¢, so the credit is 5 x 740 = $3,700 less brokerage of $50 for a net of $3,650. If BHP is above $21.00 at expiry the options expire worthless and we pocket the $3,650.

Defensive Strategy

The options are likely to be exercised if BHP falls below $21.00. Taking into account the option credit of $3,650 and total exercise brokerage costs of $200, this equates to 69¢ per share. Consequently a loss is incurred if we have to take delivery at $21.00 and sell the shares below $20.31.

To alleviate this loss we could roll the option down by repurchasing the 21.00 options, and writing the new at-the-money options.

Roll Down After Two Weeks

Suppose two weeks after we write the options BHP falls to $20.50, and we think it prudent to lower the exercise price to 20.50. Table 7.3 shows that when BHP falls from $21.00 to $20.50, the 21.00 put option rises from an initial 74¢ to about 91¢, for a loss of 91 – 74 = 17¢. The new at-the-money option is 20.50 strike price and has a value of 63¢, so writing five new options converts the loss to a credit trade of about 63 – 17 = 46¢ per option.

Risk-Return for Writing Put Options

We summarise the risk-return for the above three option cases by listing the profit against the safety margin, as shown in Table 7.4 overleaf. The safety margin is the amount that BHP shares must fall for our initial put options to be exercised at a loss, taking into account brokerage on accepting the shares from the option exerciser, and then selling the shares.

The safety margin for the 2nd and 1st out-of-the-money cases comprises exercise price leeway plus time premium, while the at-the-money safety margin comprises only time premium so is a riskier proposition.

The values used in the illustrative examples above suggest the 2nd or 1st out-of-the-money put options give a satisfactory compromise between risk and reward. For these options to incur a loss, the share price must move more than 130¢ or 97¢ respectively against us during the eight weeks to expiry.

Table 7.4 Safety Margin and Profit for Written Put Options

	Safety Margin (¢)	Profit per Trade ($)
2nd out-of-the-money	130	1,700
1st out-of-the-money	97	2,550
At-the-money	69	3,650

WRITING COVERED CALL OPTIONS

Some investors who own shares write call options over these shares as a major strategy (this is called writing covered call options). Alternatively, we might write puts with the intention of being exercised (and so effectively buy the shares below the current market price), or we might have puts exercised on a severe downswing. In either case we finish up holding the stock. These cases are treated separately in the following pages, as they require different call option writing strategies.

Writing Call Options to Keep the Shares

Some investors have long-term holdings of shares that they do not want to lose because of capital gains tax, or other considerations. These investors would have bought the shares at a cheaper price some years ago, and then written deep (say 2nd or 3rd) out-of-the-money call options that must not be exercised. The credits obtained on the call options supplement the stock dividend and the gradual appreciation of the stock over time.

Suppose we own 5,000 BHP shares purchased at, say, $15.00. With BHP at $21.00, we sell five 3rd out-of-the-money call options (strike price 22.50) with six weeks to expiry. Table 7.1 (on page 53) shows the price of the 3rd out-of-the-money options is 24¢, so the premium is 5 x 240 = $1,200 less $50 brokerage for a net credit of $1,150. Suppose BHP has two downtrends a year where we may be able to utilise this strategy, for a total credit of $2,300.

BHP pays annual dividends of about 50¢, so total dividend on the 5,000 shares is $2,500. Adding the option premium of $2,300 gives a gross return of $4,800, which effectively doubles the return on the held stock.

Defensive Strategy for 2nd Out-of-the-money Case

If BHP rises above $22.50 we are likely to be exercised, so we must buy back the options to cancel the trade. This may incur a cash loss but a paper profit. Suppose we repurchase with two weeks to expiry, when the options are at-the-money and the BSOPM gives the price as 46¢. The credit/debit situation is:

	Credit $	Debit $
Write 5 22.50 options 6-week expiry @ 24¢	1,200	
Brokerage		50
Buy 5 22.50 options 2-week expiry @ 46¢		2,300
Brokerage		50
Total	1,200	2,400
Cash loss		1,200
Value of 5,000 BHP shares @ $15.00	75,000	
Value of 5,000 BHP shares @ $22.50	112,500	
Paper profit	37,500	

Instead of quitting the trade, suppose we roll up to the new 3rd out-of-the-money option (strike price $24.00) in the next time series that has six weeks to expiry, and again will have a price of about 24¢. The credit/debit situation is now:

	Credit $	Debit $
Write 5 22.50 options 6-week expiry @ 24¢	1,200	
Brokerage		50
Buy 5 22.50 options 2-week expiry @ 46¢		2,300
Brokerage		50
Write 5 24.00 options 6-week expiry @ 24¢	1,200	
Brokerage		50
Total	2,400	2,450
Net loss		50

By rolling up, the loss on the initial trade is recovered, and we distance ourselves a further $1.50 from the rising share price, as well as increasing the paper profit on the held shares. At some stage BHP will stop rising and the options we hold will expire worthless, or can be repurchased for the small amount of intrinsic value remaining.

When we do not want to lose our shares, it is safest to only write call options when the shares are trading in the upper half of the trend channel.

Writing Call Options to Lose the Shares

Sometimes after writing a put option trade we may choose to be exercised and buy the stock, rather than employing the defensive strategy of rolling the put options down. Such a case could be where we wrote the puts near the bottom of a trend channel, and are confident the stock will move upwards from that trend channel in the near future. Alternatively, we may have the shares put to us in a quick downswing. In either case, after being exercised our intention is to write call options on the shares, thus hoping to on-sell the shares through exercise of the call options.

Suppose BHP is trading at $21.00 and there is chart support at $20.50. Writing five 20.50 put options with eight weeks to expiry for 52¢ (see Table 7.3, page 60), gives a credit of 5 x 520 = $2,600 less brokerage of $50 for a net of $2,550.

Suppose after two weeks BHP has a sharp fall to $20.00 and we are exercised, thereby having to buy the shares at $20.50. The cost of accepting the 5,000 shares is:

	Credit $	Debit $
Option write net premium	2,550	
Option exercise brokerage		100
Net credit	2,450	

The net credit equates to 49¢ per share, so the net cost of the 5,000 shares is $20.01 per share.

At this point we could immediately write 20.00 call options which are at-the-money and have six weeks to expiry. We choose this option as our intention is to be rid of the shares as quickly as possible. If the share price rises the options become in-the-money, and are almost certain to be exercised. Further, the at-the-money option commands the highest time premium. Table 7.1 shows the 21.00 at-the-money call option with six weeks to expiry is valued at 77¢, so we use this value for the 20.00 at-the-money option also. If the call options are exercised the full transaction costs are:

	Credit $	Debit $
Write 5 20.50 put options 8-week expiry @ 52¢	2,600	
Brokerage		50
Purchase 5,000 BHP shares @ $20.50		102,500
Brokerage		100
Write 5 20.00 call options 6-week expiry @ 77¢	3,850	
Brokerage		50
Sell 5,000 BHP shares @ $20.00	100,000	
Brokerage		100
Total	106,450	102,800
Net credit	3,650	

If the call options are not exercised, the net profit from writing the call options is 3,850 – 50 = $3,800 or about 76¢ per share. Thus the effective purchase price of the shares becomes $20.50 – 0.49 – 0.76 = $19.25.

CALL BEAR SPREAD FOR FALLING STOCK

The comparative advantages, and disadvantages, of using a spread to limit losses in a losing trade are detailed in the case of a call bear spread. A call bear spread consists of writing a lower strike price call option, and simultaneously buying a higher strike price call option. This spread will be profitable if the stock price falls, but if the stock rises, the loss is limited.

Suppose BHP is trading at $21.00 and the 21.00 and 21.50 call options with eight weeks to expiry are priced about 90¢ and 67¢ respectively (see Table 7.1 on page 53), so writing a 21.00 call and buying a 21.50 call gives a credit transaction of 23¢. We open this trade as a spread, i.e. write the 21.00 call option and buy the 21.00 call option simultaneously. Table 7.5 overleaf lists the possible outcomes at expiry expressed in cents.

Thus, if we pick the market direction correctly and BHP at expiry is below $21.00, then our maximum profit is 23¢ per option pair. If we trade five options this equates to a profit of 5 x 230 = $1,150, less two lots of $50 brokerage to open the spread, for a net profit of $1,050. Both options expire worthless so no brokerage is incurred in closing the spread.

Table 7.5 Profit and Loss Values for Call Bear Spread

BHP expiry ($)	21.00 call	Profit/loss	21.50 call	Profit/loss	Total profit/loss
20.00	0	90	0	-67	23
20.50	0	90	0	-67	23
21.00	0	90	0	-67	23
21.50	50	40	0	-67	-27
22.00	100	-10	50	-17	-27
22.50	150	-60	100	33	-27

Closing a Losing Call Bear Spread

The advantage of the call bear spread, as against simply writing a call option, is that the loss is fixed no matter how far the stock moves against us. However, in order to crystallise this loss we need to understand the mechanics of closing the trade when the price does move against us.

Option brokers claim that bought options which are in-the-money are nearly always exercised, with the exercise taking place during the last week before expiry. However, if the stock moves strongly in favour of the buyer of the option, he or she may decide to exercise early. We have opened the trade as a spread, and should close the trade as a spread, and not allow our written calls to be exercised.

As we have written 21.00 call options for 90¢, we need to consider taking defensive action if BHP rises above, say, $22,00 to avoid being exercised. We do this by instructing our broker to buy back the spread, i.e. to buy the written 21.00 call and sell the bought 21.50 call. On closing the spread we crystallise the loss of $270 per option pair, and also incur two further sets of brokerage.

Thus the total loss in having to close out the spread is (5 x 270) + (2 x 50) = $1,450.

If the concept of spreads seems appealing, it is necessary to work through the profit and loss sums carefully, taking account of brokerage, and compare this with a simple buy or write strategy.

Appendix II gives a detailed comparison between various spread strategies.

STRANGLES FOR RISING OR FALLING STOCK

Another strategy which uses a spread of two options is called the "strangle". In a so-called bought strangle, we buy a call option and a put option with the same expiry time, but with different strike prices.

Suppose BHP is trading at $21.00 and is due to make a market report which is likely to move the share price, but we are unsure of the direction the move will take. To execute the strangle we decide on a four-week time frame and 1st out-of-the-money options. Thus we buy a 21.50 strike price call option for 40¢ (see Table 7.1) and also buy a 20.50 strike price put option for 33¢ (see Table 7.3), for a net cost of 73¢ per option pair. Table 7.6 below lists the possible outcomes of the strangle at expiry expressed in cents.

Table 7.6 Profit and Loss Values for Strangle

BHP expiry ($)	21.50 call	Profit/loss	20.50 put	Profit/loss	Total profit/loss
19.50	0	-40	100	67	27
19.77	0	-40	73	40	0
20.00	0	-40	50	17	-23
20.50	0	-40	0	-33	-73
21.00	0	-40	0	-33	-73
21.50	0	-40	0	-33	-73
22.00	50	10	0	-33	-23
22.23	73	33	0	-33	0
22.50	100	60	0	-33	27

In this example, if BHP moves $1.50 *either way* from the initial $21.00 value, then the strangle shows a profit of 27¢, while a $2.00 move up or down equates to a profit of 27 + 50 = 77¢ (not shown in the table). The downside for this strategy is that a loss results if BHP is between $19.77 and $22.23 at option expiry, while the maximum loss is 73¢ which translates to $730 per option pair, plus two lots of brokerage for a gross loss of $830.

Once again, the strangle strategy looks attractive, but we need to do our sums carefully before employing it.

The name "strangle" comes from the fact that the price is strangled in the range $19.77 to $22.23. For stock prices outside that range at expiry, a profit can be achieved by selling the profitable option, and letting the other option expire worthless.

Chapter 8

SELECTED SHARE PRICE PATTERNS

CHARTS OF THE 12 major option stocks are given in Figures 8.1 to 8.12. Most of the charts are displayed as weekly bar charts spanning four years from mid 1996 to September 2000. The chart for the more recently listed AMP spans a little over 12 months, while Telstra is displayed as a daily chart spanning 14 months. All of the charts are drawn with a linear price scale, and are included to show how volatile these blue chip stocks can be, and consequently, the trading opportunities they present.

NCP Price Pattern

The weekly bar chart for News Corp is shown in Figure 8.1 overleaf. NCP is a fascinating stock, having been on the verge of bankruptcy in 1991, to now being the highest capitalised stock on the ASX. From its darkest days, the stock has mostly risen on the back of astute business deals, and expansion in many facets of media and entertainment, with a high exposure to sport.

NCP is not a stock for the unwary, as it is prone to sudden sharp unexpected moves caused by a waxing and waning of market sentiment towards the company. Items like the box-office returns of its latest film production affect the price. The falls in September 1998 were attributed to the shelving of plans to float part of its Fox Entertainment Group, and also to news of Rupert Murdoch's divorce. The subsequent rise in the following month was due to a firmer tone in world markets, but also to the announcement that the Fox float would now proceed. Of the industrial stocks listed here, NCP has the highest volatility (see Chapter 5).

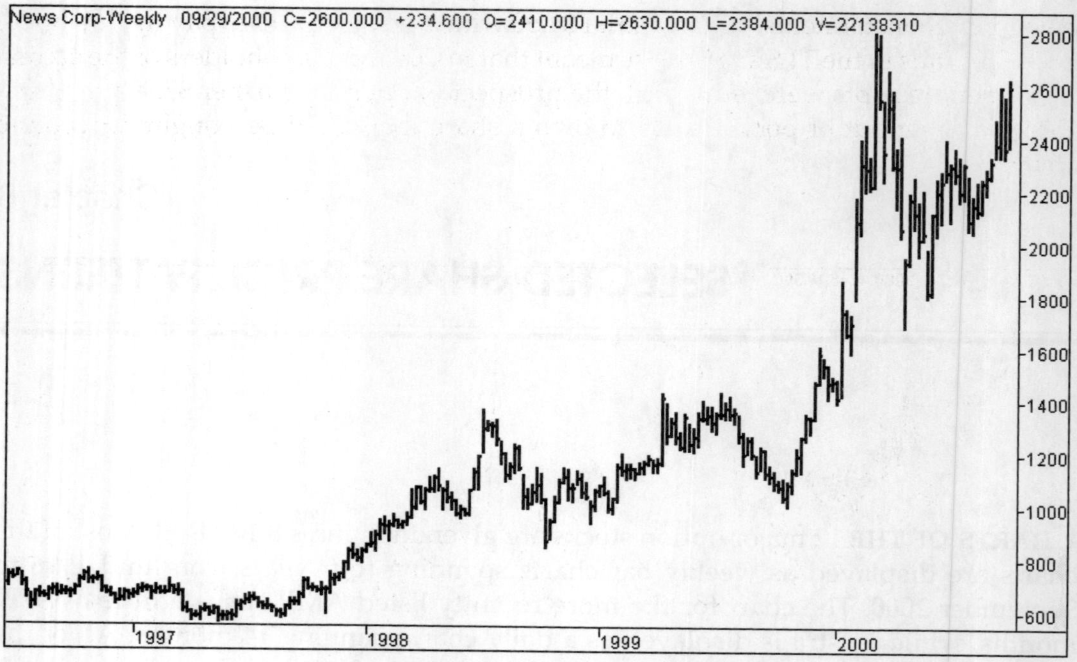

Figure 8.1 NCP Weekly Bar Chart

TLS Price Pattern

One-third of Telstra was floated in the form of *instalment receipts* on 17 November 1997, and was a glamour float, doubling from an initial application price of $1.95 to around $4.00 in April 1998. At the end of October 1998 the second payment of $1.35 per share was made, whereby the shares became fully paid, and had the ASX code TLS. The daily chart for TLS spanning the 14 months to September 2000 is shown in Figure 8.2 opposite. With the technology boom in late 1999, these shares which cost a total of $3.30 traded as high as $9.00. Since then, market sentiment has turned against the company, with the shares trading below $6.00 at the time of writing. This malaise was caused by a general cooling of the telecommunications sector, along with unfavourable sentiment towards the deal with Hong Kong based Pacific Century CyberWorks, plus the float of a second tranche of instalment receipts at an inflated price.

In October 1999 the Federal Government floated this second tranche of instalment receipts in the form of a further one-sixth of Telstra at $7.40, with payment again being in two instalments, viz. an initial $4.50 with a further $2.90 to pay in November 2000. The falls in the TLS share price meant that in October 2000, holders of the second instalment receipts were faced with the prospect of paying a further $2.90 per share, thereby being out of pocket $7.40 to own a share that could be bought for around $6.00.

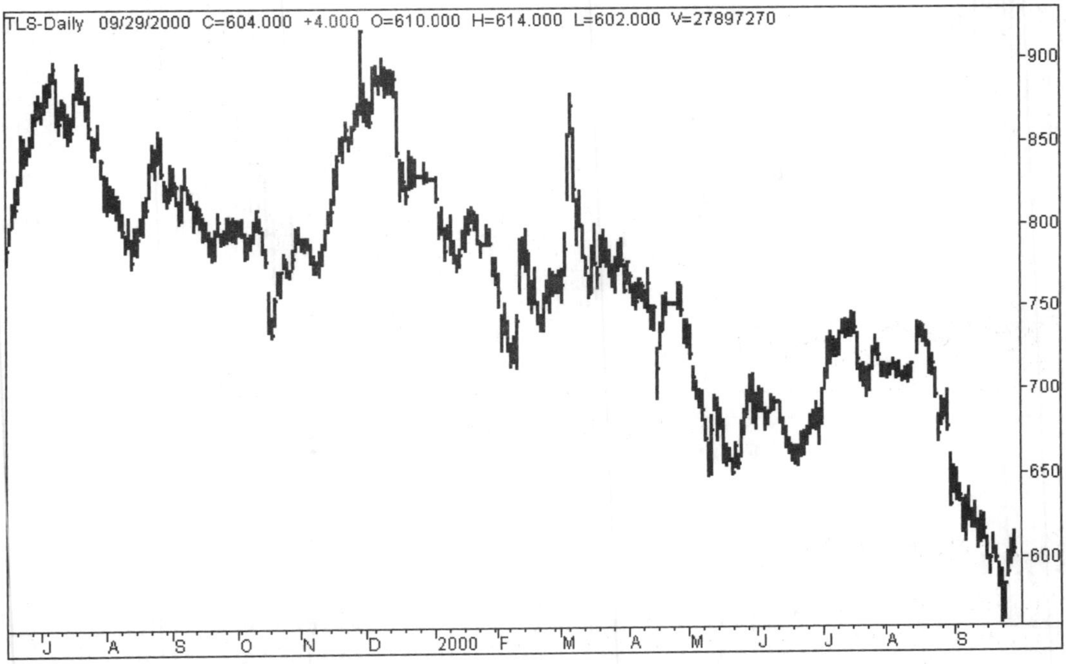

Figure 8.2 TLS Daily Bar Chart

AMP Price Pattern

The weekly bar chart for AMP is shown in Figure 8.3 overleaf. AMP floated on 15.6.98 with a remarkable day's activity, opening at $45.00 and closing at $23.00. The stock has subsequently settled down to a more normal trading pattern, taking into account its insurance, banking and portfolio management business, plus its own substantial equity, property and bond assets. However, management problems and an overpriced takeover of GIO caused a gradual erosion of the share price to below $14.00. At the time of writing the share price seems to be responding to better management of the company assets.

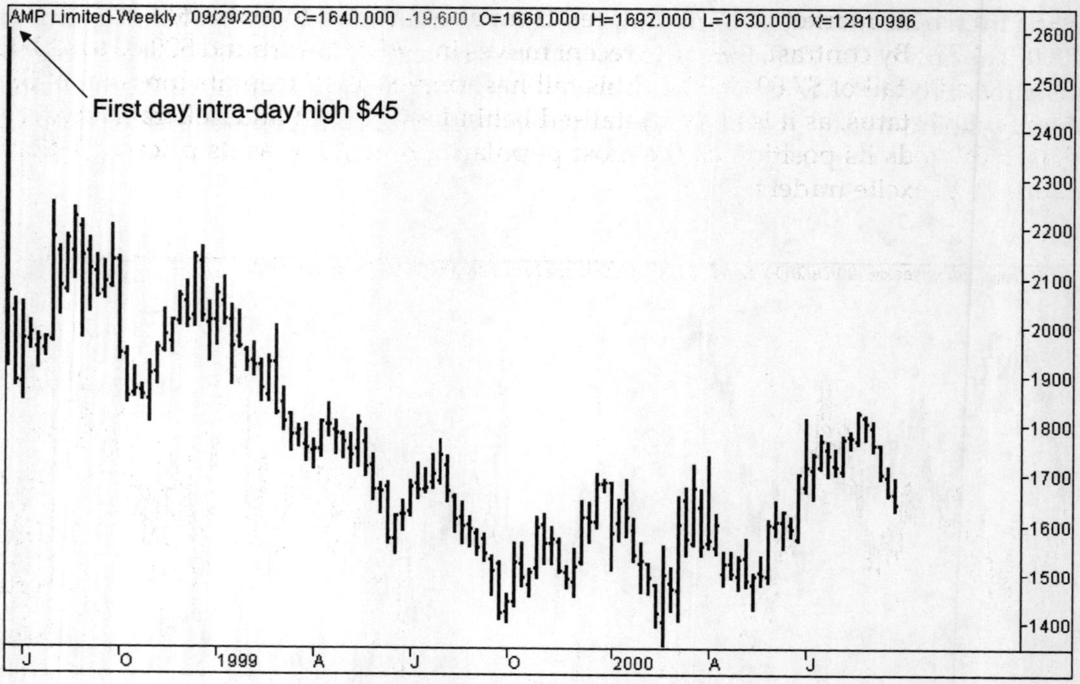

Figure 8.3 AMP Weekly Bar Chart

BHP Price Pattern

The weekly bar chart for BHP is shown in Figure 8.4 opposite. It is seen that the share price is never static, but is always responding to commodity prices and the fortunes of its global interests, comprising primarily steel, oil and minerals. The fall below $17.00 in September 1996 was caused by the collapse of the copper price, resulting from the Sumitomo Corp futures debacle. The share price recovered, but the prolonged fall in the second half of 1997 was the result of a series of financial problems involving the Magna Copper purchase at inflated prices, plus a number of other project overspends. This downtrend culminated in the October 1997 mini-crash. The recovery in early 1998 was aborted with continuing low commodity prices and the resignation of some senior management. The recovery which started in early 1999 was partly in response to respected new management, but also to a better tone in world commodity markets. Experience shows that BHP's price often moves about $1.00 in the space of one or two weeks, and that medium-term trends are typically six to ten weeks in duration.

It is useful to know the magnitude of the falls in BHP over the past decade. During the October 1987 crash BHP fell from about $9.70 to about $6.00, a fall of $3.70 or 38%, and in the bear market of 1992 BHP fell from about $15.10 to about $11.00, a fall of $4.10 or 27%. By contrast, the more recent moves in 1997 from around $20.00 to $13.00 constituted a fall of $7.00 or 35%. This fall has toppled BHP from its long-held "Big Australian" status, as it is now capitalised behind NCP, NAB and Telstra. However, BHP still holds its position as the most popular option stock, as its price variations continue to excite traders.

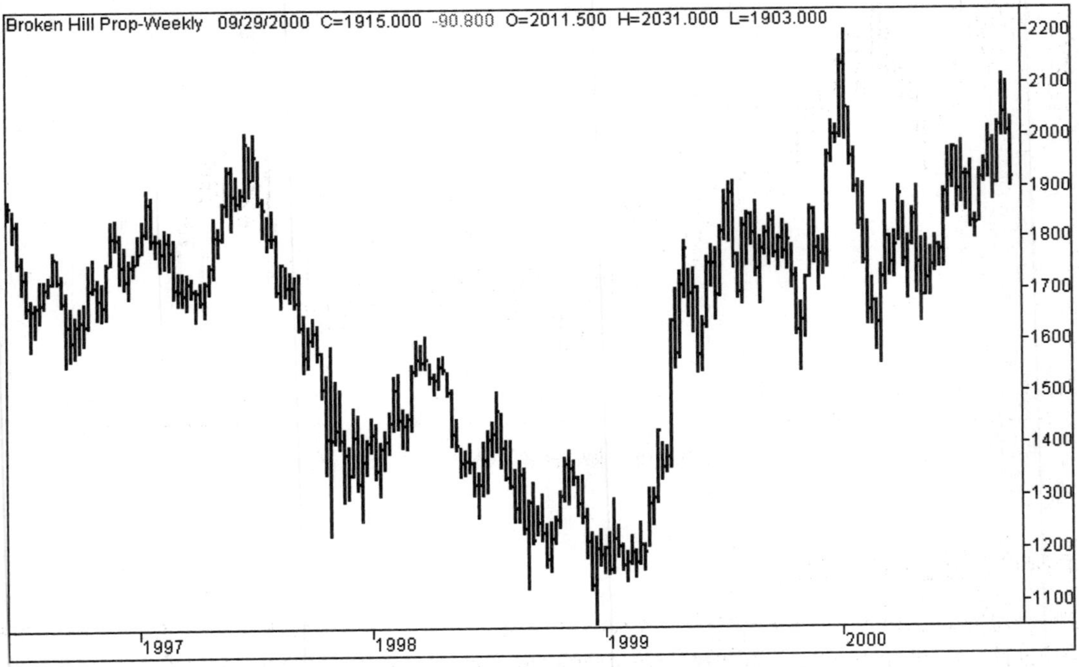

Figure 8.4 BHP Weekly Bar Chart

RIO Price Pattern

The weekly bar chart for RIO is shown in Figure 8.5 overleaf. Like BHP, RIO is a worldwide resource company, so its fortunes are also subject to commodity prices. It is interesting to compare the charts of the two companies. Close inspection of Figures 8.4 and 8.5 shows that BHP and RIO have peaks and troughs at the same time, though the magnitude of the moves between peaks and troughs can vary. Further, both BHP and RIO had highs in mid 1997, and both fell about $7.00 at the worst of the October mini-crash. Whereas BHP has continued to languish, RIO has benefited from long-term resource investors swapping from BHP to RIO, and consequently supporting RIO's price.

More recently, BHP and RIO both had new highs in late 1999, followed by big falls in early 2000. At the time of writing BHP has recovered well, whereas RIO is held back by its hostile takeover of North Limited, along with its takeover bid for Ashton Mining.

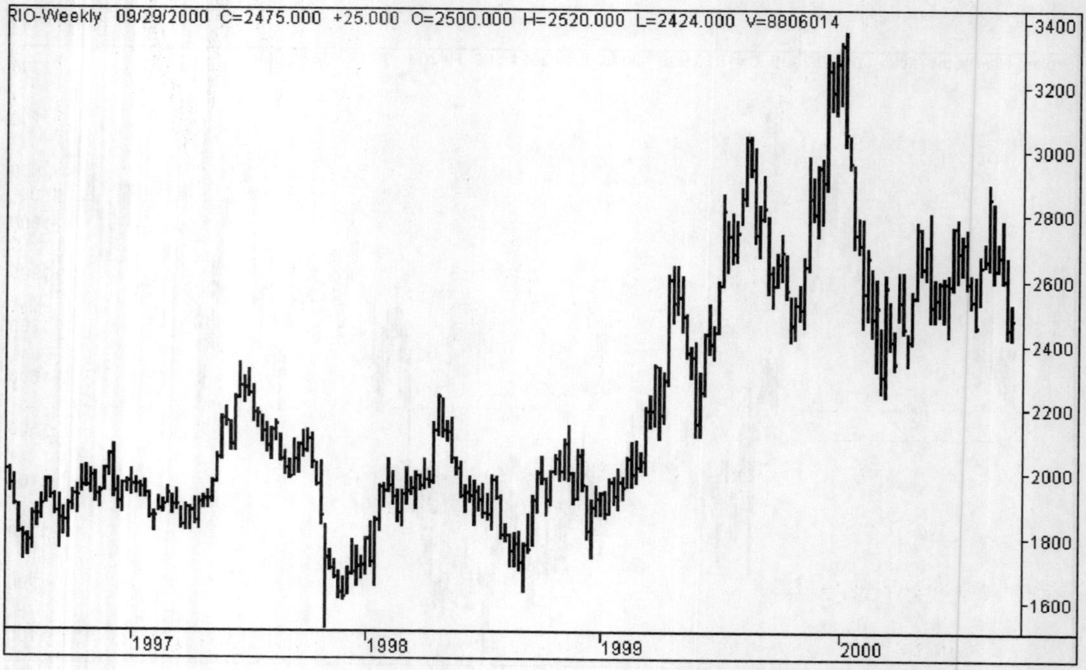

Figure 8.5 RIO Weekly Bar Chart

WMC Price Pattern

The weekly chart for WMC is shown in Figure 8.6 opposite. Like BHP and RIO, WMC is a well-respected worldwide resource company, and is a popular options stock. Comparing the three charts shown in Figures 8.4 to 8.6, we see that WMC price moves follow BHP quite closely, but avoided the continued fall which BHP endured in 1988.

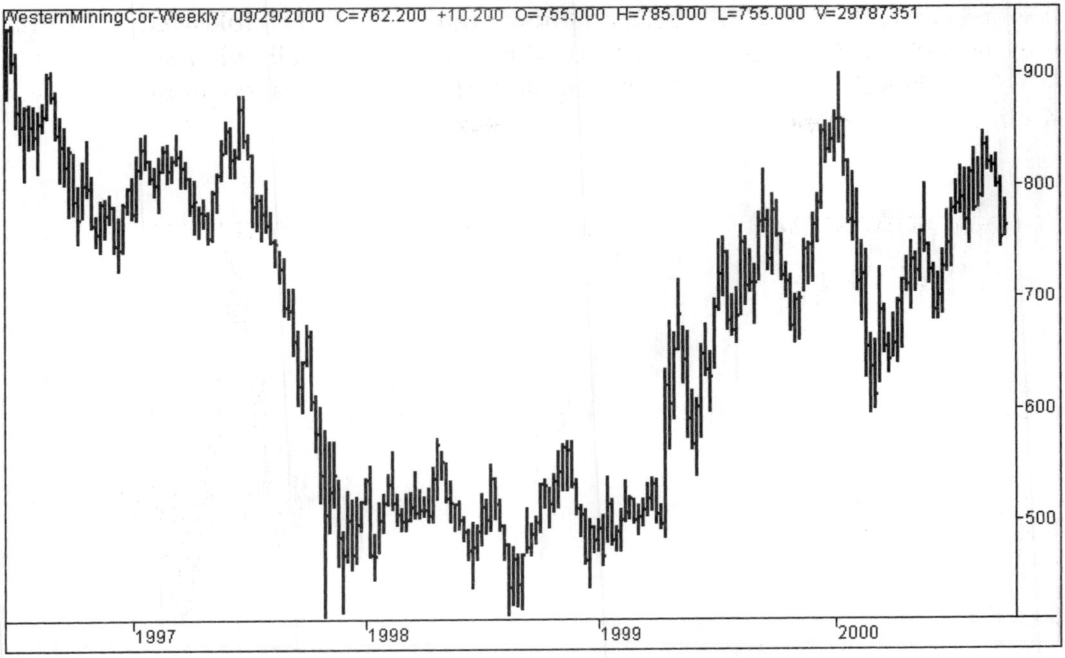

Figure 8.6 WMC Weekly Bar Chart

NDY Price Pattern

The weekly bar chart for Normandy Mining is given in Figure 8.7 overleaf. NDY is Australia's largest producer of gold, with production of 1.97 million ounces in 2000, and reserves increased to 21 million ounces. NDY hedges part of its gold production and reserves, but the share price still fluctuates in line with the physical price of gold. The company also has lesser interests in zinc and industrial minerals.

Traditionally, gold is a safe haven in times of high inflation and financial uncertainty, as the price of gold tends to rise at these times. However, during the Asian currency crisis of late 1997 gold continued to fall, reinforcing once again the fickleness of the financial markets, but also the complex relationship between the price of gold and the world economic system.

In August 1998 the price of gold traded around $US275, before climbing to $US300 in October. These variations caused NDY to move from a low of about $1.00 to around $1.55. Subsequent gold prices below $US270 in 2000 resulted in NDY trading at $0.85, but the price has since rallied to around $1.10 on takeover speculation.

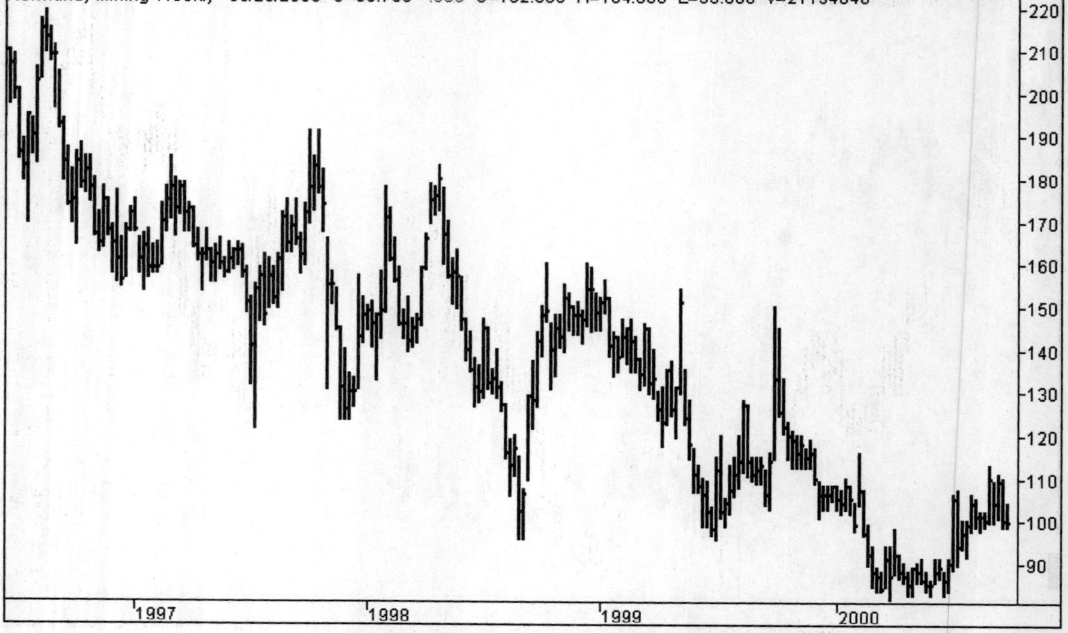

Figure 8.7 NDY Weekly Bar Chart

WPL Price Pattern

The weekly chart for Woodside is shown in Figure 8.8 opposite. For the 18 months to September 2000, crude oil prices have risen from around $US12/barrel to $US35/barrel. At the time of writing the jury is out as to where oil prices will be cum 2001, with estimates varying between $US25/barrel to $US50/barrel. WPL is Australia's premier oil stock and its price moves in sympathy with the oil price. Trading options in WPL is one way of taking a view on the future price of oil.

At September 2000, WPL was being buoyed by the crude oil price, the signing of major new gas contracts with Japanese buyers, and a merger/takeover proposal from Shell.

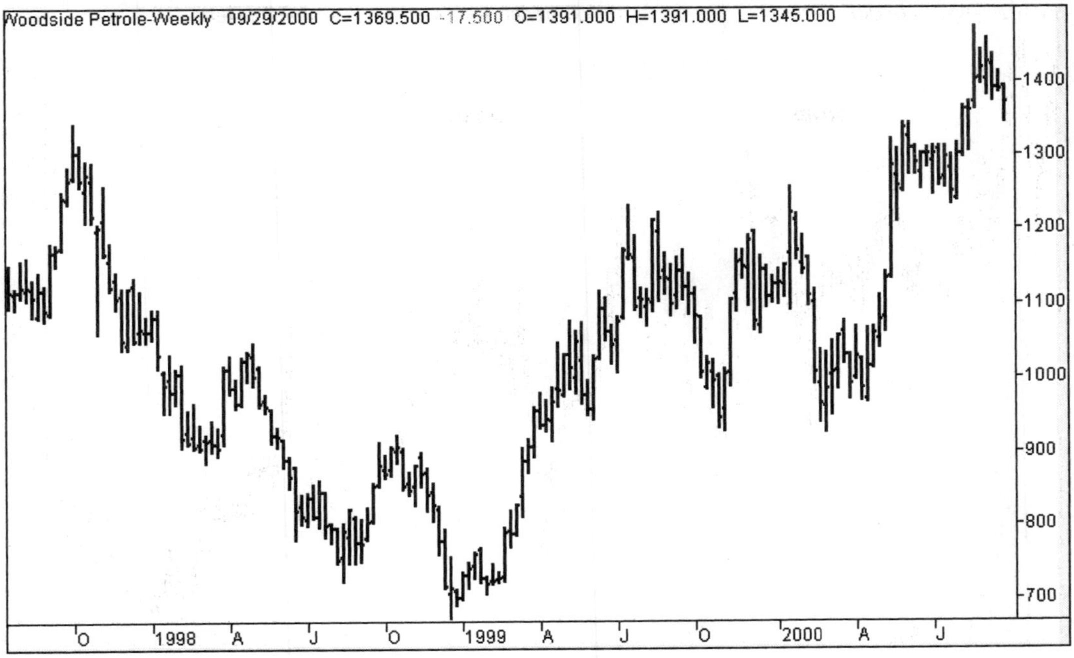

Figure 8.8 WPL Weekly Bar Chart

ANZ Price Pattern

The weekly bar chart for ANZ is shown in Figure 8.9 overleaf. From a low of just under $4.00 in late 1994 (not shown in the figure), the stock enjoyed a sustained rise through to late 1997. This price rise was the result of improving profits, falling interest rates, as well as sporadic takeover speculation.

The mini-crash in October 1997 triggered by the Asian crisis deflated the price for several months, before new highs near $12.00 were reached in April 1998. The stock then executed a classic double top formation, prior to falling back to support levels around $8.50. Since then the price has moved upwards, albeit within a trend channel about $2.50 wide.

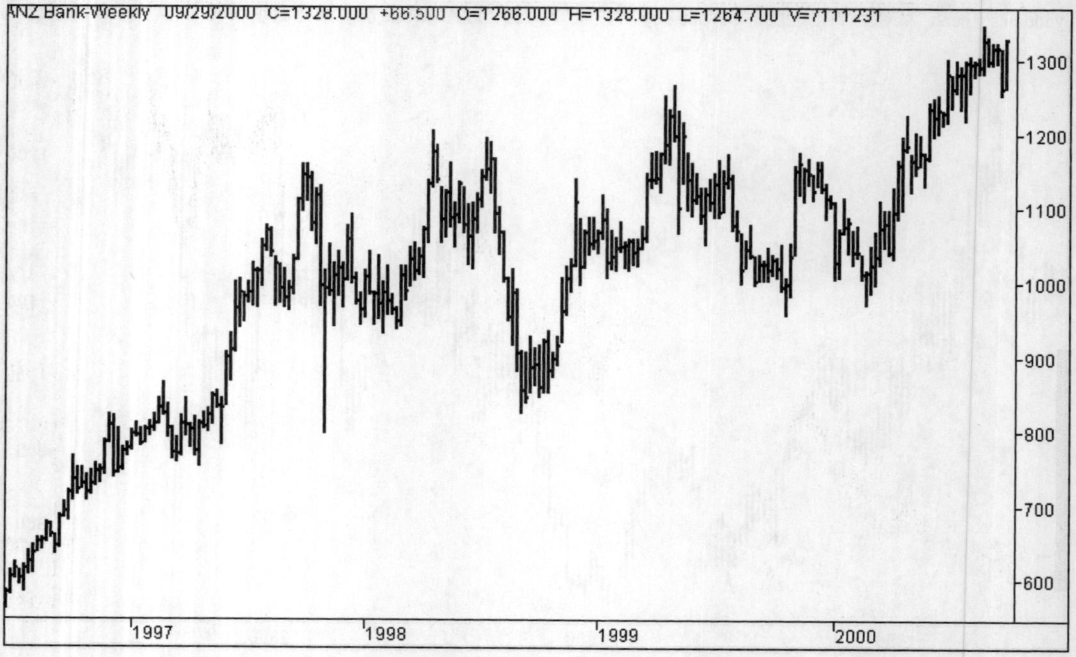

Figure 8.9 ANZ Weekly Bar Chart

CBA Price Pattern

The weekly bar chart for CBA is shown in Figure 8.10 opposite, and shows a steady rise as the bank's efficiency improved and profits continued to increase. The second tranche of government shares were floated in July 1996, and were preceded by several months of flat prices.

Figure 8.10 CBA Weekly Bar Chart

NAB Price Pattern

The weekly bar chart for NAB is shown in Figure 8.11 overleaf. NAB did not run up massive bad debts in the late 1980s and early 1990s as some banks did, so during 1995-96 its share price was more stable. In 1996-97 increased profits and an improving economy caused NAB's price to accelerate. After the October 1997 mini-crash, the price consolidated between $19.00 and $23.00, before running to new highs above $30 in early 1999. The Asian currency crisis pulled NAB's price down during 1999. The subsequent price recovery during 2000 was halted by the large damages case filed against NAB by John Maconochie for breach of Ausmaq intellectual property.

During the October 1987 crash NAB fell from about $7.00 to about $6.00, a fall of $1.00 or 14%, but unlike the miners, NAB reached a new high within a few weeks of the crash.

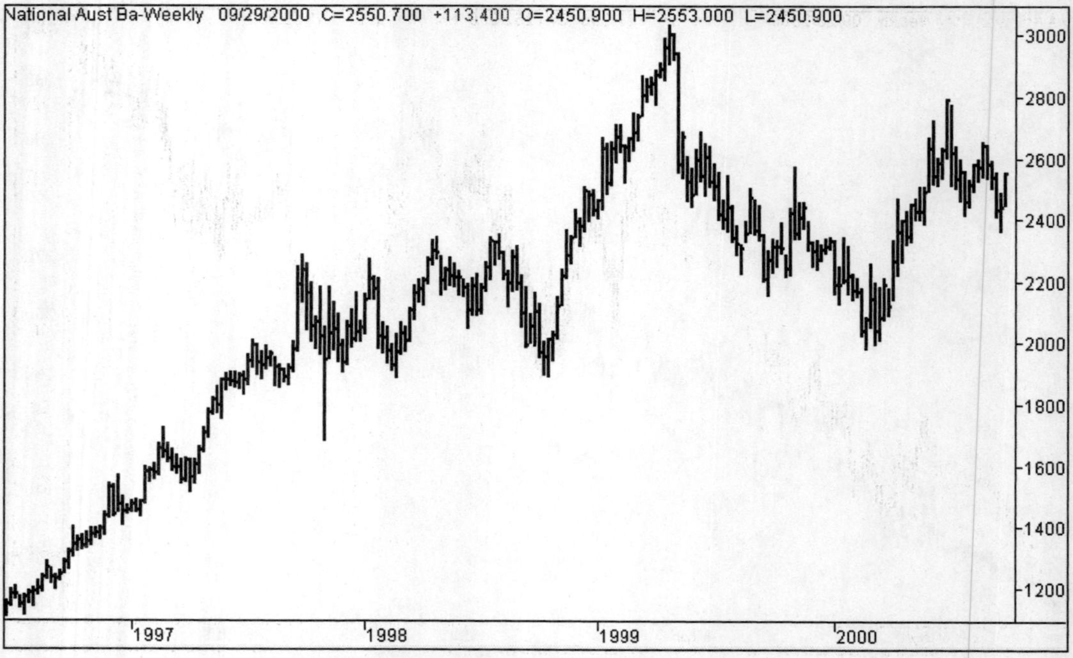

Figure 8.11 NAB Weekly Bar Chart

WBC Price Pattern

The weekly bar chart of WBC is shown in Figure 8.12 opposite. WBC has risen steadily from a trough of $2.70 in 1992, when the board stabilised and a new CEO was appointed in the wake of bad loans and bad publicity. At September 2000 WBC has achieved new highs around $13.00, having been driven by rising profits and occasional bouts of takeover speculation.

Just as the three global resource companies BHP, RIO and WMC show similar macro chart patterns but differ in the fine detail, so too do the four Australian "Big Banks" show similar macro chart patterns, but again differ in the fine details. Thus the banks all fell steeply in May 1999, staged a partial recovery in October 1999, fell again in March 2000 and, with the exception of NAB, have since achieved new highs.

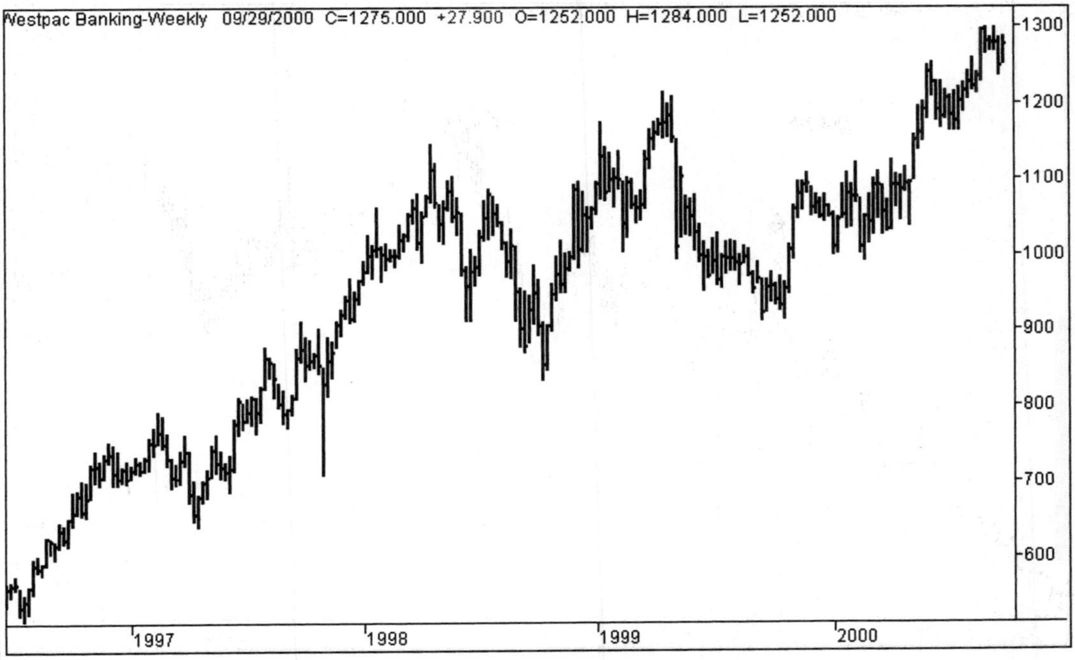

Figure 8.12 WBC Weekly Bar Chart

Chapter 9

TECHNICAL ANALYSIS

TECHNICAL ANALYSIS IS based on the premise that the future price and behaviour of a stock can be predicted by analysis of the stock's past price patterns and volume.

Before personal computers became available, technical analysis mainly comprised charting and moving average techniques. The art of charting was very refined, as is evident in the benchmark works by Gann, and Edwards and Magee, which were published prior to 1950.

The advent of the personal computer, and its ready availability and acceptance in the 1980s, led to a boom in the development of mathematically-based technical indicators. Many of these technical indicators have proved to be useful, and have gained a following among traders and investors in both the futures and the stock markets. Further, the development of stock price databases which can be accessed via a telephone modem, along with readily available analysis software, makes it possible for traders to have a powerful suite of technical indicators for their own use.

Technical indicators take the raw price data, perform a number-crunching algorithm, and produce a graph that is intended to show in some way when the stock trends change—and consequently, opportune times to enter and exit the market.

It is easy to be overwhelmed by the number of technical indicators available, but they can be made more manageable by reducing them to the broad groupings of:

1. Indicators based on price data.
2. Indicators based on volume data.
3. Charting techniques.
4. Cyclical patterns.

Most of the technical indicators fall into the price grouping, and these can be sub-grouped further as:

a) Trend-following (lagging).

b) Oscillators (leading).

c) Bands and envelopes.

d) Sundry others.

If we intend using technical indicators to give the entry and exit signals for our trading, then it is necessary to be familiar with the mathematics and rationale behind the popular indicators, and to test these against the stocks we choose to trade.

Our option and warrant strategy is to trade the medium-term one to three-month trends in heavyweight stocks, so the indicators chosen must be capable of determining these trends with a high probability of being correct.

The indicators I find useful with daily data are the Moving Average Convergence Divergence (MACD), the Directional Movement Indicator (DMI) and Average Directional Movement Index (ADX), the momentum, and the Relative Strength Index (RSI). For weekly data I use weekly RSI and weekly MACD. If several of these indicators show an entry or exit signal, I check time cycles, point and figure charts and general chart pattern procedures for confirmation.

Each of these indicators is discussed in the following pages. In Chapter 10 they are applied to a selection of BHP data; which shows how to use our trading strategy and gives some profit/loss results.

A comprehensive discussion of technical indicators is given by Kaufman, while LeBeau and Lucas, and several of the other references, cover the more popular technical indicators.

STOCK BEHAVIOUR AT A TURNING POINT

Inspection of each of the stock price charts of Figures 8.1 to 8.12 in the previous chapter shows a series of successive uptrends and downtrends, along with some periods of sideways movement.

Technical analysis attempts to define the start and end of the trends, and so indicate the times to trade the stock for a profit. The problem arises at the end of the trends, when the price often churns about as the buyers and sellers mull over their opinions on the prospects and price of the stock. Sometimes the change in market sentiment is a gradual process over several weeks or months, which results in a saucer-shaped pattern on the chart as the prevailing mood changes. At other times the mood changes very quickly, with the release of new data on the company or a sudden change in market sentiment, which produces a "V" formation. A selection of price patterns that occur at the end of stock trends are discussed in the Charting section later in the chapter.

TECHNICAL INDICATORS

The task for the technical analyst is to determine the true time of the trend change, no matter which price pattern the stock goes through while the trend changes direction.

Single Moving Average

One of the simplest, yet most useful, technical indicators is the Single Moving Average (SMA). For daily data the SMA is calculated as:

$$SMA = \frac{\text{sum of N close prices}}{N}$$

where:

N = number of data being used in the SMA

(Thus, if today's close price is 100¢ and the previous trading days' close prices are 98, 102, 103 and 102, then today's 5-day SMA is 101.)

The main feature of the SMA is that it smooths the price variations, and clearly indicates the changes in the trend directions. The SMA is a lagging indicator, as it changes direction after the stock trend has changed.

The value chosen for N is typically 5 to 30, and the larger the value of N, the greater the smoothing effect on the prices, and the further the SMA lags the price moves.

Figure 9.1 opposite shows the 9-day and 18-day SMA for BHP, and the smoothing of the price data is clearly seen.

The SMA is generally not used by itself, but is combined into a double or triple moving average system.

Figure 9.1 Chart of 9-day and 18-day SMA for BHP

Double and Triple Moving Averages

It is customary to use a Double Moving Average (DMA), where a shorter duration SMA is used with a longer duration SMA. When the shorter SMA crosses above the longer duration SMA an uptrend is indicated, while when the shorter SMA crosses below the longer duration SMA a downtrend is signalled. A popular combination is 9 days and 18 days for the two SMAs.

Experience shows that the 9,18 DMA crossing is always a few days after the actual start of a fresh leg. This few days of delay acts as an effective filter, as when the SMAs eventually cross the new trend is usually underway, and will continue for some time (see Figure 9.1).

The end of the trend occurs when the prices turn over from their peak/trough values. We want to quit the trade as soon as possible after the peak/trough occurs, otherwise too much of the available profit is lost from the leg. The 9,18 day DMA combination is too slow for this purpose, and it is customary to use a faster 4,9 day DMA combination. An uptrend is terminated when the 4-day SMA crosses below the 9-day SMA, while a downtrend is terminated when the 4-day SMA crosses above the 9-day SMA.

Exponential Smoothing

Single moving averages have the disadvantage that each piece of data "wags the average twice"; firstly, when it is introduced into the average, and secondly, when it is dropped out of the average.

Exponential smoothing, or Exponential Moving Average (EMA), is an alternative procedure which effectively uses all data to calculate the smoothed value, but discounts the older data. Exponential smoothing can be calculated mathematically as an iterative procedure whereby each new smoothed value is calculated by adding a portion of the new data to the preceding smoothed value.

Thus, for the data stream $P_1, P_2 \ldots P_n$ with P_1 being the most recent, the smoothed values are $S_1, S_2 \ldots S_n$, where:

$$S_1 = S_2 + \kappa(P_1 - S_2)$$

Rearranging and expanding gives:

$$S_1 = \kappa P_1 + (1 - \kappa)S_2$$
$$= \kappa P_1 + \kappa(1 - \kappa)P_2 + \kappa(1 - \kappa)^2 P_3 + \ldots \kappa(1 - \kappa)^{n-1} S_n$$

and:

$$\text{smoothing factor } \kappa = \frac{2}{1 + N}$$

where:

N is the number of data in the calculation

As $\kappa < 1$, then older data is exponentially discounted.

Exponential smoothing is used in exactly the same way as the double and triple SMAs discussed above. Thus, 4, 9 and 18-day EMAs are calculated, with the start of the trend signalled by the 9-day EMA crossing the 18-day EMA, and the end of the trend signalled by the 4-day EMA crossing the 9-day EMA.

The iterative exponential smoothing is mathematically more elegant than the SMA calculation. Many studies have been done to compare the effectiveness of the two methods in trading systems, and the results seem to favour the SMA for overall profitability and minimising whipsaws.

Moving Average Convergence Divergence

The MACD is a useful extension of exponential smoothing developed by Gerald Appel in 1979. The 12-day and 26-day exponential smoothing values are calculated as EMA_{12} and EMA_{26}, and the difference obtained as $EMA_{12} - EMA_{26}$. This difference is the MACD line, which moves above and below zero as the stock trend moves up and down. When the two smoothed curves cross over, the MACD line = 0, so this is essentially the same concept as the double moving averages discussed above.

However, the MACD line is now exponentially smoothed using 9-data smoothing, and this is called the signal line. The MACD line crosses up and down through the signal line, and these crossovers are taken as the start and finish of the stock trends. Thus, when the MACD line crosses above the signal line the trend is up, while when the MACD line crosses below the signal line the trend is down.

The MACD plot is usually constructed to show both the MACD line and the signal line, and the difference between these two lines in histogram form. Figure 9.2 overleaf shows the daily chart for BHP spanning eight months with several uptrends and downtrends. The MACD plot is shown at the bottom of the chart, with the MACD line drawn as the lighter trace. When the MACD line is above the signal line the histogram is above zero, and when the MACD line is below the signal line the histogram is below zero. It is easier to see on the MACD plot where the histogram crosses the horizontal zero line, rather than where the MACD line crosses the signal line. This leads to an alternative way of stating the rules for the MACD:

1. An uptrend begins when the histogram moves above zero.
2. A downtrend begins when the histogram moves below zero.

The complete notation for the MACD indicator is MACD (12,26,9) where the numbers 12 and 26 refer to the initial two exponential smoothing calculations, and the 9 refers to the smoothing to produce the signal line. Values other than 12, 26 and 9 can be used, but these are the most common values which have been found to work well.

The MACD can be expressed as:

$$\text{MACD line} = EMA_{12} - EMA_{26}$$

Signal line = 9-data exponential smoothing on MACD line

with exponential smoothing as defined previously.

Experience shows that the MACD performs well when the stock is trending, but in common with other trend-following systems, it gives many whipsaws if the stock is listless and moving sideways.

A useful filter to use with the MACD that inhibits some of the sideways whipsaws is:

> Take up trades only when the MACD line crosses above the signal line, *and the crossover occurs below zero*. Take down trades only when the MACD line crosses below the signal line, *and the crossover occurs above zero.*

Figure 9.2 shows that for well-defined trends the MACD line crosses the signal line several days before the MACD line crosses zero. Using charting software it is possible to show the daily MACD, the 9,18-day DMA and the 9,18-day EMA plots on the same screen. Inspection of various stocks shows that the MACD (12,26,9) crossovers consistently occur before the DMA crossovers, which in turn are before the EMA crossovers.

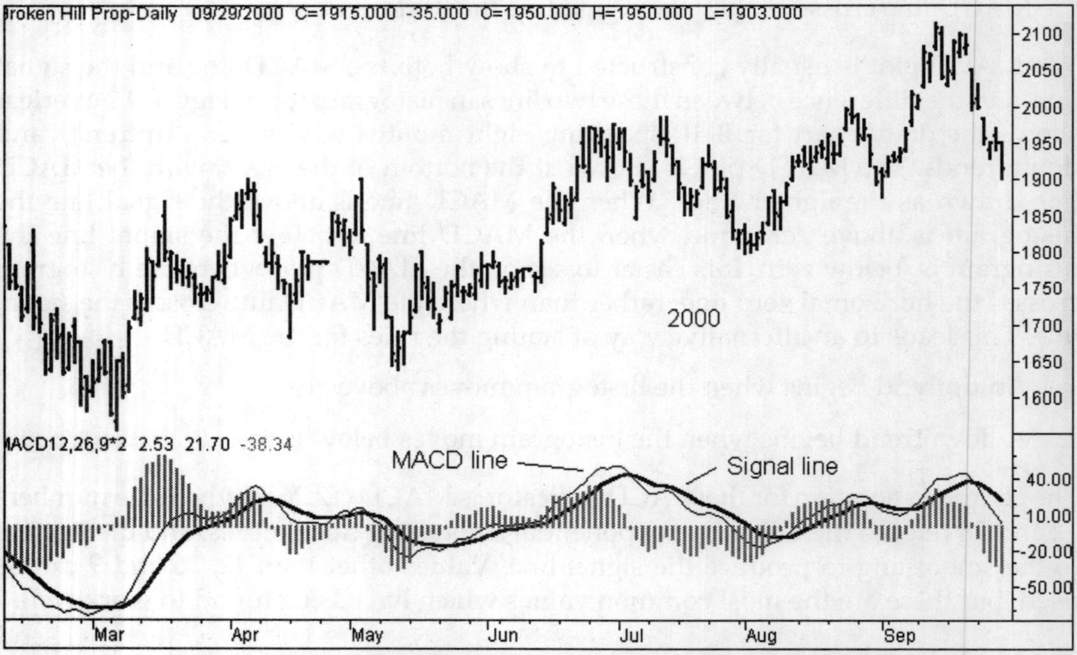

Figure 9.2 Chart of Daily MACD (12,26,9) for BHP

Directional Movement Indicator (DMI) and Average Directional Movement Index (ADX)

The DMI and ADX are related indicators developed by Welles Wilder Jr in 1978. The DMI is a trend-following system which gives signals that indicate the start and end of stock trends, while the ADX is derived from the DMI and indicates the strength of a trend. If the trend is strong then trend-following indicators (like the MACD, moving averages, etc.) should produce a profit, while if the trend is weak it is better to stand aside from that trade, as whipsaws are the likely result.

The concept and calculation of the DMI and ADX differs from other price-based indicators, and consequently can be used either alone, or more usually as a reliable independent filter on other trending indicators.

To calculate the DMI it is first necessary to understand the concepts of "directional movement" and "true range". When the trend is up, today's high should be above yesterday's high, and their difference is the "up" directional movement, defined as +DM. Similarly, when the trend is down, today's low should be below yesterday's low, and their difference is the "down" directional movement, defined as -DM.

Directional movement is the largest part of today's range that is outside yesterday's range, and the various possibilities are shown in Figure 9.3 overleaf.

The true range (TR) is the largest of:

Today's high – today's low

Today's high – yesterday's close

Yesterday's close – today's low

Each day has a directional index (DI) defined as $\frac{DM}{TR}$. These values are normally calculated over 14 days and then separated into up DM days and down DM days. The resulting 14-day up DI is $+DI_{14}$ and the down DI is $-DI_{14}$ where:

$$+DI_{14} = \frac{+DM_{14}}{TR_{14}}$$

$$+DI_{14} = \frac{-DM_{14}}{TR_{14}}$$

Note that by convention the $-DM_{14}$ values are positive. Thus, when the $+DI_{14}$ and $-DI_{14}$ are plotted together they form crossovers. When the $+DI_{14}$ crosses above the $-DI_{14}$ an uptrend is signalled, while when the $-DI_{14}$ crosses above the $+DI_{14}$ a downtrend is signalled. The $+DI_{14}$ and $-DI_{14}$ terms comprise the DMI.

The ADX is calculated as:

$$ADX_{14} = \frac{|\,(+DI_{14}) - (-DI_{14})\,|}{(+DI_{14}) + (-DI_{14})}$$

The ADX_{14} is a measure of the strength of the trend. When the stock is moving sideways there will be little difference between $+DI_{14}$ and $-DI_{14}$. However, as the stock develops either an uptrend or downtrend, the difference between $+DI_{14}$ and $-DI_{14}$ will widen and the ADX_{14} will increase in value. When the trend starts to turn over the $+DI_{14}$ and $-DI_{14}$ will converge again, and the ADX_{14} will fall.

Each of $+DI_{14}$, $-DI_{14}$ and ADX_{14} is multiplied by 100, so they are all plotted within the scale 0 to 100.

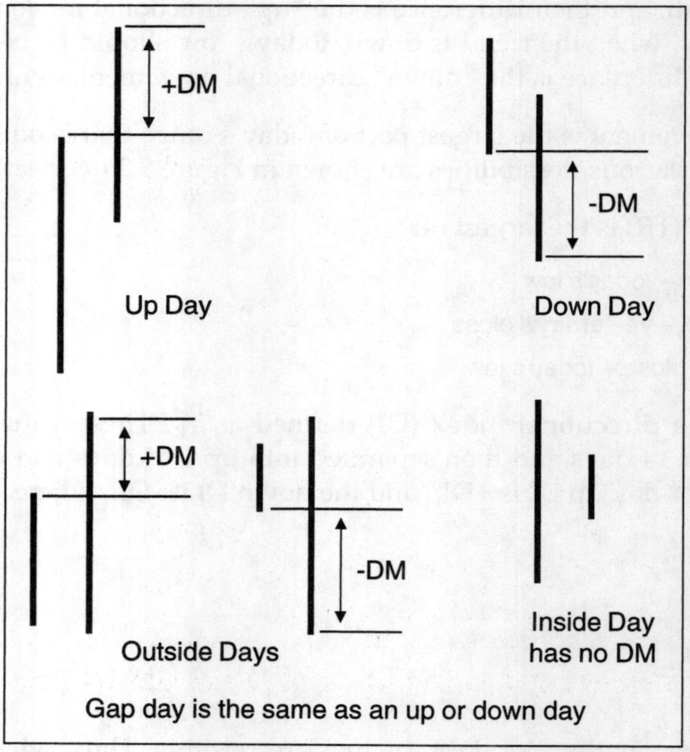

Figure 9.3 Definition of Directional Movement

Figure 9.4 opposite shows a daily chart for BHP spanning eight months. The DMI and ADX plots are shown at the bottom of the chart, with the ADX the heavy line. In late April -DI crossed above +DI and the ADX turned upwards (having been below both +DI and -DI), giving a confirmation of a downtrend. Similarly, in late October a similar set of conditions applied but with +DI crossing above -DI, confirming an uptrend.

The ADX is used as a filter to select only the +DI and -DI crossovers where the ADX is below both +DI and -DI and is moving upwards, as this indicates the beginning of a sustainable trend. Similarly, when the ADX is above both the +DI and -DI and turns down, this indicates that the present trend is weakening, and is an opportune time to quit a trade. It can also be a profitable time to write options, as some price consolidation can be expected prior to a reversal of the previous trend.

The primary interpretation of the ADX is that a rising ADX infers a trend is strengthening, while a falling ADX infers a trend is weakening or becoming a sideways move.

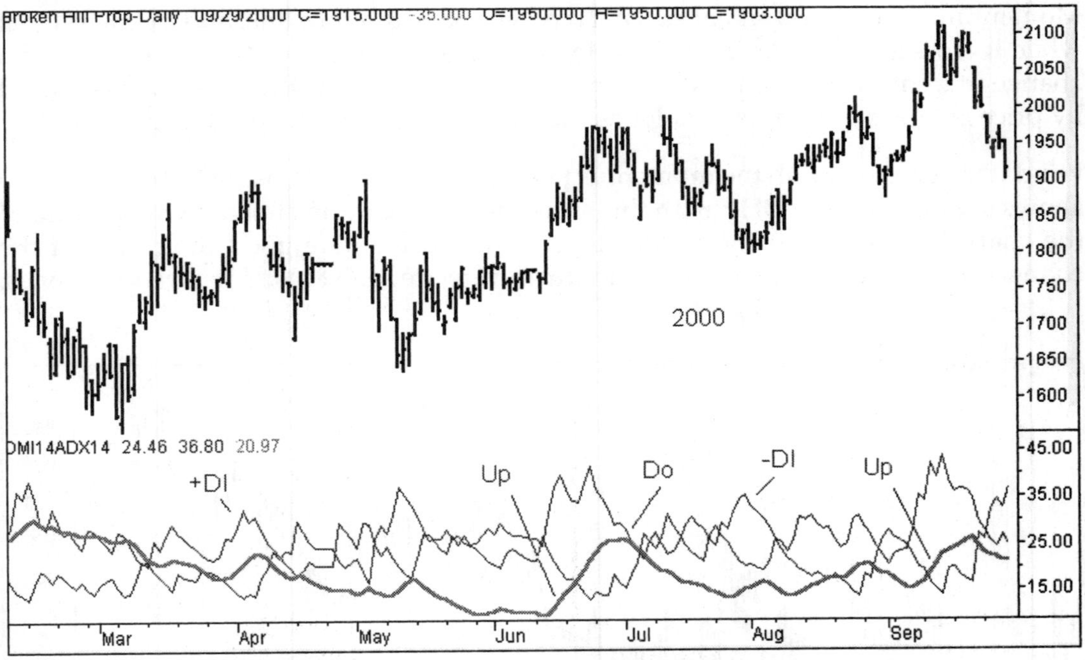

Figure 9.4 Chart of 14-day DMI and ADX for BHP

Momentum

Momentum is a popular and versatile indicator which can be used either as a leading indicator, an overbought/oversold oscillator or to determine a trend. Momentum M is defined as:

$$M = P_t - P_{t-n}$$

where:

P_t = today's close price P_{t-n} = the close price n data ago

For daily data, the value of n is usually selected as 10.

Momentum moves up and down around a zero line as prices move from uptrends to downtrends.

A typical uptrend will last for several weeks and then lose its drive, flatten out and turn down. In the early part of the uptrend, momentum will move above zero and rise. As the trend runs out of steam and moves into a consolidation phase the momentum will turn over and head towards zero. When the trend reverses the momentum will become negative.

Momentum gives an up signal when it crosses above the zero line, and a down signal when it crosses below the zero line. Momentum also gives an advance warning of a change in trend when it turnss over prior to crossing zero, as this turn-over is caused by price changes becoming smaller as the trend approaches its peak or trough.

I find it useful to smooth the momentum values over two data using SMA. Figure 9.5 shows a daily chart for BHP with this smoothed momentum shown at the bottom of the chart. It is seen that the momentum zero crossings are good indicators of the change in trend, while the momentum turn-overs are seen to lead the trend changes.

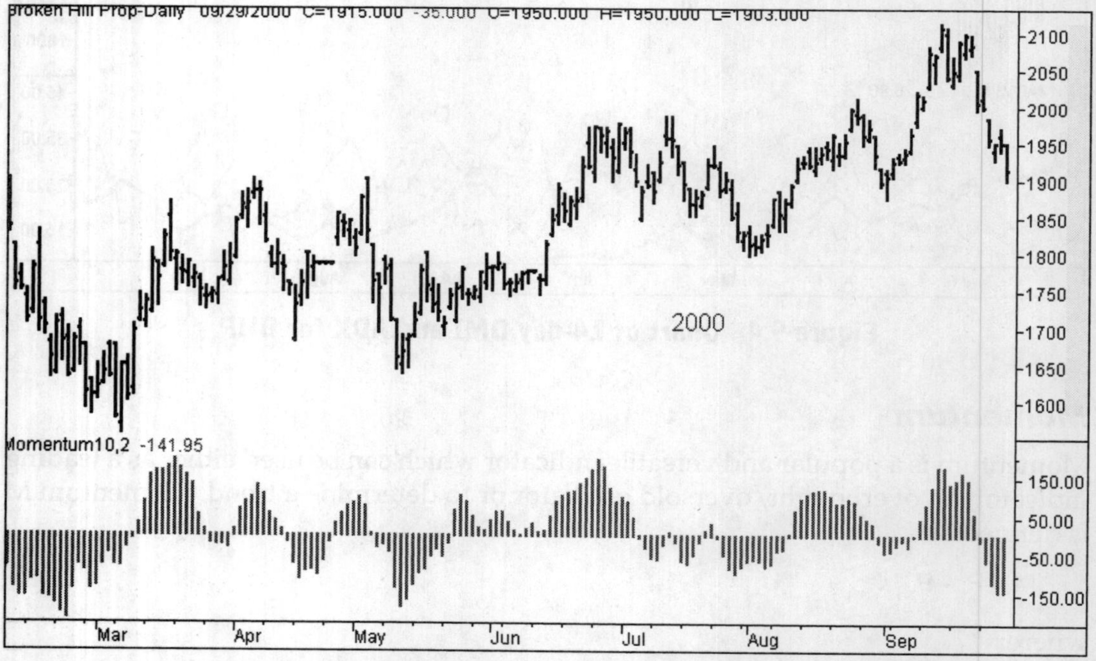

Figure 9.5 Chart of 10-day Smoothed Momentum for BHP

Rate of Change Indicator

The Rate of Change (ROC) indicator is an alternative representation of the momentum indicator, with ROC being defined as:

$$ROC = 100 \times \frac{P_t}{P_{t-n}} - 100$$

where:

P_t = today's close price P_{t-n} = the close price n data ago

To show the equivalence between the ROC and momentum indicators, Table 9.1 lists a set of close prices, with the corresponding momentum and ROC values when n = 10.

Table 9.1 Momentum and ROC Values

Data number	Close Price	Momentum	ROC
1	200		
2	205		
3	210		
4	215		
5	220		
6	225		
7	230		
8	225		
9	220		
10	215		
11	210	-10	-4.8
12	205	0	0
13	200	10	5
14	195	20	10.3
15	190	30	13.2
16	200	25	12.5
17	210	20	9.5
18	215	10	4.7
19	220	0	0
20	225	-10	-4.4

Table 9.1 shows that both the momentum and ROC values cross through zero at the same time (data numbers 12 and 19), while their peak values both occur at data number 15.

When the momentum and ROC values are plotted they display similar patterns, and have identical zero crossings, but their charts have differing vertical scales.

Bollinger Bands

Bollinger bands are statistically-defined bands above and below a short-term moving average, and are useful in showing overbought and oversold situations.

A 9-day SMA is calculated on the daily close data, and the standard deviation of the close price away from this average is calculated for the past nine days. An upper and lower band is drawn two standard deviations away from the average. As the standard deviation is calculated from a small number of samples, it responds rapidly to variations in price. Thus, when the stock is moving sideways in a congestion phase the bands contract, while when a trend develops the bands expand.

When stock prices move in a narrow trading range, as occurred in June in Figure 9.6 opposite, the Bollinger bands contract towards each other. When the stock price breaks out of this band it has significance, and is often the start of a new major move in that direction.

Further, when prices are close to, or penetrating, the upper band the stock is overbought, and when prices are close to, or penetrating, the lower band the stock is oversold. Bollinger bands are not used by themselves, but in conjunction with other indicators to confirm a trade.

Figure 9.6 shows Bollinger bands for daily BHP based on 9-day SMA and two standard deviations, and the overbought/oversold regions are clearly seen at the end of the stock trends.

Figure 9.6 Bollinger Bands for BHP

Relative Strength Indicator

The Relative Strength Indicator (RSI) is an overbought/oversold indicator, and was the forerunner of a family of such indicators. The RSI was also developed by Welles Wilder Jr and published in 1978. The value of the RSI always lies between 0 and 100, with values >70 indicating an overbought situation, and values <30 indicating an oversold situation.

RSI values above 70 also occur during a strong uptrend, while RSI values below 30 also occur during a strong downtrend. This leads to problems in applying the RSI to strongly trending stocks, as is noted later.

One formulation of the RSI is:

$$RSI = 100 - \frac{100}{1 + RS}$$

where:

$$RS = \frac{\text{exponential moving average of N days up closes}}{|\text{ exponential moving average of N days down closes }|}$$

An alternative formulation of the RSI is to use simple moving averages in calculating RS. In this case algebraic manipulation of the RSI formula results in the simplified expression:

$$RSI = \frac{100 \times U}{U + D}$$

where:

U = sum of up closes over last N days

D = sum of down closes over last N days

Wilder limited his initial analysis to N = 14-day periods. Other analysts have extended the RSI to cover both daily and weekly data, and looked at data periods other than 14. Experience shows that for best results, the RSI data period must be matched to the price behaviour of the stock, and the period will typically be in the range 7 to 21.

When using weekly data, the RSI calculations may be performed on the weekly close data. Alternatively, it is possible to use other measures of weekly price movement, and I also use the weekly $\frac{(high + low)}{2}$ value for calculating the RSI, which I call the "average" RSI.

I use a 7-week period for BHP and calculate both the weekly close RSI and the weekly "average" RSI. Figure 9.7 opposite shows the corresponding RSI charts for BHP.

A stock is overbought when the RSI is above 70, and is oversold when the RSI is below 30. These regions are easily seen from the RSI plot, yet being overbought or oversold does not in itself indicate a change in trend, but rather that a stock is due for a correction. It is necessary to wait for a double top or double bottom to form, as that is the RSI signal. Thus the trading rules are:

An up signal occurs on the formation of a double bottom, with each of the bottoms below 30, and the RSI then rising above 30.

A down signal occurs on the formation of a double top, with each of the tops above 70, and the RSI then falling below 70.

These double formations should occur within the space of about eight data to be valid.

Figure 9.7 for BHP weekly data shows that both the close price RSI and "average" RSI have several double tops and double bottoms, and sometimes only one RSI shows the double formation. It can be seen that the RSI gives a reliable signal for entering trades.

I find the 7-week RSI to be a useful indicator for the resource stocks that execute regular cycles. However, when stocks execute long trends the RSI can stay above 70 or below 30 for considerable periods of time, and give multiple (false) signals during that time. Bank stocks exhibit these trends, so the RSI is best avoided with these stocks.

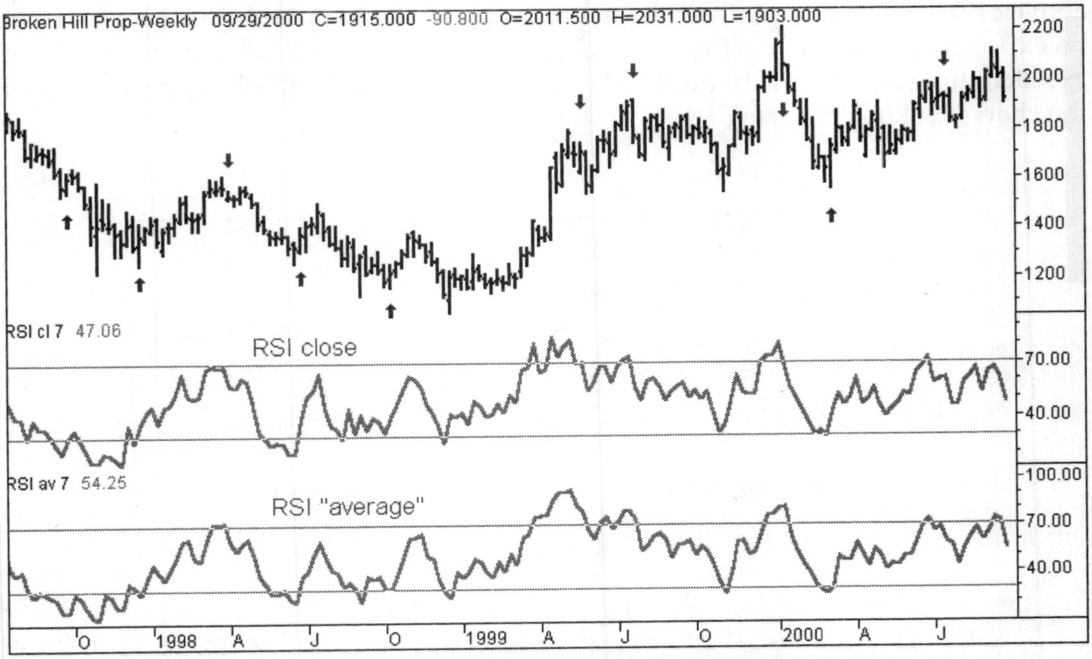

Figure 9.7 Chart of 7-week Close and "Average" RSI for BHP

CHARTING

The classic text on charting, *Technical Analysis of Stock Trends*, by Edwards and Magee has been reprinted many times since it first appeared in 1948. Four much shorter, but very helpful, books on the topic are by Meani, Hull, Armstrong and Krastins.

It is necessary to have a general understanding of charting principles, and to use charts to confirm or complement the technical indicators discussed above. The assumption here is that the reader has a general knowledge of charting. If this is not the case, then Regina Meani's concise book is recommended, as it covers the fundamentals well.

In this section we consider some specific topics of interest in our trading strategy.

Confirmation and Pullbacks

Figure 9.8 below shows two common chart reversal patterns, the double top and the symmetric triangle. When the stock breaks through the XX support line, some chart theory recommends to wait for a 3% confirmation at A before entering the trade. Thus if XX occurs at $1.00, we would wait for the price to drop below $0.97 or move above $1.03. Furthermore, chart theory states that a pullback to the XX breakout can be expected within the next three weeks, and when the pullback occurs, this is an excellent time to enter the trade. Similar confirmation and pullbacks apply to most of the chart breakout patterns.

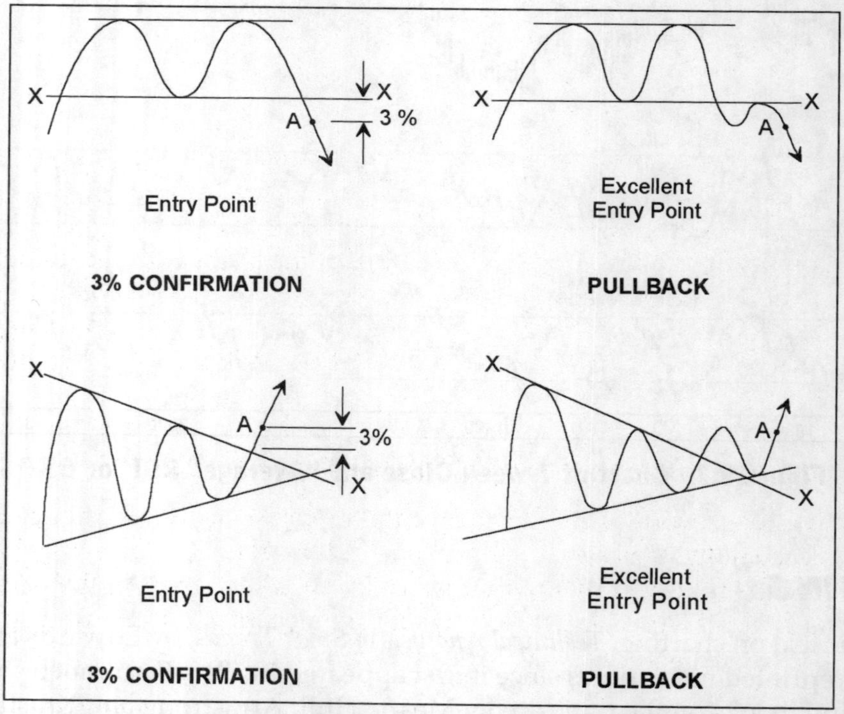

Figure 9.8 Chart of 3% Confirmation and Pullbacks

Volume

Daily and weekly price charts need to be read in conjunction with their volume of sales, as volume is the driving power in the market.

The basic rules are:

Rising prices with rising volume is bullish

Rising prices with falling volume is bearish

Falling prices with rising volume is bearish

Falling prices with falling volume is bullish

Many of the chart patterns have associated volume patterns, and the two need be read together for correct interpretation.

The option stocks of interest to us have regular heavy volume. However, such volume is frequently biased by the expiry of options at the end of the month, and by the institutions re-weighting their portfolios.

Point and Figure Charts

Point and figure charts are a favourite charting tool used by analysts to complement the technical indicators. A point and figure chart is a series of vertical x and o symbols on a sheet of squared paper, with the x symbols indicating rising prices, and the o symbols representing falling prices. The feature of the point and figure chart is that it takes no account of time, as price is the only parameter in the chart. The patterns generated in point and figure charts give rise to a variety of buy and sell signals, and support and resistance lines, and are covered in charting texts (see Meani and Armstrong).

Price Retracements and Projections from Ranges

W. D. Gann wrote several classic texts on chart theory. He showed that prices tend to move in a reasonably consistent manner. In a bull market, an uptrend is followed by a reversal, that is followed by another uptrend, etc. Furthermore, the price move in the reversal and the subsequent uptrend are related to the price range of the first uptrend. The opposite applies in a bear market.

Figure 9.9 overleaf shows an uptrend with a price range R. The likely retracement amounts are $\frac{R}{3}$, $\frac{R}{2}$ and $\frac{2R}{3}$. The $\frac{R}{3}$ value is a minimum to expect, while $\frac{R}{2}$ is the normal amount, and $\frac{2R}{3}$ is the maximum retracement. Retracements larger than $\frac{2R}{3}$ are likely to signal the reversal of the original trend.

Once the stock has turned around from the retracement to continue its previous direction, the likely move is $\frac{R}{2}$ or R above (below) the previous top (bottom). The Gann retracement ratios expressed in decimal form are 0.33, 0.5 and 0.67. Another choice for reversals are the Fibonacci ratios of 0.38, 0.5 and 0.62 (see also page 103).

The two sets of numbers are close to one another, and analysts often mark both sets on their charts.

The safest place to enter the market is often at the end of the reversal when the stock resumes its previous trend.

Inspection of stock charts will confirm Gann and Fibonacci retracements and targets. It is customary to draw bar charts using a semilog scale as this allows straight line trend lines to be drawn. Some software displays the Gann and Fibonacci retracements only on a linear scale, so we need to check our software capability, and possibly only display these retracements on charts drawn to a linear scale.

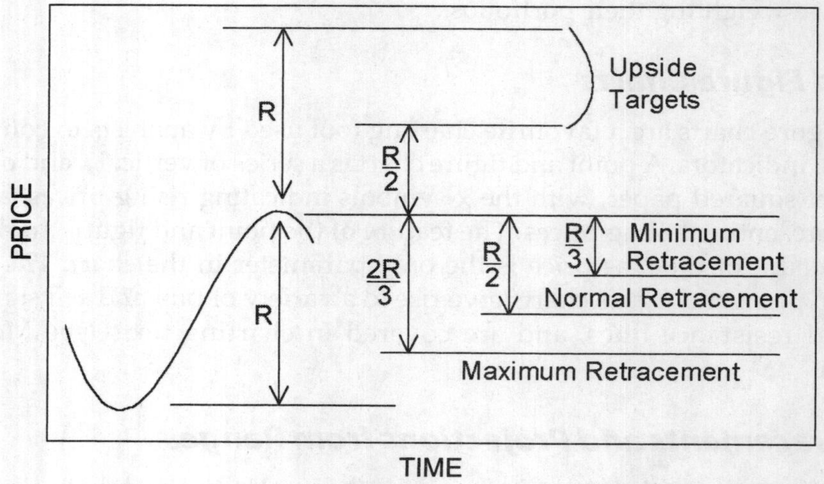

Figure 9.9 Gann Retracements and Targets

TIME DURATION AND THE ANNUAL MARKET CYCLE

This section may seem a little ethereal in a chapter on technical indicators which are precise mathematical algorithms. However, time duration analysis has stood the test of time, and is another indicator to check before making a final decision on executing a particular trade.

Gann was one of the first analysts to use time as a factor in analysis. He divided the year into calendar day segments or cycles of roughly 360, 180, 90, 45, 30 and 15 days and observed that these time cycles occur frequently in the duration of stock trends and reversals. Some of Gann's work has been simplified and refined by McLaren.

Time Durations and Projections

Gann determined that trends tend to have a specific duration, and that important trend changes frequently occur at specific times after a major top or a major bottom. Both these times correspond to his calendar day segments or cycles. Converting from days to weeks gives:

Days	360	180	90	45	30	15
Weeks	52	26	13	7	4	2

Gann considered the 7-week, and particularly the 13-week, trend to be a prime candidate for a reversal. Measuring forward 26 and 52 weeks from major tops and bottoms often shows a trend reversal occurs at these times. Once again, inspection of weekly stock charts confirms Gann's theory.

Time analysis cannot be used by itself, but is another useful tool to monitor and use as a confirmation when other indicators indicate a change in trend.

Time analysis can be a bit confusing, because another choice of values is the Fibonacci numbers 1,1,2,3,5,8,13,21,34,55,89,144... for the length of the trends. However, the two sets of numbers have a correspondence in the important regions of 7,8 and 13,15. The Fibonacci ratios of 0.62 and 0.38 listed on page 101 are derived by dividing the current number in the series into the previous number, and the current number into the number two increments ago, i.e. $\frac{89}{144} = 0.62$ and $\frac{55}{144} = 0.38$.

Annual Cycle in the Australian Market

Gann's detailed study of the market allowed him to highlight particular months and dates when important tops and bottoms had occurred, and so had a high probability of happening again on those dates in the future. These days, computers and databases make time analysis a straightforward exercise, but Gann did not have this luxury.

Appendix I lists the important dates in the year when Gann determined a change in trend often occurs, which are included for interest and some surprise.

Statistical studies on the Australian stock market show that it has an annual cycle, which can be partitioned into monthly behaviour.

June's weakness is caused by the end of the Australian financial year with tax losses being taken, and is also the time of summer holidays in the Northern hemisphere. July is strong with portfolio buying at the start of the new financial year, as well as the anticipation of half-yearly earnings reports. The Christmas rally is due to the optimism associated with a new year, and also expectations of half-yearly earnings reports.

We need to be aware of the October + November/December + January and June/July couplets and be alert to the trading opportunities they present.

There is a rough correspondence between the Australian annual cycle and Gann's annual cycle listed in Appendix I.

January	Strong month
February	Weak month, i.e. small gains to small losses
March	Weak month—journalists trot out "beware the ides of March" story
April	Weak month
May*	Federal Budget and market can respond either way
June	Worst month
July	Strong month
August, September	Weak months
October	The month for crashes and crashettes
November	Weak month
December	Start of Christmas and New Year rally

*Sometimes the Federal Budget is handed down in August

COMPARISON OF SIGNALS FROM TECHNICAL INDICATORS AND CHARTING

Technical indicators and charting both use the same price data stream, so the question arises, "Do they give signals at the same time?" The answer is yes, they often do.

It is a simple matter to generate a data file representing, say, a double top formation, and run this through the RSI and stochastic indicators. (The stochastic is another popular oscillator-type indicator.) By optimising each indicator to the time span of the double top formation, an overbought single or double top pattern can be produced, along with a signal to indicate the start of a downtrend.

I have generated data files for the common chart major top and bottom formations listed by Meani: double top/bottom, triple top/bottom, head and shoulders, horn, inverted V and saucer; and for the minor formations: triangle, flag, pennant and wedge. In each case, the RSI and stochastic indicators give a single or double top/bottom pattern and a signal to indicate a trend reversal.

By the same token, charts can show signals that are missed by the indicators, while the indicators can show signals that are not evident in the charts. Thus, charts and technical indicators can give complementary information from which to make trading decisions.

THE HARD PART OF TECHNICAL TRADING

As we become more experienced in trading, we find that it is relatively easy using technical indicators to decide when to open a trade.

The hard part comes in making the decision to close the trade, because our emotions may get the better of us. The correct course of action is to follow our trading strategy, and to be particularly disciplined in the way we close our trades. If we have a profit we are apt to close too early. We pat ourselves on the back for a day or so, but when the trend we have quit continues unabated we feel somewhat cheated. Conversely, if we have a loss we are loath to close the trade, but keep hoping that the market will turn in our favour—usually it does not, and again we feel the market has cheated us.

The feeling is akin to the golfer who loves the game but not the score, yet can't wait to play another round. These issues of emotional discipline are discussed further in Chapter 15.

Chapter 10

PROFIT PROFILE FOR BHP USING TECHNICAL TRADING SYSTEMS

THIS CHAPTER DEVELOPS a trading system for BHP using the MACD technical indicator to indicate the trends, and shows the need to use some form of filter so that only those trades with a high probability of success are opened. The trades are closed on a predetermined profit move, or on the MACD closing signal if the profit is not achieved.

The four cardinal rules of trading are:

1. Follow the trend.
2. Let the profits run.
3. Cut the losses.
4. Manage the money to stay in the game.

The MACD trading system obeys the first two rules of following the trend and letting the profits run, while rules 3 and 4 relate more to discipline and risk management and are discussed in Chapter 14.

Using a database of past prices and charting and analysis software, it is a simple matter to back-test the MACD indicator on BHP and determine the profit or loss in the trades.

RESULTS FOR BHP USING MACD

In order to demonstrate the trading system in a variety of conditions, the period from February 1996 to January 1997 is selected as a representative set of data. The first three months were flat trading conditions, even though March produced some volatility due to the Australian Federal Election which resulted in a change in government. From May onwards BHP executed several well-defined and profitable trading trends.

Table 10.1 (on page 109) lists the trading legs using the following rules:

1. BHP daily close price data used with the MACD (12,26,9) indicator.
2. Close down trades and open new up trades on the day the MACD line crosses above the signal line, i.e. when the histogram moves above zero.
3. Close up trades and open new down trades on the day the MACD line crosses below the signal line, i.e. when the histogram moves below zero.

For simplicity, all profit and loss values are calculated using the close price on the day of the MACD signal. In practice, the trade would be taken sometime on the following day. (Some traders would take the trade about 30 minutes after the market opens, while others prefer to wait until just before the close of trading, and then take the trade if BHP has moved in the direction of the trade.)

In Table 10.1 columns 1 and 2 are the leg number and direction. Columns 3 and 4 are the date and close price stop and reverse (SAR) days at the start and end of the leg, and these dates specify the leg turning points (TPs). Columns 5,6 are the leg move from TP to TP in cents and in days. (All the "days" listed in the table are trading days, and not calendar days.) Columns 7,8 are the leg maximum move in the correct direction from starting TP to peak (or trough) in cents and days. Columns 9,10 are the leg draw-down (from starting TP to maximum move in the wrong direction) in cents and days. Finally, column 11 is the amount of profit the leg gives back before the signal to quit is given, i.e. maximum move – leg move, while column 12 is the number of days after the peak/trough that the leg ends, as defined by the closing TP.

These various parameters are shown in Figure 10.1 overleaf.

The first five legs in Table 10.1 are all short time duration trades with no profit. We show later that the DMI and ADX indicators used as a trading filter keep us out of these trades, so their full leg values are not included in Table 10.1.

Table 10.1 demonstrates clearly the best and worst features of a trend-following system, viz. we get on-board every up and down leg and so catch the big ones (legs 6,7), but we are always late getting in and getting out of the leg (as evidenced by the maximum move always being much greater than the leg move, so the peak or trough has well passed before the system gives a signal to quit).

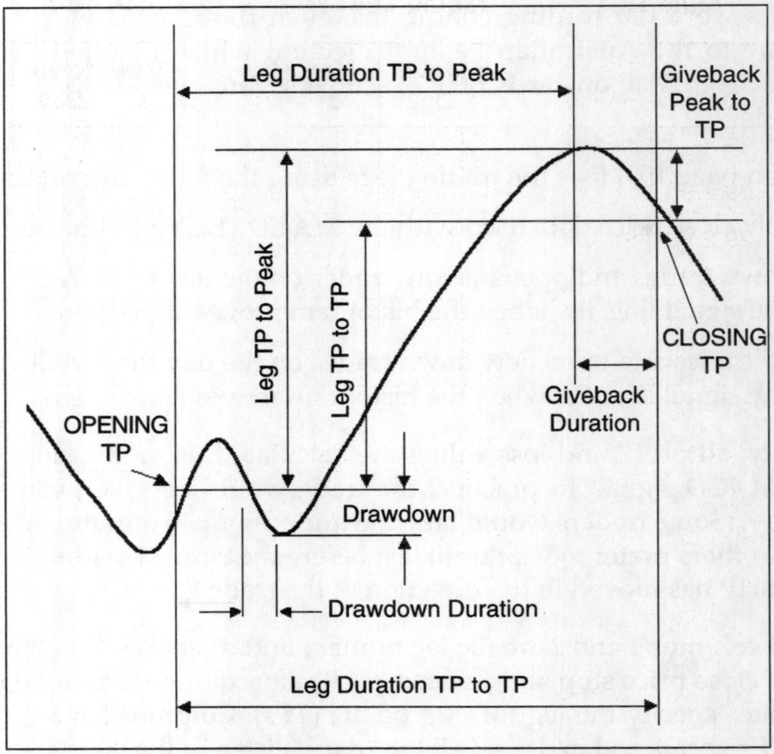

Figure 10.1 Definition of Trading Leg Terms

Considering legs 6 to 14, columns 5,6 show the profit in the legs if we enter and exit the trades on the TP signals, and 7 of the 9 legs show a profit. Notice that these 7 legs have a time duration from 17 to 52 days (except leg 12, which has a 13-day duration), while the loss legs have shorter time durations of 13 and 16 days.

Columns 7,8 show that there is a profit in every trade, if we have a crystal ball to pick the peak or trough day. These profits range from 29¢ in leg 11 to 352¢ in leg 7. Eight of the legs have a peak or trough profit >66¢, while six of the legs are >90¢. (More extensive analysis shows that 90¢ is an optimal profit move for BHP, so we quit warrants at this point.)

Because our trading strategy involves writing options, we are interested in the leg draw-down figures, as this determines when we may need to buy back our options to avoid being exercised. Leg 11 has identical figures in columns 5,6 and columns 9,10, which indicates that the maximum draw-down of 73¢ occurs at the end of the leg. Legs 8 and 10 have the next worst draw-downs of 38¢ and 23¢ respectively.

Table 10.1 BHP Trading Legs With MACD Indicator

Leg No.	Dir.	Date	Close Price	Leg Move ¢	Leg Move Day	Max. Move ¢	Max. Move Day	Draw-down ¢	Draw-down Day	Give-back ¢	Give-back Day
1	DO	20.2.96	1849								
		29.2.96	1895	-46	7						
2	UP	29.2.96	1895								
		8.3.96	1867	-28	6						
3	DO	8.3.96	1867								
		21.3.96	1869	-2	9						
4	UP	21.3.96	1869								
		22.3.96	1808	-61	1						
5	DO	22.3.96	1808								
		2.4.96	1835	-27	7						
6	UP	2.4.96	1835								
		9.5.96	1942	107	24	158	22	16	2	51	2
7	DO	9.5.96	1942								
		23.7.96	1658	284	52	352	48	0	0	68	4
8	UP	23.7.96	1658								
		2.9.96	1720	62	29	106	23	38	1	44	6
9	DO	2.9.96	1720								
		27.9.96	1635	85	19	138	15	3	2	53	4
10	UP	27.9.96	1635								
		29.10.96	1679	44	22	117	19	23	8	73	3
11	DO	29.10.96	1679								
		15.11.96	1752	-73	13	29	7	73	13	102	6
12	UP	15.11.96	1752								
		4.12.96	1762	10	13	66	9	0	0	56	4
13	DO	4.12.96	1762								
		30.12.96	1780	-18	16	69	10	1	34	87	6
14	UP	30.12.96	1780								
		23.1.97	1808	28	17	90	13	7	3	62	4

Column 11 shows that 8 of the 9 legs give back >50¢ of profit before the leg is terminated by the MACD rules. Column 12 shows that the legs terminate between two and six days after the peak/trough has occurred.

In summary, Table 10.1 shows that MACD has potential as a trading system for BHP, particularly if we can quit the trades somewhere near the leg peaks and troughs.

Anatomy of a Trade

Leg 7 of Table 10.1 is the ideal trade. On 9.5.96 we open the trade by writing 1st or 2nd out-of-the money call options, and buy put warrants. When the leg terminates 52 days (10 weeks) later, the call options will have expired worthless, while we would sell the put warrants as soon as BHP falls 90¢. Columns 9,10 list values 0,0 which mean that the stock price falls from the opening day, so the written call options are always in profit.

Leg 8 is a more typical trade. On 23.7.96 we write 1st or 2nd out-of-the-money put options and buy call warrants. Columns 9,10 show that one day later the stock has a draw-down of 38¢ and the 1st out-of-the-money option is close to being in-the-money, and causing concern lest the share price falls any more, but it does not. We quit the call warrants when BHP rises 90¢. The leg terminates on the 29th day (6 weeks) with a profit of 62¢. The written put options can be bought back for a few cents, as their time premium is eroded, and the share price rise makes the options deeper out-of-the money.

Leg 11 is the exception that occurs in any trading system, and strikes a note of caution against expecting every trade to be a winner. On 29.10.96 we write 1st or 2nd out-of-the-money call options and buy put warrants. Columns 7,8 show that the maximum profit occurs 7 days later and is only 29¢. The leg terminates on the 13th day with a loss of 73¢, and on this day we buy back both the call options and the put warrants at a loss.

Leg 13 demonstrates the advantage of writing options, whereby a small move in the stock against us can still result in an option profit. On 4.12.96 we write 1st or 2nd out-of-the-money call options and buy put warrants. Columns 5,6 show that the leg terminates 16 days later with a 18¢ loss. Calculations done at the time show that the 1st or 2nd out-of-the-money BHP call option with 8 weeks to expiry loses about 5¢ per week of time premium. If the stock price rises from \$18.00 to \$18.50 the value of the 2nd out-of-the-money option rises from about 28¢ to 46¢ (a rise of 18¢ giving a delta of $\frac{18}{50} = 0.36$).

Thus for leg 13, the rise in stock price of 18¢ would cause the option to rise about 18 x 0.36 = 6¢ while the passage of 16 days (3 weeks) would cause the option to fall about 3 x 5 = 15¢ for a net fall of 15 – 6 = 9¢. (In fact, the 2nd out-of-the-money Jan 18.50 call option written on 4.12.96 at 28¢ could be bought back on 30.12.96 at 19¢ for a profit of 9¢).

Filtering MACD Signals with DMI and ADX Indicator

Chapter 9 showed that the MACD indicator is prone to whipsaws during sideways price congestion, but that the DMI and ADX indicators can be used as a filter, enabling us to keep out of trades during this time.

Figure 10.2 below shows the daily chart for BHP covering the time period from Table 10.1, and includes the MACD (12,26,9) and 14-day DMI and ADX indicators. While the ADX is below both the DMI lines BHP is trending sideways and no trades can be taken. The strong uptrend in BHP in April moves the ADX, and from then on each of the ADX peaks and troughs have patterns which validate the MACD signals as being the start of worthwhile trends.

Figure 10.2 Chart of Daily BHP with MACD, DMI and ADX Indicators

On the subject of filters, when taking signals from daily data, it is often prudent to use a weekly indicator as a filter. This may seem contradictory, as we would expect the weekly indicator signal to occur much later than the daily indicator, and so be of little use. However, the weekly MACD is a suitable filter, as its histogram turns over before the MACD line crosses the signal line. Thus, for an uptrend, when the weekly MACD histogram has peaked and is declining the trend is weakening and ready to reverse. Similarly, for a downtrend, when the weekly MACD histogram has bottomed and is increasing the trend is weakening and ready to reverse. Using charting software it is easy to confirm this effect. Elder considers the MACD weekly histogram used in this way to be the most reliable of all the weekly indicators.

Recap of Trading Strategy Rules

Chapter 6 defines the general trading strategy while Chapter 9 discusses the need to use the MACD in conjunction with a filter such as the DMI and ADX indicators.

Thus, our trading strategy for BHP becomes:

In a down market open trades signalled by daily MACD and confirmed with DMI and ADX and weekly MACD, in the following ways:

1. Write out-of-the money call options with six to ten weeks to expiry.
2. Buy put warrants with preferably six months to expiry.

In an up market open trades signalled by daily MACD and confirmed with a filter such as the DMI and ADX and weekly MACD, in the following ways:

1. Write out-of-the money put options with six to ten weeks to expiry.
2. Buy call warrants with preferably six months to expiry.

The results from Table 10.1 imply the rules for closing BHP trades as:

1. Quit bought put and call warrants on a stock move greater than 90¢.
2. Buy back open options and warrants on the daily MACD signal.

Profit from Writing Options

Chapter 7 discusses the various profits to be expected from trading five BHP put and call options. The maximum profits arise when the options expire worthless. In January 1997 when BHP was trading around $18.00 and volatility was about 21%, the 1st out-of-the-money written call options with eight weeks to expiry resulted in profits up to $2,210, while the corresponding put option profits were up to $1,510.

Notice that in September 2000 with BHP trading around $21.00 and having volatility of 25%, Table 7.2 shows the corresponding call options give profits of up to $3,300, while Table 7.4 shows the corresponding put options give profits of up to $2,550. Thus in terms of profit from writing options, the rise in the value of BHP from around $18.00 to $21.00, along with the rise in volatility from around 21% to 25%, results in the option profits rising some 50%.

Profit from Buying Call Warrants

Warrants are discussed in Chapter 11. We are interested here in the warrant delta, which determines the increase in the warrant price for, say, a 90¢ move in BHP.

In October 1996, BHP moved up from about $16.30 to about $17.30 (100¢). The BHP BT Securities 25.9.97 expiry call warrant (code BHPWBB and see Chapter 11) moved from around 40¢ to 60¢, or a 50% increase, and a delta of $\frac{20}{100} = 0.2$. Similarly, over the same time, the BHP BT Securities 25.6.98 expiry call warrant (code BHPWBT) moved from around 40¢ to 55¢, or a 37% increase, and a delta of 0.15.

Thus, if we trade the call warrants in parcels of, say, $4,000, the profit on a 90¢ stock rise is about $4{,}000 \times 0.50 \times \frac{90}{100} = \$1{,}800$, depending on the warrant chosen.

Profit from Buying Put Warrants

In January 1997, BHP moved down from about $18.55 to about $17.45 (110¢ fall). The BHP Macquarie Bank 26.3.98 expiry put warrant (code BHPWMP) moved from around 96¢ to 130¢, or a 35% increase, and a delta of 0.31. Thus, if we trade the put warrants in parcels of, say, $4,000, the profit on a 90¢ stock fall is about $4{,}000 \times 0.35 \times \frac{90}{110} = \$1{,}145$, depending on the warrant chosen.

RESULTS FOR BHP USING RSI

We will now look at an alternative technical trading system using an oscillator, and select the RSI as discussed in Chapter 9 using the alternative simple moving average formulation. The RSI signals can be used alone, or in conjunction with the other indicators. For simplicity, the RSI is treated here as a "stand-alone" system.

We use weekly BHP data, and a shorter 7-week RSI which gives satisfactory results. The RSI signal indicates an overbought/oversold situation which often results in a fast correction. Consequently, the strategy is to enter a trade on the signal and quit within six weeks on any reasonable price move.

Table 10.2 below lists the results obtained by applying the weekly RSI method to BHP over the 2.5-year period from June 1994 to January 1997. The signals are taken from both the weekly close RSI (termed C) and the weekly "average" RSI (termed A). Column 2 indicates whether the signal is from close or "average" RSI and column 3 shows the direction of the leg. Columns 4 and 5 are the date and price at the start of the leg. Column 6 shows the peak/trough price (¢) that occurs within six weeks of the signal. Finally, columns 7 and 8 show the leg peak/trough move and the number of weeks this occurs after the trade is opened.

Table 10.2 BHP Results for RSI and Quitting Trades Inside Six Weeks

Leg No.	Signal	Dir.	Date	Price (¢)	Peak/ Trough (¢)	Move (¢)	Weeks
1	A	DO	24.6.94	1707	1582	125	3
2	C&A	DO	9.9.94	1829	1709	120	4
3	A	DO	11.8.95	1938	1828	110	6
4	A	UP	10.11.95	1828	1933	107	5
5	C&A	DO	12.1.96	1892	1849	43	6
6	C	UP	27.9.96	1635	1752	117	4

Where column 2 lists "C&A", both the close and "average" RSI give signals on the same week.

The trading rules for the RSI system are:

1. Weekly high, low and close price data is used, and 7-week RSI values are calculated for both the close and "average" prices.
2. Monitor both these close and "average" RSI values and take signals from either system.
3. Open up trades on the formation of a double bottom, with each of the bottoms below 30, and the RSI then rising above 30.
4. Open down trades on the formation of a double top with each of the tops above 70, and the RSI then falling below 70.
5. Close the legs on a BHP move greater than 90¢.
6. If the legs do not reach the 90¢ move, close the leg after six weeks, or with the help of the daily MACD indicator.

It is preferable to open the trade just before the market closes on Friday afternoon. Using a software package it is possible to test the weekly RSI values up to Thursday's close. If we monitor the price of BHP on Friday afternoon, we have a good idea if there will be any change in the RSI value, and whether to open a trade. If in doubt, then wait until Monday to open the trade.

Table 10.2 shows that over the 2.5-year time span there are only six signals, but each give a correct move greater than 40¢, while five signals precede moves greater than $1.00 over the following six weeks.

With BHP and the RSI system, we can maintain our previous trading rules of opening trades by writing out-of-the-money put and call options, and buying put and call warrants. It is prudent to quit the trades on a stock move greater than 90¢.

SUMMARY AND WARNING ON TECHNICAL SYSTEMS

Most analysts warn against a blind reliance on technical analysis methods, as the signals they produce need to be tempered with common sense and an awareness of what is happening in the broader market. Experience shows that a particular analysis system may perform well on a stock for some time, but can deteriorate due to changes in the stock behaviour, so systems need to be monitored regularly.

Before using any technical system in the market, it is essential to back-test it with at least two years of data for the stock to be traded, and critically analyse the results. By its very nature, back-testing (see page 117) is always conducted in hindsight from a list of historic inanimate prices. In real life, investors must contend with news items, headlines and market sentiment that may alter their perception on a trade and, hence, their actions. However, a disciplined technical analyst will thoroughly test a system and, if it looks profitable, take its trades and so let the probabilities for success work over a period of time.

Several technical indicators have at least one parameter to optimise (the MACD has three, while the RSI has one). It is of interest to vary these parameters in back-testing, but it is best to stick with the tried and proven values from the various texts. LeBeau and Lucas, in particular, are strongly against fiddling with the optimising parameters.

The goal of any trading system is to be able to define the trends (whether we be interested in short, medium or long-term trends), define the peaks and troughs within these trends, and give reliable signals as near as possible to these peaks and troughs.

Some popular technical indicators, as discussed in Chapter 9, comprise moving averages and MACD to determine the trend, DMI and ADX to determine times of sideways consolidation, RSI to determine overbought/oversold situations and momentum to give advance warning of change in trends. The technical trader needs to be aware of each of these and other indicators, and choose a set to comprise a trading system for personal use. This system must be back-tested and optimised for the stocks of interest, before committing cash to the market.

General charting techniques, including point and figure charts, are also useful to determine trends, stops, breakouts and targets.

KNOWING WHEN TO BEND THE RULES

We should always check the signals from one technical indicator against other technical indicators, as sometimes this checking will tell us to not take a trade. As an example, suppose BHP completes a downtrend and is a couple of weeks into an uptrend, but then falters and the MACD indicates the start of a fresh down leg. Checking the RSI may happen to show that the uptrend is preceded by a double bottom (which is a reliable signal for BHP). This conflict of indicators would caution us to look at the broader market for any clues to BHP's future price.

This set of conditions occurred with BHP in October 1996. Earlier in the year, the price of copper dived 35% in the course of seven weeks due to the Sumitomo debacle. Over the next 20 weeks copper formed a double bottom and then rallied strongly upwards. Just prior to the copper fall, BHP bought Magma Copper at a price that was considered high by the market. Consequently, as copper slumped, so too did BHP, and come October 1996 BHP formed a double bottom along with the price of copper.

On 27.9.96, with BHP at $16.35 the MACD signalled the start of an uptrend which was the right-hand side of the double bottom. This leg peaked on 24.10.96, with BHP at $17.52, and then a downtrend was signalled by the MACD on 29.10.96 with BHP at $16.79. At this time the 7-week RSI for BHP was 57 and moving up from a double bottom. But, more importantly, the price of copper was establishing an uptrend on the right side of its double bottom, and market sentiment was for a continued rise in the price of copper.

Taking all these factors into account, we should not have acted on the MACD down signal, but anticipated a rise in BHP in the near future. This did happen; the MACD gave a fresh up signal on 15.11.96 with BHP at $17.52. (Table 10.1 shows that leg 11 starting on 29.10.96 was a loss trade of 73¢.)

At the time, I noticed CRA (since renamed RIO) was following BHP fairly closely, but was more highly favoured by the financial writers for recovery. From past trades I knew that the CRA warrant CRAWBT had a high delta. Consequently, in order to profit from this set of signals and market conditions, I chose to buy CRAWBT call warrants in early November 1996. Copper continued upwards and I quit the trade within two weeks for a net profit of 50%.

Schwager says that some of the market traders who do not use technical indicators find it difficult to specify exactly why they make a trade – they weigh up the conflicting factors in the market and then come to their own decision. So it is when it comes to bending our trading rules. The broader market gives the big picture which sometimes must be used in preference to our favourite indicators.

BACK-TESTING

Before using an indicator in the market it is essential to apply some form of back-testing, and so gain confidence in the indicator by understanding its performance, and any quirks it may exhibit. Ideally, we should have data spanning five years, or even ten years, to analyse. With five years of data, it is partitioned into three segments as: the earliest 18 months, the central two years, and the most recent 18 months. The central two years of data is analysed thoroughly by the indicator(s) we hope to use, along with any optimisation or application of filters. If the results look satisfactory, the indicator(s) are then applied to the earliest 18 months of data. If the results are confirmed, then the indicator(s) are applied to the most recent 18 months of data. Provided each of these three sets of analysis shows satisfactory and confirming results, then we are ready to use the indicator(s) in the market, as we should then understand what to expect in terms of profits and losses, and how to minimise the effect of the losses.

The analysis contained in this chapter covers the MACD results on daily BHP data from February 1996 to January 1997, and the RSI results on weekly BHP from June 1994 to January 1997. The interested reader with available software and database should extend this analysis from January 1997 onwards, and so confirm the previous results. A more detailed discussion on back-testing is contained in *Technical Analysis for Trading Index Warrants*.

Figure 10.3 overleaf shows a weekly chart of BHP from August 1997 to September 2000, along with the 7-week close price RSI and "average" RSI traces. The up and down arrows show buy and sell signals derived from these indicators, and it is apparent that the RSI system, using the rules listed on page 114, continues to work well on BHP.

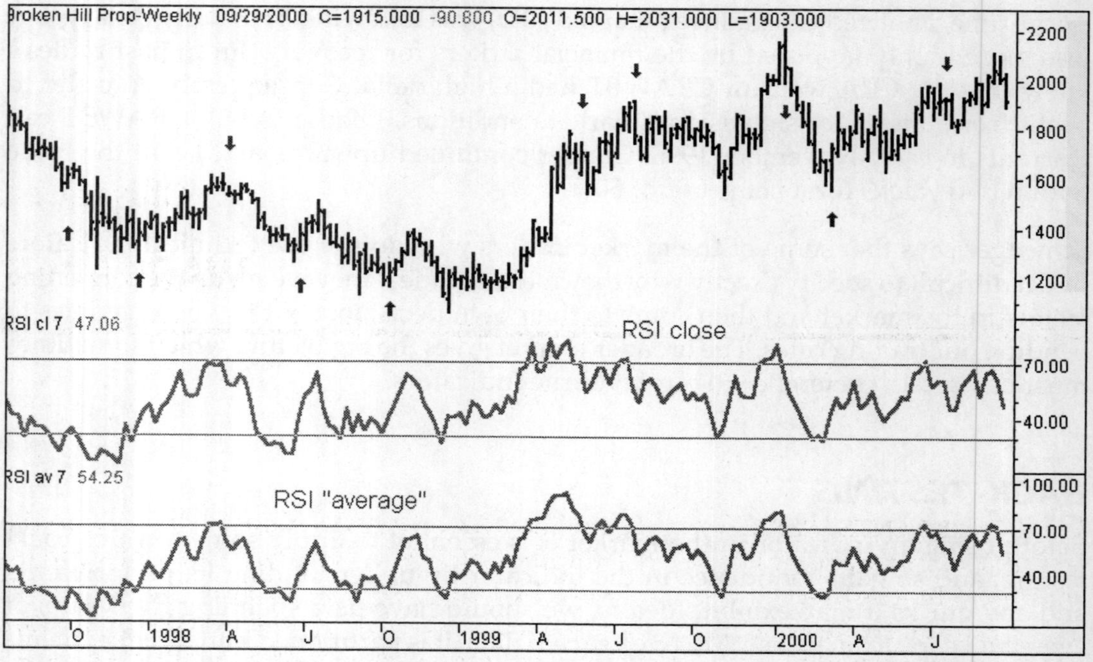

Figure 10.3 Chart of 7-Week Close and "Average" RSI for BHP

Chapter 11

WARRANTS

CALL WARRANTS WERE introduced to the ASX on a small number of stocks in the late 1980s, but in recent times the number of stocks with warrants has grown considerably. The first put warrants were introduced in 1996. In early 1997 either call or put warrants were available on some 30 stocks, while at September 2000 the number had grown to around 50 stocks. Warrants give traders and investors another leveraged way to make profits in a moving market (and losses, if we get the direction wrong).

There are several classes of warrants trading on the ASX.

1. **Equity Call Warrants**

   Equity call warrants are sponsored by a number of large merchant banks and finance institutions. These warrants have typically up to 12 months to expiry when first issued, and parcel sizes are 1,000 warrants. On exercise, one warrant normally converts to one share, but there are also many warrants which convert on the basis of two, three, four or ten warrants to one share.

   Equity call warrants are either American or European in style. American-style warrants can be exercised during the life of the warrant, while European-style warrants can only be exercised on the expiry date. The majority of equity call warrants are American-style.

2. **Equity Put Warrants**

   Equity put warrants are also sponsored by a number of large merchant banks and finance institutions. These warrants have typically up to 12 months to expiry when first issued, and parcel sizes are 1,000 warrants. The majority of equity put warrants are European-style, and convert on the basis of one, two three, four or ten warrants to one share.

3. Endowment Warrants

Endowment warrants are offered by Credit Suisse Financial Products and Macquarie Bank Ltd. Endowment warrants were first issued in 1996 with a term of ten years. Endowment warrants offer a leveraged investment in the underlying stock, but their performance is dependent upon that stock paying an increasing rate of dividend over their ten-year life.

Endowment warrants are not a part of our trading strategy.

4. Instalment Warrants

Instalment warrants, as the name implies, are call warrants which are paid for in two instalments over a period of typically two years. Instalment warrants are available on about 35 stocks, but are not a part of our trading strategy.

5. Capital Plus Warrants

Capital Plus warrants cover the purchase of a basket of shares, whereby the purchaser is guaranteed a minimum capital return at the warrant expiry which is typically five years. This minimum is normally the initial offering price, but this may not be the same as the price paid by a subsequent purchaser.

Capital Plus warrants are not a part of our trading strategy.

The following discussion relates only to equity warrants, which will be referred to simply as "call warrants" or "put warrants".

WARRANT ISSUERS

Warrants are issued by several large merchant banks and finance houses. At September 2000 the warrant issuers are as listed in Table 11.1 opposite. Each warrant series has a unique six-letter code for identification. For example, the BHP warrant BHPWMO is a call warrant having a strike price of $21.00, expiry 29.3.01, conversion ratio 3:1, is American-style and is issued by Macquarie Bank. The first three letters in the warrant code are the ASX code for the stock, the fourth letter is W to indicate an equity warrant, the fifth letter M defines the issuer (Maquarie Bank in this case), and the last letter O is the issuer code for that series, e.g. Maquarie Bank would have issued warrants A to N on BHP which covered different strike prices and expiry times, etc.

Unlike options, only the issuing companies are allowed to issue warrants, i.e. sell them to the public, but once issued the warrants can be bought and sold just like ordinary shares up to their expiry time.

In Table 11.1 below, column 1 lists the issuing company's name, column 2 is an abbreviation used in this text when discussing that issuing company, and column 3 is the single letter used in the warrant code to identify the issuing company.

Table 11.1 Warrant Issuing Companies

Company Name	Abbreviation	Defining Letter
Australia & NZ Bank	ANZ	A
Credit Suisse	CS	C
Deutsche Bank AG	DB	D
Robert Fleming	RF	F
SG Australia	SG	G
Barclays Bank Plc	BL	L
Macquarie Bank Ltd	MB	M
Natwest Markets Australia	NM	N
Citibank	CI	O
BNP Paribas	BNP	P
UBS Warburg Australia	WDR	S
Westpac	WBC	W
Merrill Lynch International	ML	X
Commonwealth Bank	CBA	Y
ABN AMRO Australia	ABR	Z

LIST OF STOCKS WITH CALL WARRANTS

The stocks with call warrants available at September 2000 are listed in Table 11.2 overleaf, along with the corresponding ASX code. Some stocks have a single call warrant, while the more popular stocks like AMP, BHP, etc. may have several different call warrants available (even as many as 12). This large number of warrant series covers different strike prices, expiry times and conversion ratios, and is made possible by several issuing companies wanting a piece of the action, as well as sometimes offering more than one warrant series.

Table 11.2 Stocks Having Call Warrants

AAPT	APT	Hutchinson	HTA	Qantas Airways	QAN
AMP	AMP	Lihir Gold	LHG	RIO	RIO
ANZ Bank	ANZ	Lend Lease	LLC	Sausage Software	SAS
BHP	BHP	Mayne Nicholas	MAY	St George Bank	SGB
Brambles	BIL	Macquarie Bank	MBL	Solution 6	SOH
C'wealth Bank	CBA	MIM	MIM	Santos	STO
CC Amatil	CCL	Nat. Aust. Bank	NAB	Tabcorp	TAH
Coles Myer	CML	Newcrest Mining	NCM	Telstra Corporation	TLS
Computershare	CPU	News Corporation	NCP	Uecomm	UEC
CSR	CSR	Normandy	NDY	Voicenet	VNA
C&W Optus	CWO	National Mutual	NMH	Westpac	WBC
Davnet	DVT	NRMA	NRM	WMC	WMC
ecorp	ECP	One.Tel	ONE	Woolworths	WOW
ERG	ERG	Oil Search	OSH	Woodside	WPL
Foster's	FBG	Pasminco	PAS	Westfield Holdings	WSF
Fairfax (John)	FXJ	Publish. & Broad.	PBL		

LIST OF STOCKS WITH PUT WARRANTS

The stocks with put warrants available at September 2000 are listed in Table 11.3 below. Once again, some stocks have a single put warrant, while the more popular stocks like NAB, NCP, etc. have several different put warrants available (even as many as six). Once again, this large number of warrant series covers different strike prices, expiry times and conversion ratios, and is made possible by several companies issuing put warrants.

Table 11.3 Stocks Having Put Warrants

AMP	AMP	C&W Optus	CWO	NRMA	NRMA
ANZ Bank	ANZ	Lend Lease	LLC	RIO	RIO
BHP	BHP	Mayne Nicholas	MAY	Telstra Corp	TLS
Brambles	BIL	National Aust. Bank	NAB	WMC	WMC
C'wealth Bank	CBA	News Corp	NCP	Woodside	WPL
Computershare	CPU				

WARRANT QUOTES

The ASX issues a complete list of warrants, showing the strike price, expiry date, conversion ratio and issuing company.

The Australian Financial Review gives an excellent coverage of all the warrants in a special section each day, while *The Australian* gives an abridged version. Figure 11.1 below is a segment from *The Australian* for Thursday 21 September 2000, and the column headings are self-explanatory. The last column headed "Vol" is the turnover for that day in hundreds, so the first AMP warrant AMPWZB had turnover of 2,000. Similarly, warrants BHPWAB each had turnover of 261,500 while CWOWSH had turnover of 1,155,000—that's healthy volume, and shows the popularity of the warrant market.

Warrants Issuers are identified by the fifth letter of the ASX code

Code	Stock	Strike	Expiry	Cnvrs	Bid	Offer	Last	Vol
Call Warrants								
AMP								
8592	AMPWZB	16.00	28/09/00	2:1	.45	.57	.47½	20
8274	AMPWDE	17.00	28/09/00	4:1	.06	.08	.06	200
AUD/USD Curr W								
8551	AXUWMC	5.70	14/06/01	1:1	.31	.33	.32	980
BHP								
8022	BHPWMN	19.00	28/09/00	4:1	.46½	.52	.48	500
8750	BHPWFE	19.50	28/09/00	4:1	.37	.39	.36	85
8457	BHPWPE	20.00	28/09/00	4:1	.27½	.28½	.25	500
6857	BHPWAB	20.00	21/12/00	4:1	.48½	.49½	.50	2615
	BHPWGA	20.00	22/02/01		1.22	1.23	1.20	200
9365	BHPWCB	20.00	29/03/01	4:1	.65	.67	.64	200
7697	BHPWPF	20.00	29/03/01	4:1	.67	.68	.63	350
Brambles								
6708	BILWPA	50.00	21/12/00	4:1	.45	.48	.46	200
9376	BILWCA	55.00	29/03/01	4:1	.62	.64	.65	40
CBA								
7944	CBAWXA	27.00	26/10/00	2:1	.51	.53	.53	1120
	CBAWPC	29.00	25/01/01	4:1	.28	.29	.28	900
Coles Myer								
	CMLWAA	7.00	22/02/01	2:1	.18½	.19½	.20	220
Computershare								
6680	CPUWCC	8.00	25/01/01	2:1	.47	.50	.47½	12
6671	CPUWCA	8.25	26/07/01	1:1	.80	.89	.80	2
C&W Optus								
9411	CWOWSH	4.50	20/12/00	2:1	.10½	.11	.11	11550
6375	CWOWXF	5.50	21/12/00	1:1	.10½	.11½	.11	3143
7897	CWOWMJ	5.25	29/03/01	1:1	.29½	.31	.29½	100
6821	CWOWAA	5.50	29/03/01	2:1	.14½	.15½	.15	260
Davnet								
9239	DVTWDB	.50	26/10/00	2:1	.30	.31	.30	310
ERG								
9134	ERGWDB	10.50	28/03/01	4:1	.37	.38½	.37½	250
Foster's Brew								
6709	FBGWMC	4.40	23/11/00	2:1	.04	.06½	.04	1100
	FBGWPC	4.50	25/01/01	2:1	.08	.08	.08	2800
Fairfax								
6182	FXJWGA	5.00	25/01/01	2:1	.15	.16	.15	374
Lihir Gold								
6773	LHGWPA	.75	22/02/01	1:1	.11½	.12½	.11½	46
LookSmart								
6958	LOKWMB	.75	25/01/01	2:1	.23	.26	.24	1200
MIM								
6842	MIMWAA	.90	26/10/00	1:1	.26	.28	.27	3570
8527	MIMWMC	1.15	26/10/00	1:1	.08	.10	.08	60
9782	MIMWDG	1.20	26/10/00	2:1	.04	.04	.04	1350
8105	MIMWCA	1.25	26/10/00	1:1	.04½	.05½	.05	300
7155	MIMWDI	1.10	25/01/01	1:1	.19	.20	.20	190
6781	MIMWPB	.90	26/04/01	2:1	.17	.18	.17½	550
6651	MIMWMD	1.00	26/04/01	1:1	.26½	.28	.26½	1050
9412	MIMWSD	1.00	26/04/01	1:1	.26½	.28	.27	200
6173	MIMWGA	1.00	28/06/01	1:1	.31	.32	.32	450
Nat Aust Bank								
8301	NABWDD	24.00	26/10/00	4:1	.29	.31	.27	200

Figure 11.1 Call Warrant Quotes

BHP WARRANTS

BHP is a popular warrant stock, with several of the issuing companies offering one or more call warrants, and also put warrants. Table 11.4 below lists all the BHP call and put warrants available at October 2000. The warrant prices are last sales for 6.10.00, and on that day BHP closed at $19.28, down 36¢ for the day. Where there is no price recorded, there were no sales for that warrant on the day.

From time to time the issuing companies release new warrant series, either as a previous series expires, or in response to demand. The trend has been to shorten the time to expiry, and inspection of Table 11.4 shows that the furthest-dated warrants are April 2001 which, at the time of writing, have seven months to expiry.

Table 11.4 BHP Warrants

ASX Code	Strike Price ($)	Expiry Date	Conversion Ratio	Price (¢)	Volatility (%)	Delta
Call Warrants						
BHPWAB	20.00	21.12.00	4:1	21.5	31	0.46/4
BHPWGA	20.00	22.2.01	2:1	69	32	0.50/2
BHPWLD	19.00	29.3.01	4:1	–	–	–
BHPWFF	19.50	29.3.01	4:1	51	36	0.57/4
BHPWCB	20.00	29.3.01	4:1	39	32	0.52/4
BHPWPF	20.00	29.3.01	4:1	–	–	–
BHPWDK	21.00	29.3.01	4:1	–	–	–
BHPWMO	21.00	29.3.01	3:1	53	39	0.46/4
BHPWXC	22.00	26.4.01	2:1	–	–	–
Put Warrants						
BHPWPT	20.00	21.12.00	3:1	48.5	33	-0.54/3
BHPWFS	17.50	29.3.01	4:1	–	–	–
BHPWMX	18.50	29.3.01	3:1	51	40	-0.35/3
BHPWCQ	19.00	29.3.01	2:1	–	–	–

Trading activity in warrants waxes and wanes as a function of overall market sentiment, and also in response to developments within individual stocks. Figure 11.1

shows that on 20.9.00, which was an ordinary sort of day, BHPWAB was the most actively-traded BHP call warrant with volume of 261,500. By contrast, the day the appointment of Paul Anderson as new CEO was announced, the most popular BHP call warrant at that time had a volume of over 1.3 million.

Table 11.4 lists nine different BHP call warrants, with several different strike prices, expiry dates and conversion ratios. Similarly, four different BHP put warrants are listed, also with differing strike prices, expiry dates and conversion ratios. Such a large number of warrants available on a single stock can be confusing. Thus, we need to comb through the choices to select the one that satisfies our requirements. Warrants behave similarly to long-term options, and for trading purposes, the main requirements are:

Time to expiry:	Preferably more than, say, six months
Strike price:	Preferably just out-of-the-money
High delta:	Leading to worthwhile profit on stock move
Popular series:	With good turnover

It is essential to check the turnover figures over several days when making the selection of which warrant to trade. When a number of warrants are available, it is customary for one or two series to command the bulk of the volume, so these series should be chosen if they meet the other requirements listed above. In late September 2000 with BHP trading around $20.00, the popular call warrant was BHPWAB, while the popular put warrant was BHPWPT, and both had a strike price of 20.00 and expiry of 21.12.00 which was about three months away.

BSOPM Example

As an example of using the BSOPM to calculate the two useful warrant parameters volatility and delta, we take warrant BHPWAB from Table 11.4. This warrant has a conversion ratio of 4:1, so the input values for the BSOPM (see Chapter 4) are:

S	1928¢
X	2000¢
r	5.0%
time to expiry	difference between 6.10.00 and 21.12.00 (during this time BHP pays a dividend of typically 25¢ in early November)

Setting C = 4 x 21.5 = 86¢ gives the volatility = 31.6% and delta = 0.46/4.

Note that the multiplication by 4, and the division by 4, in the line above is required because the warrant conversion ratio is 4:1.

Volatility

Inspection of Table 11.4 shows that the call warrants have implied volatility in the range 31% to 39%. As a cent either way in the price of the warrant can make a difference to the volatility, the market is probably using a consistent value of about 32% for each of the warrants.

The implied volatility for the put warrants is in the range 33% to 40%. Once again, a cent either way in the price of the warrant makes a difference to the volatility, particularly for those with conversion ratios above, say, 4:1.

Chapter 4 discussed the effect of volatility upon option and warrant prices, and showed that these prices are particularly sensitive to changes in volatility. Table 11.4 shows some practical figures for warrant prices and volatilities for various BHP warrants. When we buy a warrant, we obviously do not want to pay inflated prices resulting from abnormally high volatility values. We should check with our broker if the warrant price is in line with an acceptable volatility for the stock.

The BHP warrant values listed in Table 11.4 are for 6.10.00. It is interesting to note that on that day *The Australian Financial Review* list of option prices showed that the volatility being used by the RTs for a range of BHP option series sell prices was around 25% to 27%.

Delta

The deltas listed in Table 11.4 are theoretical values calculated from the BSOPM, whereas the market may operate on slightly different values. It is best to check the warrant prices in the newspaper over a couple of weeks, to see how the various warrants are behaving in the marketplace. On first sight a higher delta looks like a higher profit, but it is necessary to do the sums before making a final choice of warrant in a particular trade. The issuing companies artificially reduce both the prices of warrants and the delta by having conversion ratios greater than 1:1, as the buying public will happily pay, say, 30¢ for a warrant, but are more cautious about outlaying 60¢ or $1.00 on a warrant. The following example illustrates the fallacy in this attitude.

Example of Choice of Warrant

On 6.10.00 BHP is trading at $19.28 and we think it is about to rise its customary 90¢, and so wish to buy about $4,000 of call warrants. We look for call warrants with expiry about four to six months away, and strike price near $19.50. Looking at Table 11.4 we find that warrants BHPWGA and BHPWCB have expiry dates of 22.2.01 and 29.3.01 respectively, and both have strike prices of $20.00, so are 72¢ out-of-the-money. The first warrant has a conversion ratio of 2:1 and delta of 0.50/2 = 0.25, while the second warrant has a conversion ratio of 4:1 and delta of 0.52/4 = 0.13.

For BHPWGA trading at 69¢, the number of warrants that can be bought is 4000/0.69 = 5,797. If BHP rises 90¢ and we quit at this point, then as the warrant delta is 0.25 the warrant will rise by 90 x 0.25 = 22.5¢. The profit is 5797 x 0.225 = $1,304 neglecting brokerage.

Now for BHPWCB trading at 39¢, the number of warrants that can be bought is 4000/0.39 = 10,256. If BHP rises 90¢ and once again we quit at this point, then as the warrant delta is 0.13 the warrant will rise by 90 x 0.13 = 11.7¢. The profit is 10256 x 0.117 = $1,200 neglecting brokerage.

This example shows that for warrants with similar parameters, the resultant profit will be much the same. What is most important is to choose a warrant having consistently good turnover, so that on the days we buy and sell the warrant there are realistic, and close, bid/ask quotes.

Comparison Between BHP and Call and Put Warrant Prices

A picture is worth a thousand words.

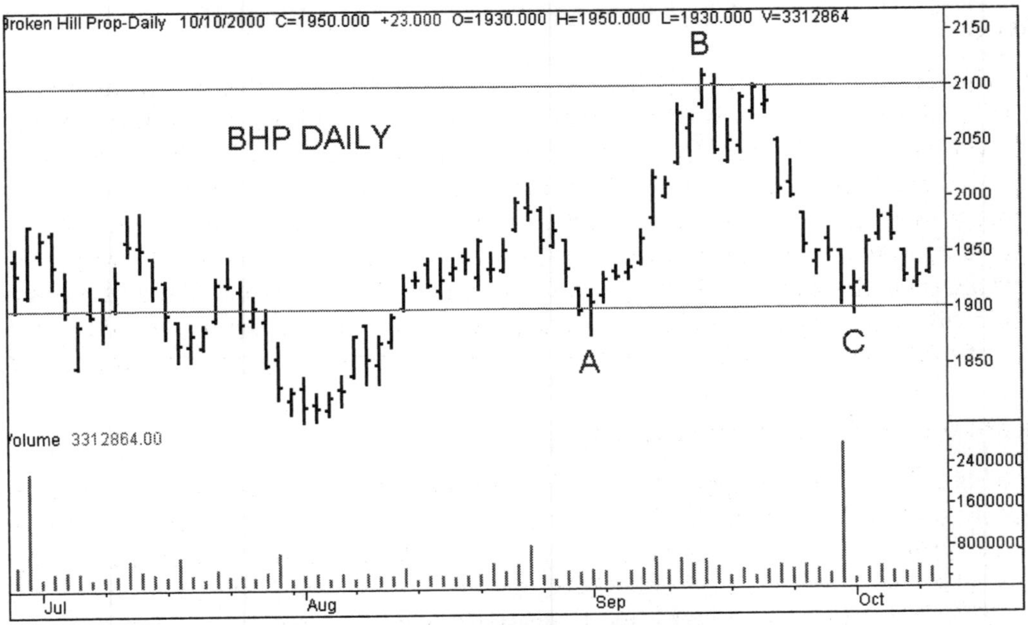

Figure 11.2 BHP Daily Bar Chart

Figure 11.2 on the previous page shows the daily bar chart of BHP spanning three months to early October 2000. During this time the price moved quite quickly from \$19.00 to \$21.00 and back to \$19.00 (see A,B,C in the figure).

Moves of this nature are ideal for trading warrants, and Figure 11.3 (a) and 11.3 (b) opposite are daily charts of the call warrant BHPWAB and the put warrant BHPWPT over the same time frame. The corresponding points A,B,C are marked on the warrant charts.

Table 11.5 below lists the dates for the BHP trough A, peak B and trough C, along with the closing prices on those days. Also listed are the call and put warrant closing prices on the same days.

The BHP prices listed in Table 11.5 show that the rise in price from \$18.96 to \$21.07 is a move A,B of 11.1%, while the move from \$21.07 to \$19.15 is a fall B,C of –9.1%. The corresponding percentage moves for the call warrant are 89.5% and –59.4%. The moves for the put warrant are naturally in anti-phase, and are –54.8% and 117% respectively. Thus BHP's 11.1% upward move A,B produces a move in the call warrant some 8 times larger, while BHP's -9.1% fall B,C produces an upward move in the put warrant some 12 times larger.

Table 11.5 Prices for BHP Call and Put Warrants

	Date A 31.8.00	Date B 14.9.00	Date C 29.9.00	% Move A,B	% Move B,C
BHP	1896	2107	1915	11.1	-9.1
BHPWAB Strike 20.00 Expiry Dec 00, CR 4:1	28	53	21.5	89.3	-59.4
BHPWPT Strike 20.00 Expiry Dec 00, CR 3:1	52	23.5	51	-54.8	117

This gearing available on the warrants is their attraction, and the spur to finding analysis methods which accurately pick the start and finish of the price trends in actively-moving stocks like BHP.

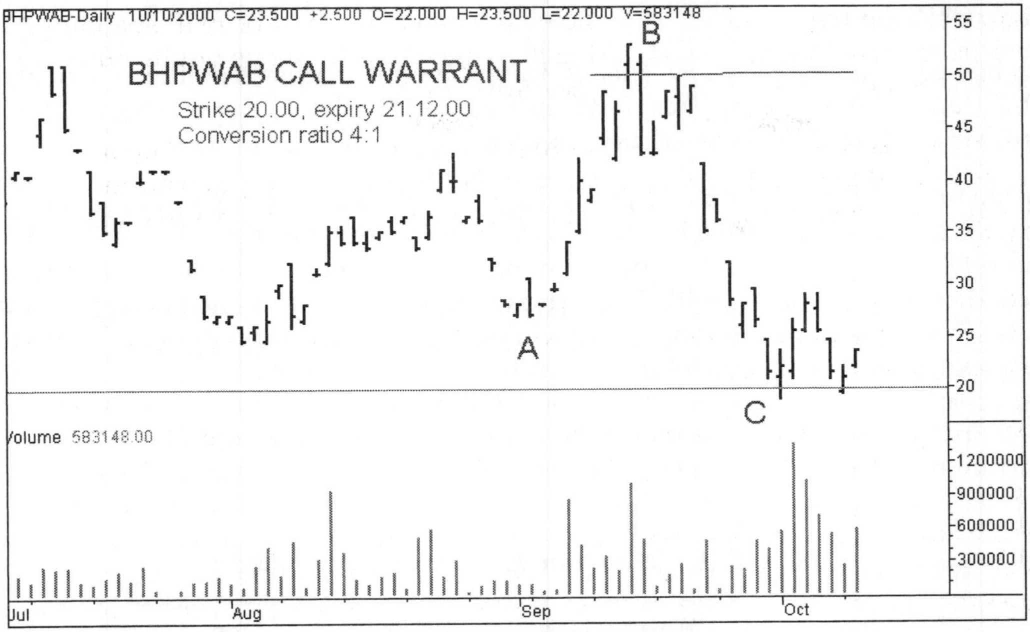

Figure 11.3 (a) Call Warrant BHPWAB Daily Bar Chart

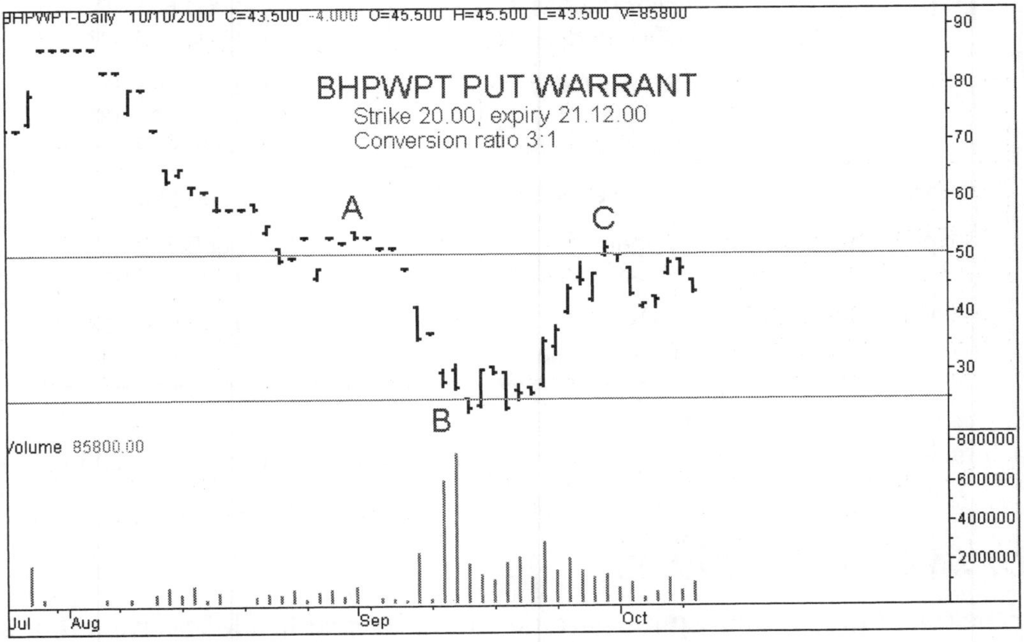

Figure 11.3 (b) Put Warrant BHPWPT Daily Bar Chart

Index Warrants

My book *Technical Analysis for Trading Index Warrants* discusses methods of analysis which are particularly applicable to indices. Index warrants available on the All Ordinaries Index are discussed along with pricing formulas.

At the time of writing, call and put index warrants are available on the Australian Share Price Index and the S&P/ ASX 200 Index, and also a number of overseas indices, and offer a simple way of trading the trends in these indices. Table 11.6 below lists the indices covered, along with the warrant issuers and their contact numbers. Notice that some warrants are American-style while others are European-style. Before trading these warrants it is helpful to obtain a copy of the "Offering Circular" from the Warrant Issuer, so we know exactly the details of the warrant we are trading. The Issuer Code listed in the table is the fifth letter of the warrant code, i.e. warrant ZQQWGQ is a put warrant on the Nasdaq 100 offered by SG Australia.

Table 11.6 Index Warrants Available on Indices

Index	Warrant Issuer	Issuer Code	Phone Number
Share Price Index	UBS Warburg	S	(02) 9324 3890
	BNP Paribas	P	1800 501 550
	SG Australia	G	1800 825 574
S&P/ASX 200	SG Australia	G	1800 825 574
	Citibank	O	1800 130 333
	Macquarie Bank	M	1800 803 010
Nasdaq 100	SG Australia	G	1800 825 574
S&P 500	Citibank	O	1800 130 333
	Macquarie Bank	M	1800 803 010
Nikkei 225	Citibank	O	1800 130 333
	SG Australia	G	1800 825 574

Macquarie Bank also offers put and call warrants on the $A versus $US exchange rate.

VOIDING OF WARRANTS

For the trader or investor, equity warrants can be likened to a long-term put or call option. However, a word of caution – whereas the integrity of exchange traded options is subject to OCH rules and regulations, equity warrants are backed by the integrity of the issuing merchant bank or finance house. Should the issuer collapse, their warrants may become void. Warrant investors should obtain a copy of the Offering Circular issued by the relevant bank or broker to the issue, which is available from stockbrokers. This document sets out the terms of the warrant and the definable events that may void the warrant. One such event is the takeover of the company on which the warrants are issued.

If our call warrants are out-of-the money, and a takeover bid is made below our warrant strike price, then the warrant may become worthless. Alternatively, the takeover bid may catapult out warrants from being out-of-the-money to being in-the-money, resulting in windfall profits. Takeovers are something to bear in mind when buying warrants. If we buy call warrants in company ABC with strike price 10.00 and a takeover is implemented at, say, $9.80, then our warrants become worthless. The major Australian companies on which warrants are available are reasonably immune to takeovers, but the unexpected can happen.

CALL WARRANTS ON NEW FLOATS

One profitable strategy of which readers should be aware is buying call warrants on the major new share floats. A discussion of major floats is contained in *Technical Analysis for Trading Index Warrants*. By way of example, from early 1997 to October 1998 there were four major floats, viz. Colonial, Telstra Instalment Receipts, AMP and TAB. Call warrants became available on each of these companies, either on the day of listing, or shortly afterwards. Past performance shows that in the case of major floats, the share price usually rises over a number of months as the market establishes a value for the company, taking into account improved efficiencies and future profitability. If we purchase call warrants on these stocks as soon as the warrants become available, substantial percentage gains can often be achieved.

Table 11.7 overleaf lists the details of the stock movements along with the call warrant movements for this time period.

The first column lists the stock, and also the code and details of the selected warrant, while the second and third columns show the date the warrant first traded, and the corresponding stock and warrant prices on that date. Columns four and five list the date of the stock's highest price since listing up to October 1998, and the corresponding stock and warrant prices. The last column lists the percentage move for the stock and the warrant between the first and highest listed prices in the table.

AMP is marked with an asterisk as the selected date of 1.7.97 is about two weeks after the float and the introduction of the warrant. Trading in the first week was hectic and a couple of weeks were needed for an orderly market to become established. (On the first day of trading, AMP opened at $45.00 before closing the day at $23.00.)

Table 11.7 shows that for Colonial, the stock maximum move was 72% while the corresponding warrant move was 385%. Inspection of the last column shows that the warrant moves are up to seven times greater than the stock moves. The percentage moves are maximum values, and we cannot expect to achieve this. However, the moves are so large that any sensible trading strategy should extract worthwhile profits.

Table 11.7 Comparison of Share and Call Warrant Moves

Stock and Warrant	Date Warrant Available	Close Price ($)	Date Max. Price	Close Price ($)	Move (%)
Colonial	18.7.97	3.48	23.4.98	5.98	72
CGHWSA Expiry Nov 98, strike 3.50		0.52		2.52	385
Telstra IR	17.11.97	2.67	5.10.98	4.81	80
TLIWDA Expiry Oct 98, strike 2.50		0.56		2.24	300
***AMP**	1.7.98	19.82	19.8.98	22.30	13
AMPWDA Expiry Apr 99, strike 18.00		1.87		2.58	38
TAB	22.6.98	2.20	30.10.98	3.05	39
TABWXA Expiry Mar 99, strike 2.50		0.165		0.64	288

Readers might like to check this warrant strategy on major new floats on companies which have floated since October 1988, such as C&W Optus, Davnet, Solution 6 and NRMA.

FILLING WARRANT AND OPTION ORDERS

When we place an order to buy or sell a particular stock, we ring our broker and ask for the current buy/sell quotes. He is able to give us this information directly from the computer monitor sitting on his desk which displays the buy and sell quotes, and the number of shares on offer at each price. This data is available via the ASX Stock Exchange Automated Trading System (SEATS), and shows the depth of the market for that stock. For example, BHP may be trading around $19.50 and the first few sell quotes are $19.50 (20 shares), $19.52 (550 shares), $19.52 (103 shares), etc. If we want to purchase 200 BHP shares and are prepared to pay up to $19.52 for them, then the broker buys the 20 shares on offer at $19.50, plus 180 shares from the first parcel of 550 on offer at $19.52.

The trading is "transparent", as we can see the price of the shares on offer to buy and to sell, and their parcel sizes. In our example, we decided to accept the asking price of the sellers. Alternatively, we might have held out for a lower price of, say, $19.45. Our order would be placed at the end of the queue of buyers at $19.45. This order would be executed when enough sellers reduced their asking price to $19.45 and satisfied the buying demand ahead of us at $19.45.

Warrants are traded on SEATS, just like ordinary shares. Consequently trading is transparent, and we know exactly what price we will pay or receive on our warrant transactions. The companies which issue warrants often make a market in their warrants, by having both a buy order and a sell order in place all the time. The buy order may be for 10,000 warrants code BHPXYZ at 45¢, and the sell order may be for 10,000 of the same warrants at 47¢. If these orders are filled, then they offer another parcel. Further, as the price of BHP varies during the day, the warrant issuers will vary their buy and sell prices. However, all this is transparent, and a private buyer or seller can see exactly what warrants are on offer at any time. The warrant market is not confined to just the issuing companies, but also comprises many private investors and traders.

This transparent feature of the warrant market contrasts to the manner of dealing in options, where the RTs play a more dominant role (see Chapter 2). Some traders prefer to buy warrants in preference to options because of this feature. However, our overall trading strategy includes both options and warrants, because private traders can write options, whereas only the warrant issuers can write warrants.

Chapter 12

TRADING WITH OTHER OPTION STOCKS

THE NUMERICAL EXAMPLES used in this section are based upon the stock prices and volatility listed below, which were typical market values in September 2000.

Stock	AMP	ANZ	CBA	NAB	WBC	TLS	BHP	WPL	RIO	WMC	NCP	NDY
Price ($)	17.00	12.50	27.00	24.50	12.50	6.00	21.00	14.00	25.50	7.50	24.50	1.00
Volatility(%)	18	19	19	20	20	25	25	29	30	34	41	45

The table ranks the stocks in order of volatility, and shows AMP and the banks have the lowest volatility, and NCP and NDY the highest.

COMPARATIVE RETURNS

The differing volatilities mean that, for the same cash outlay, a higher return is available for an investment in NCP options than for one in BHP, but the higher volatility means there is a higher risk involved. To illustrate, five BHP options control 5,000 x 21.00 = $105,500 worth of BHP stock, while four NCP options control 4,000 x 24.50 = $98,000 of NCP stock. Figures 5.1 and 5.3 (on pages 38 and 39) show BHP and NCP at-the-money call options with eight weeks to expiry are about 90¢ and 166¢ respectively. Consequently, the return from the five BHP options is $4,500 while the return from the four NCP options is higher at $6,640 (ignoring brokerage).

Some option stocks are fairly sedate in their price movements, resulting in low volatility and correspondingly small time premiums in their option prices. To profit from these options it is necessary to pick the direction and the time of the stock moves quite accurately. Usually Coles Myer and Woolworths are examples of this type of stock.

TRADING COMPLEMENTARY OPTIONS TO INCREASE RETURNS

Chapter 7 indicates the range of profits we could hope to achieve trading our strategy on BHP. The safest trades are writing 2nd out-of-the-money options, and the riskiest trades are buying warrants. Naturally, the safest trades give a lower potential profit than the riskier trades.

To achieve a higher return from our trading, there are various possibilities. Instead of trading five BHP options we could trade ten BHP call options. If we pick BHP's trend correctly on this larger trade, we can double the return on the call option trades. However, ten BHP options controls about $210,000 of stock, and places us at greater financial and emotional risk, so this is not recommended. (Deposit requirements may also be prohibitive.)

An alternate strategy is to look for a popular option stock that has a different price cycle to BHP, and to trade these two stocks simultaneously.

Chapter 8 noted that the miners and banks are driven by different market forces. The banks often have an inverse relation to the ten-year bond rate while the miners are directly dependent on metals prices and expectations.

Suppose we choose NAB as a stock to complement BHP in our trading. Sometimes BHP and NAB move together, while other times they move in opposite directions. Consequently, sometimes the written option trades in the two stocks will both be puts, or both calls, but there will be times when one trade is a written put and the other trade is a written call.

Once we broaden our horizons to include several stocks, a variety of trading possibilities occur. Using a database and charting software it is easy to monitor all the option stocks with a few proven indicators like MACD, DMI and ADX, RSI, stochastic and momentum. Trend lines drawn on a logarithmic scale should also be monitored, as they give a simple visual picture of the behaviour of the stock prices. The resource stocks go through regular tradeable price cycles, while the industrials are generally more sedate, but at times give classic indicator signals which lead to profitable trades.

Figure 12.1 below shows a chart of weekly NAB drawn to a semi-log scale. A series of trend lines are drawn from mid 1998 to September 2000 which clearly define a sequence of up, down and uptrends. Also shown is the MACD indicator, along with the 10-week DMI and ADX indicators. These indicators confirm the trends as defined by the trend lines. Trend lines, MACD and DMI/ADX are three independent methods of finding the start and end of stock trends. When they all agree, there is a high probability that a new trend has begun.

Having mastered the technical indicators and trading strategy, it is a matter of personal preference, time available for monitoring the market, cash reserves and money management, as to how many stocks to trade at any one time.

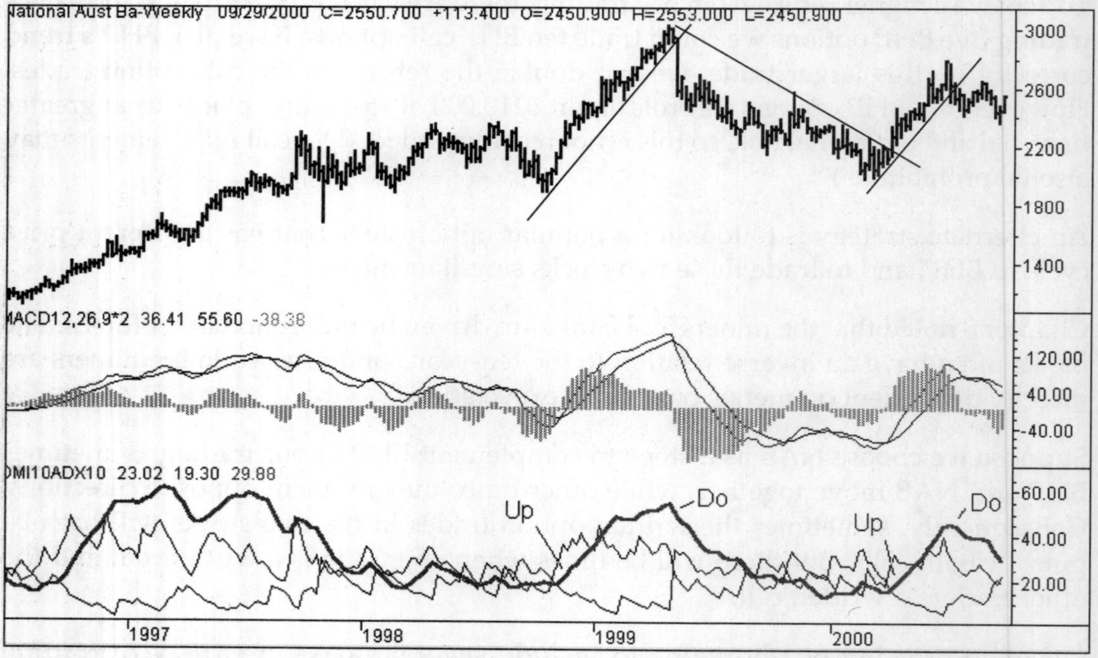

Figure 12.1 Chart of Weekly NAB with MACD, DMI and ADX Indicators

OPTION BEHAVIOUR WHEN BANKS GO EX-DIVIDEND

The banks have a high dividend yield of about 4% to 5% p.a., so twice a year when they go ex-dividend the stock price falls about 2.5% overnight. This is a larger move than the normal day-to-day variations, so we would expect some movement in the options at this time. The example given below is for NAB in mid 1996, and is chosen as it shows a classic price pattern (but some years the pattern is not so precise).

NAB Call Option Price Behaviour

On 13.6.96 NAB went ex-dividend 43¢. Table 12.1 below shows the option prices and number of option contracts open for the July series with about six weeks to expiry.

Table 12.1 NAB Call Option Prices and Open Positions

Date	NAB ($)	Strike Price 11.00 (¢)	No. Open	Strike Price 11.50 (¢)	No. Open	Strike Price 12.00 (¢)	No. Open
11.6.96	11.57	57	1,255	14	3,603	5	3,806
12.6.96	11.61	58	1,355	13	3,703	5	3,806
13.6.96	*11.10*	*36*	*63*	*13*	*4,033*	*5*	*3,716*
14.6.96	11.16	34	151	13	4,026	4	3,516
.... to							
24.6.96	11.60	53	166	31	4,021	9	3,751

On the ex-dividend day 13.6.96 NAB fell 51¢, which was more than the dividend amount of 43¢. The in-the-money 11.00 option fell in price from 58¢ to 36¢, but notice the fall in the number of open contracts from 1,355 to 63. This means that on 12.6.96 the holders of these in-the-money call options converted their options to shares, to receive the 43¢ fully-franked dividend.

Prior to NAB going ex-dividend the 11.50 option was slightly in-the-money and the 12.00 option was out-of-the-money. Table 12.1 shows that neither of these options were affected in price nor in open interest as a result of NAB going ex-dividend.

It is quite common for stocks to quickly regain their ex-dividend price, and on 24.6.96 NAB had recovered back to $11.60, and each of the 11.00, 11.50 and 12.00 options were trading with appreciable gains from their 13.6.96 ex-dividend prices.

NAB Put Option Price Behaviour

The corresponding put option prices are listed in Table 12.2 overleaf. Table 12.2 shows that NAB going ex-dividend and falling 51¢ has no effect on the put option prices, as the ex-dividend fall is a known event that is factored into the option price.

Table 12.2 NAB Put Option Prices and Open Positions

Date	NAB ($)	Strike Price 11.00 (¢)	No. Open	Strike Price 11.50 (¢)	No. Open
11.6.96	11.57	19	1,556	48	2,552
12.6.96	11.61	17	1,586	48	2,529
13.6.96	*11.10*	*17*	*1,637*	*47*	*2,531*
14.6.96	11.16	13	1,677	42	2,810
.... to					
24.6.96	11.60	4	1,734	16	2,939

Notice that on 24.6.96, when NAB had recovered back to $11.60, the put options were trading with appreciable falls from their 13.6.96 ex-dividend prices.

Bank Ex-Dividend Months

The usual months that the four major banks go ex-dividend and the half-yearly dividends they paid in 2000 are:

ANZ	29¢	June, December
CBA	72¢	February, August
NAB	59¢	June, December
WBC	26¢	June, December

Before opening bank option trades it is necessary to check the next ex-dividend date, and take that into account in determining strategy.

The Australian Dividend Handbook 2000-01 by N.E. Renton contains a wealth of information on company dividends and dates, plus other related topics.

DIVIDEND STRIPPING

When companies pay dividends, their share price falls on paying the dividend, but usually recovers to the original price within a few weeks. If the stock is in an uptrend at the time the dividend is paid, the price frequently recovers to its original value in a matter of days.

Some traders buy bank or other high-yielding stocks just prior to the dividend payment, collect the franked dividend, and then sell the stock when it recovers to a profitable level.

As an example of dividend stripping, consider the set of NAB prices listed in Table 12.1. Suppose we buy 2,000 NAB shares on 11.6.96 at $11.57. Two days later the stock goes ex-dividend and we are entitled to a dividend payment of 2,000 x 0.43 = $860. Two weeks later the price recovers to $11.60 and we complete the trade by selling the shares.

The full transaction costs are:

	Credit $	Debit $
Buy 2,000 shares @ $11.57		23,140
Brokerage		70
Dividend	860	
Sell 2,000 shares @ $11.60	23,200	
Brokerage		70
Total	24,060	23,280
Net profit	$780	

The dividend is $860 with brokerage of $140, so the trade is only profitable on larger parcels of shares. If we are patient and NAB continues to rise, then this technique could be an even more profitable proposition.

The tax rules relating to dividend stripping were changed in 1997. It is now necessary to hold shares for at least 45 days to claim any franking credits available in the dividends. Readers should seek advice from their tax accountants on this matter.

Chapter 13

ANNUAL EVENTS FOR TRADING BHP AND NAB

BHP IS THE LARGEST of the resource stocks on the ASX, and in September 2000 comprised about 5.4% of the All Ordinaries Index. Similarly, NAB is the premier bank stock and comprises about 5.8% of the All Ordinaries Index. BHP options are the most actively traded of the option stocks, while NAB options are the most popular amongst the bank stocks.

It is useful to know the corporate calendars for BHP and NAB, as these events can affect the share price and also the option price. This combined calendar is shown opposite.

Month	BHP	NAB
January		AGM Options expire*
February		
March	3rd quarter report Options expire*	
April		Options expire
May	Ex-dividend 25¢	Interim report
June	Annual report Options expire	Ex-dividend 59¢
July		Options expire
August		
September	AGM 1st quarter report Options expire	
October		Options expire
November	Ex-dividend 25¢	Annual report
December	2nd quarter report Options expire	Ex-dividend 59¢

* These are the BHP and NAB major option expiry months. Both stocks also have options that expire in each of the other months, but these options have a maximum time duration of six weeks.

Chapter 14

RISK AND MONEY MANAGEMENT

TRADING IS A BUSINESS, and needs to be treated as a business. Great care must be taken with its major asset—the cash. Market risk and money management need to be carefully thought out and guidelines adhered to.

Warren Buffett says that building wealth has more to do with controlling losses than making profits. Larry Hite of Mint Investment Management Company says to never risk more than 1% of total equity on any trade. Ed Seykota (one of the wizard traders interviewed in the book, *Market Wizards)* limits his risk to 5% of equity on any trade. Other writers and wizards have risk limits somewhere between the 1% and 5% values; Daryl Guppy, for example, recommends 2%. What is important is to determine a risk figure and to understand its implications to each trade. With a trading kitty of, say, $100,000, applying the 1% rule to a straight stock transaction works as:

	Credit $	Debit $
Buy 1,000 BHP @ $21.00 (including $70 brokerage)		21,070
Sell 1,000 BHP @ $20.14 (including $70 brokerage)	20,070	
Loss on trade		1,000

The loss represents 1% of the total equity but 4.7% of the cash committed to the trade.

Our trading strategy involves options and warrants which are geared to the underlying stock, which means their prices move a larger percentage amount than an actual move in the stock. Thus, to stipulate a percentage figure for risk management, it is necessary to look at some typical price moves in the stock, and find the corresponding price moves in the options and warrants.

Van Tharp in *Market Wizards* says that how we close a trade has far greater importance than how we open a trade. He recommends a protective stop always be used to safeguard profits and limit losses. Using this technique, as soon as a trade is opened we calculate the option or warrant price corresponding to a loss of, say, $500 or $1,000, and monitor the prices just before the day's close so as to quit the trade if this pullback occurs. Further, when the trade moves in our favour, each evening we calculate the price corresponding to a $500 or $1,000 pullback, and quit just before tomorrow's new market close if this pullback occurs.

Protective stops are the normal way of trading in the futures markets, but much less common in the stock market. Most stockbrokers accept only fixed-price buy or sell orders. To implement the stop-loss method we have to monitor the market each afternoon on all our open positions. Stockbrokers Hogan & Partners of Perth—phone number (08) 9321 2366—are one of a small number of stockbrokers which do accept stop-loss orders.

Being stopped out of a trade within a few days of opening is a chastising experience, and causes us to be very careful to obey all our rules in opening trades. Most winning trades move into profit after a few days, so the monitoring of prices becomes the more pleasant task of protecting profits, rather than cutting losses.

LOSS ON 3% ADVERSE MOVE

Figure 9.8 (page 100) shows two common chart reversal patterns. When the stock breaks through resistance XX it is customary to wait for a 3% confirmation at A before entering the trade. Furthermore, chart theory states that a pullback to the XX breakout can be expected within the next three weeks, but if the pullback is larger than this original 3% it is likely to negate the new move.

We will calculate the loss involved in our trading strategy if we quit trades on a 3% adverse move.

Writing Call Options for Down Move

Consider the double top pattern shown in Figure 9.8 and suppose the XX line for BHP is $21.00. We decide to open a trade on the 3% confirmation which is a move of 63¢. Thus, when BHP reaches $20.37 we write five 21.00 calls with eight weeks to expiry. These calls are 1st out-of-the-money and priced at about 67¢ (see Table 7.1, page 53), so we have a net credit after $50 brokerage of $3,300. Two weeks later BHP executes a pullback to $21.00 and the options become at-the-money with six weeks to expiry, and rise to about 77¢. At this point our paper loss is 5,000 x (0.77 – 0.67) = $500 plus $100 brokerage for a total loss of $600. Any further rise in BHP puts the options in-the-money with a likelihood of being exercised, and probably negates the downtrend.

Writing Put Options for Up Move

Applying the same reasoning to a put option trade, suppose we have a double bottom pattern with the XX line for BHP at $21.00. We decide to open a trade on the 3% confirmation which is a move of 63¢. Thus when BHP reaches $21.63 we write five 21.00 puts with eight weeks to expiry. These puts are 1st-out-of-the-money and priced at about 52¢ (see Table 7.3, page 60), so we have a net credit after $50 brokerage of $2,550. Two weeks later BHP executes a pull-back to $21.00 and the options become at-the-money with six weeks to expiry, and rise to about 65¢. At this point our paper loss is 5,000 x (0.65 – 0.52) = $650 plus $100 brokerage for a total loss of $750. Any further fall in BHP positions the options in-the-money with a likelihood of being exercised, and probably negates the uptrend.

Buying Call Warrants for Up Move

It is prudent to buy warrants in lots of about $4,000, as smaller lots involve a heavy percentage brokerage fee ($120 total for buying and selling), and larger lots involve too high a proportion of our trading funds if the trade goes sour.

Suppose BHP completes a double bottom and gives the 3% confirmation of an up move, and this confirmation occurs with BHP priced at $19.28 (the value used in Chapter 11, page 126). We buy 18,600 warrants at 21.5¢ (code BHPWAB and with a delta of 0.46/4 = 0.11, see also Chapter 11). If BHP falls 3%, or 58¢, then the warrants will fall to about 21.5 – (58 x 0.11) = 15.1¢. If we sell the warrants at this point, the full trade is:

	Credit $	Debit $
Buy 18,600 warrants @ 21.5¢		3,999
Sell 18,600 warrants @ 15.1¢	2,809	
Buy and sell brokerage		120
Net loss		1,310

Thus, for this particular warrant trade, a fall of 3% in the price of BHP results in a net loss of $1,310.

Buying Put Warrants for Down Move

Table 11.4, page 124, lists the BHP put warrant BHPWPT, which has a delta of -0.54/3 = -0.18 and is priced at 48.5¢ with BHP at $19.28. If BHP rises 3%, or 58¢, then the warrant will fall to 48.5 – (58 x 0.18) = 38¢. If we buy 8,250 warrants and then sell them on the 3% adverse move, the full trade is:

	Credit $	Debit $
Buy 8,250 warrants @ 48.5¢		4,001
Sell 8,250 warrants @ 38¢	3,135	
Buy and sell brokerage		120
Net loss		986

Thus, for this particular warrant trade, a fall of 3% in the price of BHP results in a net loss of $986.

Comments on Losses

These examples demonstrate how to calculate the risk associated with options and warrant trades, as recommended in our strategy. It is shown that if we close the trades on an adverse price move in BHP of 3%, then each of our typical trades (written put or call option, bought put or call warrant) result in a loss ranging from about $600 to about $1,300. If we have a trading kitty of $100,000 this represents a loss of about 1%.

Working from a smaller kitty of, say, $10,000, this dollar loss on a single trade is too great. With a smaller kitty we must strike a balance between risk and reward. For example, reducing the parcel sizes to one-tenth the full size to contain our losses also means that our profits are minuscule.

With a smaller kitty it is prudent to take only the safest trades, but in parcel sizes that will return profits of, say, $500 upwards if the stock moves as we anticipate. In this case, it is imperative to use rigid stop-loss procedures to limit losses to, say, $500 to $1,000. Without stop-loss protection we are at risk of being decimated on a single bad trade.

WHEN WE ARE AWAY

While discussing risk it is necessary to point out the dangers of being away from the market and still have written option trades open. If we know that we are going on holidays to Europe in two months time, it is unlikely that we will want to be bothered with monitoring the Australian market during the night. Should the market move against us and the written options become in-the-money, it is almost certain that the options will be exercised. It is safest to manage option trades so that none are open at times we are away from the market for any length of time.

Chapter 15

KNOW YOURSELF

THE PSYCHOLOGY OF the market, and our own emotional factors in trading the market, is an intriguing topic.

Psychologists say fear and greed drive the market, and the market gyrations are the result of fear and greed acting upon each of the thousands of participants operating in the market at any time.

Every good book on trading states the four cardinal rules as:

1. Follow the trend.
2. Let the profits run.
3. Cut the losses.
4. Manage the money to stay in the game.

This sounds so simple, yet is difficult to master. Larry Livermore, alias Edwin Lefare, in *Reminiscences of a Stock Operator* says:

> The speculator's chief enemies are always boring from within. It is inseparable from human nature to hope and to fear...The successful trader has to fight these two deep-seated instincts. He has to reverse what you might call his natural impulses. Instead of hoping he must fear; instead of fearing he must hope. He must fear that his loss may develop into a much bigger loss, and hope that his profit may become a big profit. It is absolutely wrong to gamble in stocks the way the average man does.

(As a sobering aside, Livermore's book is much-quoted as essential reading for an understanding of the markets, and was first published in 1923. Livermore tells how he made and lost millions several times, starting from trading in the "bucket shops" around 1900. Gann was a contemporary of Livermore's who loaned him money at a time that his luck had run out, and Livermore subsequently traded his way back to further millions and repaid the loan. Gann recounts, in *45 Years in Wall Street*, that Livermore "committed suicide and died practically broke").

Jacob Bernstein discusses the psychology of successful investing in commodities and stocks. He gives a test sheet to determine how we rate in emotional factors and knowledge of the market. He makes the interesting point that if we score well in the test, yet are not making consistent profits, then it is time to look at using a different trading system (a different set of indicators and strategies).

Bernstein recommends keeping a record of each trade made, and enter the indicator signals used in opening and closing the trade, the result, and any other factors taken into account in that trade. Over a period of time this becomes a useful record to show our strengths and weaknesses. We may find, looking back over the trades, that our losses frequently happen when we use indicator "Y" but do not wait for confirmation of the signal, etc. Alternatively, our losses may consistently come from not closing out losing trades at, say, a predetermined dollar loss, but hoping they will recover.

Some writers recommend paper trading as a prelude to real trading, while others scorn the idea because it takes no account of mastering emotion when our money is riding on our decisions. In our strategy it is necessary to back-test the technical indicators on the stocks we want to trade, and to learn chart patterns and techniques. Once we are confident of our indicators and charting techniques, we are ready to commit money to the market.

The put or call option buyer can only lose the initial purchase money if the market moves the wrong way. The loss is annoying but the amount is known when entering the trade. Because our strategy involves writing naked call and put options, our maximum profit is known on entering the trade, but the amount of any loss is not known and could be large in a severe adverse move, though our money management and defensive strategies should limit the loss to acceptable limits.

If the reader has never written put or call options, then it is prudent to start with a small trade of one or two BHP options. We want this trade to be a winner and a confidence-builder, so write an option that is at least $1.00 out-of-the-money in order to have a big stress buffer. If the market turns against us, then buy the option back at a loss should it become at-the-money.

We gradually become emotionally accustomed to having open naked option positions, and it need be no more stressful than owning ordinary shares.

HISTORY REPEATS ITSELF (?)

Because history tends to repeat itself, it is useful to know what happened last time a particular event occurred, as the markets may respond in a similar way the next time.

I keep a record of major world events that affect the market, such as local and overseas elections; strikes at major mines; natural disasters like the earthquake in Kobe, Japan; political unrest; major scandals like those involving Nick Leeson of Barings Bank and the Sumitomo Corp copper price plunge; any shock moves in interest rates, gold or oil, etc.

This data is kept in a text file called FEVENTS (Financial Events), and records for each event the date, the Dow and the Australian All Ordinaries Index, and the price of the most affected commodities such as gold, oil, copper or whatever. If we record the date of the event, it is a simple matter to look up the charts of that time at some later date. Knowing how the markets reacted last time around gives some confidence that they may respond in a similar (though not identical) way again, and so we should not be panicked into hasty actions based on emotion.

To illustrate the usefulness of this record, during the European currency crisis in July and August 1993 I recorded that the price of gold peaked at $US406 on Monday 2nd August, and fell $US22 in a single day a couple of days later.

Looking back at the charts we find that one week before the peak the gold price was $US392 and one week after the peak was $US383. During this two-week span the Australian gold index jumped from 2081 to 2472 and back to 2148. Six weeks after the peak the gold price bottomed at $US345 and the gold index bottomed at 1703.

Knowing how the market responded to the currency crisis in 1993, what actions do we take during the next currency hiatus? Since that time various put and call warrants have become available on some major gold stocks, so they may be part of our trading.

I also keep a diary called FORWARD CALENDAR, and here enter the dates of coming events of importance—such as meetings of the US Federal Reserve Bank, and our RBA; company reporting dates; ex-dividend days; drilling program dates; US holidays; election dates, etc. As I read of these events in the media, they get entered into the FORWARD CALENDAR. Each week or so I check the coming events, to see if there is anything there which may influence my trading decisions.

Chapter 16

SPECIFICATIONS FOR A TECHNICAL SYSTEM

THIS CHAPTER PULLS together all the threads from the preceding chapters to define a technical system, which includes the technical trading system and the trading strategy.

Cash Required:

$10,000 upwards.

A kitty of $10,000 allows five BHP call options, or five BHP put options, to be written.

The deposit requirements change from time to time, and in times of high volatility some brokers may require full cash cover to write options.

Goal:

With a larger kitty of, say, $100,000 committed to the stock market, to make above-average returns.

Alternatively, with a kitty of $10,000, to take whatever profits come our way.

Strategy:

To trade options and warrants on the option stocks—

primarily the heavyweight resource stocks BHP, RIO, NDY, WMC, WPL, the major banks ANZ, CBA, NAB, WBC plus NCP, TLS and AMP.

Technical Tools:

MACD, DMI and ADX, momentum and RSI, volume, point and figure charts, weekly and daily bar charts.

Risk Management:

Open trades only when the indicator signals have a high probability of success—i.e. the market is trending and not moving sideways.

Money Management:

Limit losses to—

$1,000 per trade on $100,000 kitty; or $500 on $10,000 kitty.

Quit winning trade on a pullback of $500 to $1,000.

Hardware:

486 computer or better (typically Pentium series), modem and printer.

Software:

Charting and technical analysis software.

Price Data:

Close of day price data from a provider.

Cardinal Rules:

1. Follow the trend.
2. Let the profits run.
3. Cut the losses.
4. Manage the money to stay in the game.

Trading Rules:

1. On a valid signal to open a down leg:
   a. Write out-of-the-money call options with six to ten weeks to expiry.
   b. Buy put warrants with preferably six months to expiry.
2. On a valid signal to open an up leg:
   a. Write out-of-the-money put options with six to ten weeks to expiry.
   b. Buy call warrants with preferably six months to expiry.
3. Sell the bought warrants into a fast stock price move (typically 90¢ for BHP).
4. Try to hold the written options to expiry when they will either expire worthless, or can be bought back at a profit, but quit at a loss if the options become in-the-money.
5. Quit all trades when the indicators signal the end of the leg.

CHECKLIST BEFORE OPENING A TRADE

Table 16.1 opposite lists the items that should be checked before opening a trade. When each item has been carefully considered, and a positive conclusion reached, then it is safe to enter the trade knowing we have done our homework.

The reader may want to add more items, or delete others. Working through Table 16.1 can be tedious, but it is a useful discipline to avoid taking spur-of-the-moment long shots that are a recipe for disaster.

The filled-out tables are a record of each trade, which are useful to monitor from time to time to see any selection patterns in winning or losing trades.

Table 16.1 Checklist Before Opening a Trade

Stock Date and price Report date Dividend and date Annual cycle	
Opening details Daily indicators MACD DMI ADX Momentum Volume Weekly indicators MACD histogram RSI Gann times Gann targets Chart pattern Point and figure	
Option opening details Number and price Stop-loss price	
Warrant purchase details Number and price Stop-loss price	
Closing details Date and price Indicators	
Profit/loss	
Comments	

Chapter 17

CONCLUSIONS

THIS BOOK IS intended for the serious investor or trader who is prepared to manage their own portfolio, with the intent of achieving a steady positive return on the funds committed to the stock market.

To define the uptrends and downtrends it is necessary to use a selection of technical indicators and charting techniques. This can be done efficiently using a modern personal computer along with analysis and charting software, and a stock price database.

The performance of the indicators must be back-tested using historic price data, and a set of logic rules defined to trade particular stocks with particular indicators, along with charting techniques. This back-testing gives us experience with the indicators and charts, and an awareness of the stock conditions that lead to profits and to losses.

When back-testing can demonstrate consistent paper profits on particular stocks, then it is safe to start trading, being careful to implement risk management and money management procedures.

The strategy involves trading options and warrants on the option stocks, but particularly the heavyweight resource and major bank stocks, and also NCP, TLS and AMP. Emphasis is placed on writing put and call options, as these trades profit from a stock move in the required direction, and also when the stock moves sideways or slightly against us. We take only those trades where the indicator signals have shown a high probability of success in the past.

The book discusses all the above topics, and gives references for further reading to assist in a general understanding of options and warrants, technical indicators and charting, and in selecting software and database providers.

Setting up a computer-based trading system can be quite a challenge, depending where we start on the learning curve. When the system is up and running, and showing consistent profits on historic data, then we are ready to "take the current when it serves, or lose our ventures".

Chapter 18

RESOURCES

BOOKS

There are scores of books available on the stock market, and the discerning reader will discover that many books contain a "common core", plus further material particular to each author. We need to understand this core, as it is a distillation of the techniques and technical indicators that have proven to be successful over a period of time, and consequently have a high probability of continuing to be profitable in the future.

Because of this overlap of material covered, the books listed as references are grouped alphabetically within categories, to help the reader select one or two from each category to more quickly further their knowledge.

I have found the books by Livermore, Schwager, Tate, Meani, Guppy, Harper, LeBeau and Lucas to be particularly helpful in my style of trading.

General Stock Market

Donnelly, A. *Sensible Share Investing*, 3rd Edition, Wrightbooks, Elsternwick, Victoria, 1999.

Gann, W. D. *45 Years in Wall Street*, Lamberet Gann Publishing Co. Inc., Pomeroy, Washington, 1976.

Renton, N.E. *The Australian Dividend Handbook 2000-01*, Information Australia, Melbourne, Victoria, 2000.

Livermore, J. L. (pen name Lefare, E.) *Reminiscences of a Stock Operator*, Fraser Publishing Co., Burlington, Vermont, 1993.

Schwager, J. D. *Market Wizards*, HarperBusiness, New York, 1993.

General Options and Options Theory

Denning, H. *Equity Options*, Longman Professional, Melbourne, Victoria, 1991.

Harper, W.S. *Speculating on the Australian Sharemarket*, 2nd Edition, Wrightbooks, Elsternwick, Victoria, 2001.

Lee, C. F., Finnerty, J. E., Worth, D. H. *Security Analysis and Portfolio Management*, Scott, Foresman Company, Glenview, Illinois, 1990.

Tate, C. *Understanding Options Trading in Australia*, 2nd Edition, Wrightbooks, Elsternwick, Victoria, 1997.

Charting

Armstrong, M. *How to Chart Your Way to Success on the Stock Market*, Rydge Publications Pty Ltd, Sydney, NSW, 1984.

Edwards, R. D., Magee, J. *Technical Analysis of Stock Trends*, 6th Edition, John Magee Inc., Boston, Massachusetts, 1992.

Hull, A. *Charting in a Nutshell*, Wrightbooks, Elsternwick, Victoria, 2000.

Meani, R. *Charting: An Australian Investor's Guide,* 3rd Edition, Wrightbooks, Elsternwick, Victoria, 1999.

Technical Indicators

Elder, A. *Trading for a Living*, John Wiley and Sons Inc., New York, 1993.

LeBeau, C. Lucas, D. W. *Computer Analysis of the Futures Market*, Business One Irwin, Homewood, Illinois, 1992.

Pring, M. *Market Momentum,*
Toppan Co. Ltd, Tokyo, Japan, 1994.

Wilder, J. W. Jr *New Concepts In Technical Trading Systems,*
Hunter Publishing Co., Winston-Salem, North Carolina, 1974.

Technical Indicators and Charting

Guppy, D. *Share Trading: An Approach to Buying and Selling,*
Wrightbooks, Elsternwick, Victoria, 1996.

Harper, W.S. *How to Handle a Bear Market.*
Wrightbooks, Elsternwick, Victoria, 1998.

Kaufman, P. *New Commodity Trading Systems,*
John Wiley and Sons Inc., New York, 1987.

Krastins, I. *Listen to the Market,*
McGraw Book Co., Sydney, NSW, 1990.

McLaren, W. *Gann Made Easy,*
Gann Theory Publishing, Overbrook, Kansas, 1986.

Market Psychology

Bernstein, J. *The Investor's Quotient,*
John Wiley & Sons Inc., New York, 1993.

The Internet

Roth, M. *The Internet for Investing and Personal Finance,*
Wrightbooks, Elsternwick, Victoria, 1998.

MAGAZINES

Several magazines are available which give a commentary on various aspects of the stock market. Readers who are interested in technical trading will find the following three helpful:

Shares This very popular monthly magazine is published by BRW Media, and is available from newsagents. Each copy contains helpful articles on the application of technical analysis in the selection of companies to trade or for investment.

Your Trading Edge	The magazine for traders in futures, options, forex, stocks and commodities. Available from the Sydney Futures Exchange, Level 3, 30-32 Grosvenor St, Sydney, telephone (02) 9256 0555 or 1800 641 588.
Australian Technical Analysts Association Journal	Inquiries directed to GPO Box 2774, Sydney, NSW, 1043 (see also page 162).

SOFTWARE AND DATA SUPPLIERS

Technical analysts usually have their own charting and analysis software, which they update each day with current values using a price data feed. There are a number of Australian suppliers of charting and analysis software and data feeds, and magazines like *Shares* and *Personal Investor* always carry advertisements for a variety of software and data vendors. As these products differ considerably in cost and performance, novices need some help in trying to select a software package and data feed to suit their particular requirements. To this end, *Shares* and *Personal Investor* from time to time carry useful articles explaining, and comparing, the various software and data on offer. (A hunt through copies held at the local library should prove rewarding.) The ATAA (see page 162) from time to time conduct extensive comparisons on software and data feeds, which are available on request. (In January 2001, *Your Trading Edge* in conjunction with the ATAA published the *Annual YTE/ATAA Electronic Trading Guide 2000*, which gives a comprehensive list of software and data vendors, along with capabilities and costs.)

Four popular software packages are Ezy Charts, Insight Trader, Metastock and SuperCharts. Having made an initial choice of software, it is usually possible to buy a demonstration disk, or download a demonstration version of the software from the supplier, and thereby confirm that the software meets our requirements prior to purchase.

A software package covers four main areas:

1. Display charts.

   A variety of chart types can be displayed, including line charts, bar charts, candlestick charts and point and figure charts. Time frames can be daily, weekly or monthly, and the vertical price scale can be linear or logarithmic.

2. Technical indicators.

   A wide range of technical indicators is available. Most software provides the popular indicators such as moving averages, MACD, directional movement, relative strength, momentum, stochastic and Bollinger bands, along with Fibonacci and Gann analysis.

Different software packages contain various extended sets of indicators for advanced analysis (or for confusion!).

3. Signal alerts (or search engine).

   It is possible to set a variety of logic conditions and test a selection of stocks against these conditions. This allows stocks which are initiating new price moves to be quickly found.

4. Portfolio management.

   Portfolio management allows a record to be kept of buy and sell transactions, along with dividend payments, etc., which makes life a bit easier at tax time. The entries may be tied to the database, thereby allowing easy access to the value of the portfolio at any time.

Metastock and SuperCharts cover the first three areas well, and allow users to build their own technical indicators and do back-testing. Neither have a portfolio management module.

Ezy Charts and Insight Trader cover all four areas but are limited to a set of (comprehensive) pre-programmed technical indicators.

The data feed is available in various time frames:

1. Real-time data.

   This data is also called "live data" and is similar to that available to stockbrokers during the trading day. This live data may also include depth of market data showing the number of buyers and sellers for a stock along with their bid and ask prices. Real-time data is essential for day traders who trade on an intra-day time span.

2. Delayed data.

   This data is typically close-of-day data, and is suitable for people other than day traders.

Data providers supply a complete package of all ASX stocks, indices, warrants and futures, plus a selection of overseas indices and commodity prices. A smaller selection can be chosen at a lesser cost. Similarly, option prices can be had at an extra cost.

Each data provider can either deliver data in compatible formats for each of the listed software packages, or provide conversion software for this purpose. They also provide historic data going back typically ten years or more, for a fee.

Some data providers deliver the data via a phone modem, others via the Internet or email. Again, some data providers use different cost rates, depending on whether the data is provided before or after midnight for each trading day, with after midnight being cheaper.

We get what we pay for, and service and reliability are important factors in selecting a data provider.

As mentioned previously, there are many charting and analysis software packages, data feeds and suppliers. Online Trading Systems (OTS) is a popular supplier of software and data, and indicative prices are listed below:

Software	**$**
Demonstration pack (covering Ezy Group, Metastock, and SuperCharts)	11
Ezy Chart V4	379
Ezy Professional Pack (includes modules for charting, indicators, signal alerts and portfolio manager)	654
Metastock V7	654
SuperCharts V4.0	759
Insight Trader V8	545
Data	**$ p.a.**
All ASX stocks, warrants, ASX and world indices and historic data back to 1987	600
Top 150 ASX companies, ASX and world indices and historic data back to 1987	360
Sydney Futures Exchange and data back to 1987	290
World futures exchanges and data back to 1987	790
Combined package	**$**
Ezy Professional Pack software and two months of data for all ASX stocks, warrants, ASX and world indices	1,095

For enquiries contact: OTS, Level 1, 457 St Kilda Rd, Melbourne
Phone 1300 366 887
Email sales@ezycast.com Website www.ezycast.com

ATAA

The Australian Technical Analysts Association (ATAA) is a national forum for learning and exchanging ideas. It holds monthly meetings in Adelaide, Brisbane, Canberra, Melbourne, Perth, Sydney, Newcastle and Toowoomba. Its address is listed in the Magazine section on page 159. The ATAA also publishes a bi-monthly journal containing informative articles, covering a variety of stock market and futures-related topics.

The contact phone number is (02) 9667 0983. An information pack, including a free copy of the *Journal*, is available on request.

HARDWARE

The current state-of-the-art personal computer goes under the generic name "Pentium", and is a powerful beast. A Pentium III 500 with Windows 2000, a monitor and telephone modem costs around $1,500 upwards (depending on make), while a colour bubble jet printer costs around $250 upwards.

Appendix I

GANN'S ANNUAL DATES AND CYCLES

LISTED OVERLEAF ARE Gann's annual dates and cycles. These cycles are time cycles only, based on the physical time periods of the solar system, and are used to determine dates when changes in the market frequently occur. The reference to seasons in Gann's books naturally applies to North America.

Australia is part of the Global Village, so our market tends to follow Wall Street.

Notice that the listed important dates usually indicate a change in trend, rather than the market always turning specifically bullish or specifically bearish around that date.

The dates in **bold** are the more important ones within the table.

The table shows that 8 November is an important date. Readers will remember the November 2000 US election, with contenders George W. Bush and Al Gore continuing their battle in the courts after the primary voting proved inconclusive. The broader S&P 500 market started falling in the second week of November, which is consistent with Gann's cycles in election years.

Date	Comments
Dec 22	Start of winter quarter.
Jan 4-5	15 days from Dec 22 and the start of the market new year. Stocks often make extreme highs or lows on these dates and a change in trend occurs. If stocks make a low near Dec 22 the rally will last till Jan 3-7 and sometimes run till Jan 20-21.
Feb 5	Minor trend changes.
March 21	Sun crosses the equator and spring begins. Spring rally begins around this date or, if stocks have been advancing, culminates around now.
May 6	135 days from Dec 22— important changes in trend around this date.
June 22	Opposite Dec 22 and start of summer.
July 7	Advances or declines often culminate around this date.
August 8	Important date for change in trend— watch for tops or bottoms.
Sept 23	Sun crosses equator and fall begins. Important changes in trend.
Nov 8	In US election years a change in trend often occurs early in the month. In other years low prices often occur late in the month.
Dec 22	Start of winter and important changes in trend.

Other pointers

- July 27 to the first week of August has a bullish bias.
- August has a high probability of being an up month.
- September has a high probability of being a down month.
- Friday has a high probability of being an up day.
- Monday has a high probability of being a down day.

Appendix II

SOME OPTION STRATEGIES ON STOCKS AND INDICES

IN THIS APPENDIX we look at a selection of the more common options strategies used by traders, and point out their pros and cons. The strategies include buying options and writing options, and also straddles, strangles, spreads and ratio spreads. The strategies cover both put and call options, and bull and bear conditions. Each strategy is explained, and the pay-off diagram is drawn, as these diagrams show visually the result of the trade when held to contract expiry. Each strategy has a different risk/reward ratio (the potential loss compared to the potential profit), and includes the cases of limited loss/unlimited profit, unlimited loss/limited profit and limited loss/limited profit.

Each strategy is applied to options on the London FTSE 100 index, and numerical values are given for a particular day, to allow a comparison between the relevant strategy's profit/loss if held to expiry.

FTSE 100 INDEX AND OPTIONS

The Sydney Futures Exchange (SFE) trades futures and options on the Australian Stock Exchange (ASX) benchmark indices (see page 5), i.e. contracts over the All Ordinaries Index and the new S&P/ASX 200 Index. The London stock market major index is called the Financial Times Stock Exchange (FTSE) 100 Index (which covers 100 leading stocks), and has comparable futures and options which trade on the London International Financial Futures Exchange (LIFFE). These LIFFE derivatives are popular with traders from all around the world, resulting in heavy turnover. Because of their popularity, these LIFFE options are used in this Appendix to illustrate the various options trading strategies.

The relevant specifications for the FTSE 100 options contract is:

Contract size in BPD (£):	10 x FTSE 100 Index expressed in points
Unit if trading:	1 point valued at BPD 10
Strike price intervals:	50 points
Style:	American
Expiry months:	Every month up to four months ahead
Expiry:	Third Friday of each month
Settlement:	Cash

For an exchange rate of, say, BPD 1 = AUD 2.5, then a 1-point move in the FTSE 100 index translates to a AUD 1 x 10 x 2.5 = $25 move in price. (In this chapter Australian dollars will be designated simply as $.)

For brevity we refer to the FTSE 100 index as the FTSE index, and options on the FTSE 100 index are referred to as FTSE options.

Deposits and Margins

As discussed in Chapter 2, a deposit is required before we can write naked options on stocks. Further, at the close of each day, holders of losing positions face a margin call, while holders of a profit position receive a credit margin. These daily margin moves are known in financial circles as *variation margins.*

A similar situation applies to written FTSE options, as both written puts and written calls are of the naked type. Thus if we write a FTSE call (put) option and the market moves upwards (downwards), then margin calls are required. Before writing a FTSE option, a deposit of around $5,000 needs to be paid to the broker, and is available for margin calls as they arise.

Holding a written naked option can be a distinct embarrassment when the market turns against us. Several of the option strategies discussed later offer the advantage of not invoking margin calls when the market turns contrary.

Settlement Price

When FTSE options expire, the clearing house allocates an official settlement price to them, for the purpose of settling open contracts. This settlement price is calculated by taking an average of a selection of index values prior to the time designated for expiration of the options.

RECAP ON TERMINOLOGY

There are four sets of terms which are part of futures and options trading jargon, so they are defined to avoid confusion.

Bull, bullish, bull market: Pertaining to a rising market, or a point of view that the market will rise.

Bear, bearish, bear market: Pertaining to a falling market, or a point of view that the market will fall.

Long: Holding a position that will profit from a rising market.

Short: Holding a position that will profit from a falling market.

OPTIONS TRADES

Options can be either put or call, and can be either bought or written. Consequently combining these choices gives rise to a variety of option strategies.

We look at the four basic option situations and draw the corresponding pay-off diagrams. In order to make numeric comparisons between option strategies, actual option close prices on a given day in mid November 1999 are used. That day was a fairly steady day, and the FTSE index closed at 6551 points, and the options chosen are the December series with four weeks to expiry. At that time the exchange rate was close to BPD 1 = $2.5, so each 1-point move in the option prices equated to a move of $25.

The absolute value chosen of 6551 points is not important, and other days and prices could have been used. The benefit of the analysis is to be able to compare the various option strategies as "apples versus apples". As always, the principles involved are of more interest than the absolute values.

A weekly bar chart of the FTSE index is given in Figure A.1 overleaf. It can be seen that in mid November 1999, the market paused for a couple of weeks in a prolonged uptrend.

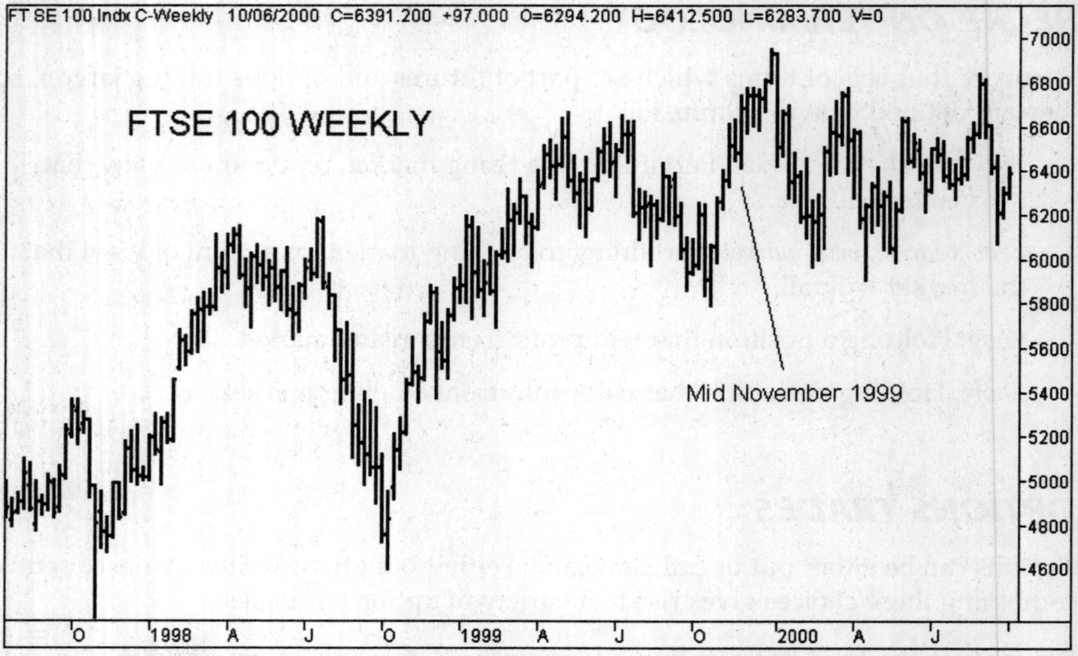

Figure A.1 Weekly Bar Chart of FTSE 100 Index

Call Options

Bought Option

The FTSE index is trading at 6550 points and we anticipate a strong price increase. To capitalise on this rise we buy call options with strike price 6650 points (i.e. 100 points out-of-the-money) for 95 points. The pay-off diagram is shown in Figure A.2 (a) opposite. If the FTSE index at settlement is above 6745 points the trade shows a profit, and the higher the index the greater the profit. The loss is limited to 95 points.

Written Option

The FTSE index is trading at 6550 points and we anticipate a sideways to slightly down trend to develop. To generate a profit from this listless move we write deep out-of-the-money options with strike price 6850 points for 31 points. The pay-off diagram is shown in Figure A.2 (b) opposite. If the FTSE index at settlement is below 6881 points the trade shows a profit, with maximum profit limited to 31 points. The loss is unlimited, and the higher the index, the greater the loss.

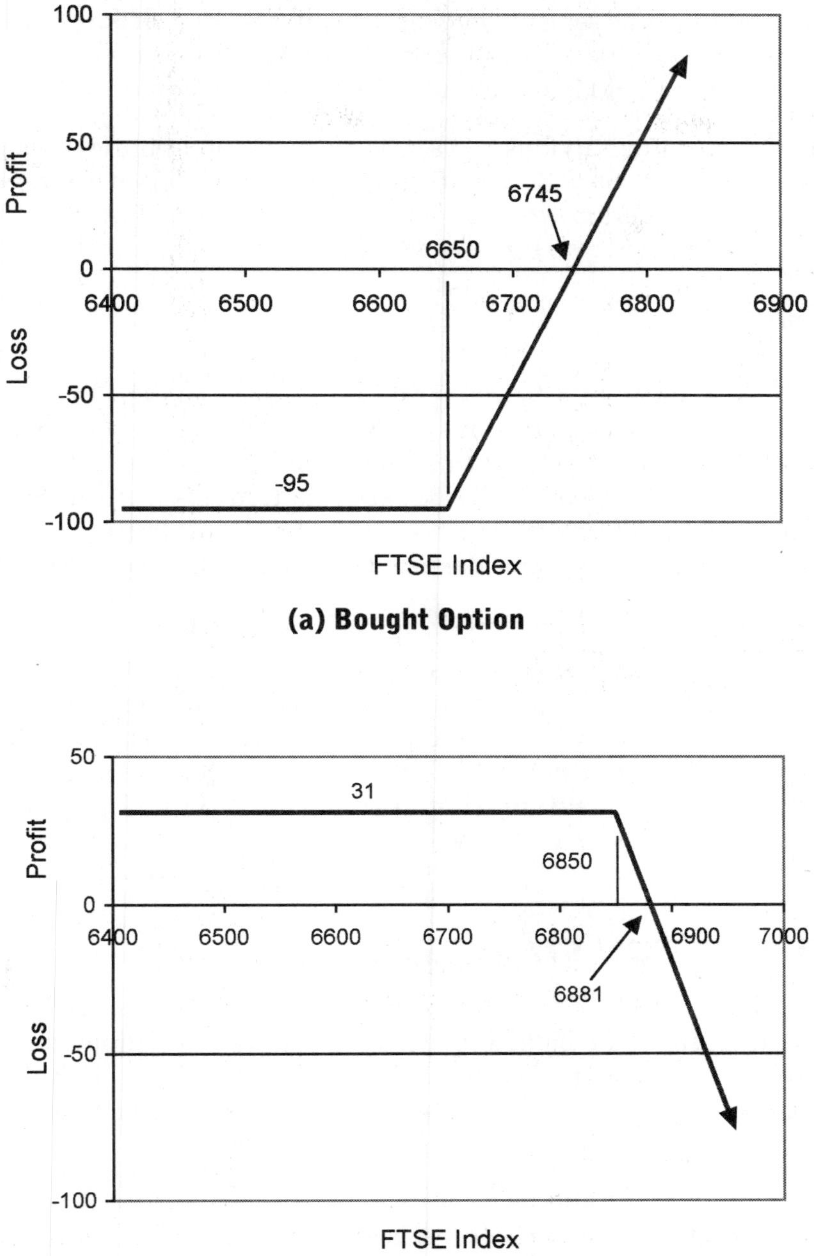

(a) Bought Option

(b) Written Option

Figure A.2 Call Option Pay-Off Diagrams

When buying options it is safest to choose an option with a strike price close to the value of the index . Thus the option chosen above is 100 points out-of-the-money. An in-the-money option would be safer, but is correspondingly more expensive to buy.

Conversely, when writing options it is safest to choose an option with a strike price some distance from the value of the index. Thus the option chosen above is 300 points out-of-the-money. An option which is 500 points out-of-the-money would be safer, but has a lesser value, and also has lower turnover.

Put Options

Bought Option

The FTSE index is trading at 6550 points and we anticipate a sharp fall in the price. To capitalise on this fall we buy put options with strike price 6450 points (i.e. 100 points out-of-the-money) for 87 points. The pay-off diagram is shown in Figure A.3 (a) opposite. If the FTSE index at settlement is below 6363 points the trade shows a profit, and the lower the index the greater the profit. The loss is limited to 87 points.

Written Option

The FTSE index is trading at 6550 points and we anticipate a sideways to slightly up trend to develop. To generate a profit from this listless move we write deep out-of-the-money options with strike price 6250 points for 38 points. The pay-off diagram is shown in Figure A.3 (b) opposite. If the FTSE index at settlement is above 6212 points the trade shows a profit, with maximum profit limited to 38 points. The loss is unlimited, and the lower the index, the greater the loss.

VERSATILE OPTION STRATEGIES

The above option strategies can be very profitable when the market moves in one direction as anticipated. The flexibility available with options allows strategies to be developed which produce profits from a variety of market conditions. Some of the more straightforward of these versatile strategies are discussed below.

Straddle

A *long straddle* consists of buying both a call option and a put option simultaneously, with both options being at-the-money and having the same expiry date.

A *short straddle* consists of writing both a call option and a put option simultaneously, with both options being at-the-money and having the same expiry date.

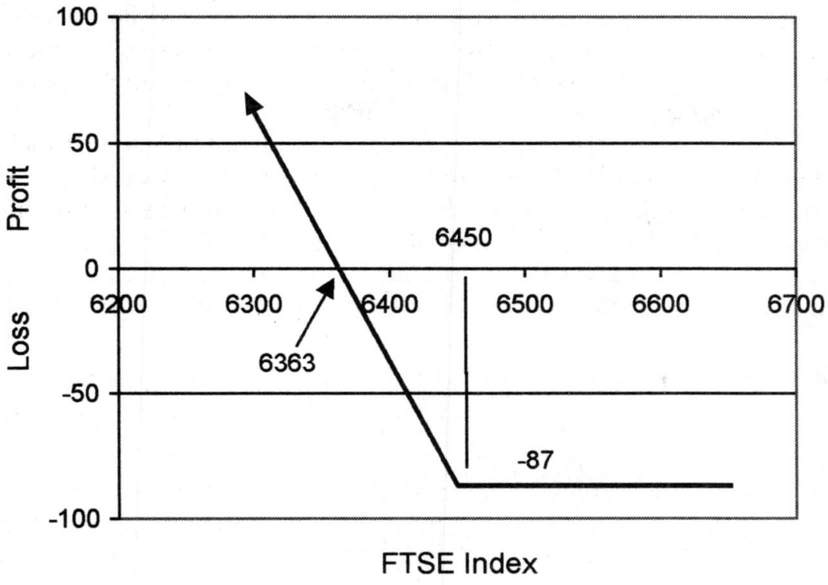

(a) Bought Option

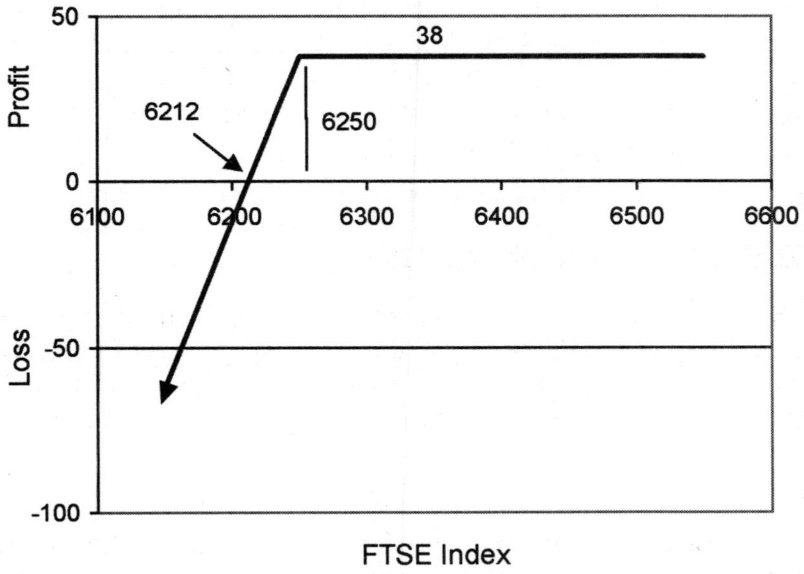

(b) Written Option

Figure A.3 Put Option Pay-Off Diagrams

Long Straddle

Suppose market conditions are such that we expect a sharp move to occur, but are unsure which direction the move will take. Such occasions could be, say, times of general elections where the outcome is uncertain, major pronouncements on interest rates, the close of a day when the market has made a sharp move, etc.

As a simple example, suppose the FTSE index is 6550 points, and we buy a FTSE call option with 6550 strike price for 144 points, and simultaneously buy a FTSE put option with 6550 strike price for 130 points. The total cost of buying the straddle is 274 points or 274 x 25 = $6,850. The options are expensive because they are at-the-money. The pay-off diagram is shown in Figure A.4 (a) opposite, and it is seen that a profit is made if at option expiry, the FTSE index has moved up or down more than 274 points, i.e. is outside the trading band from 6276 to 6824 points. The further away the FTSE index is at settlement, the greater the profit.

If the market just moves sideways, we stand to lose the total cost of the purchase.

Short Straddle

Suppose we expect the market to drift sideways for a while. We can capitalise on a listless market through selling a short straddle.

Using the same values as for the long (bought) straddle, suppose with the FTSE index at 6550 points, we write a FTSE call option with 6550 strike price for 144 points, and simultaneously write a FTSE put option with 6550 points strike price for 130 points. The total premium from selling the straddle is 274 points or $6,850. The pay-off diagram is the reverse of the long straddle, and is shown in Figure A.4 (b) opposite. A profit is made if at option expiry, the FTSE index is within the band 6276 to 6824 points. A loss is made if the FTSE index is outside this band, and the further away the FTSE index is at settlement, the greater the loss.

The strategy is called a straddle, because it is centred (or straddled) upon the single at-the-money option strike price.

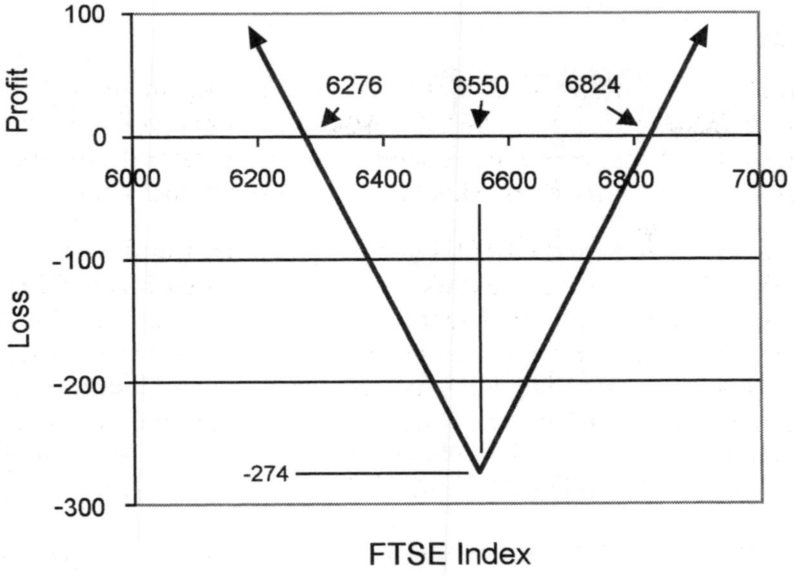

(a) Long Straddle

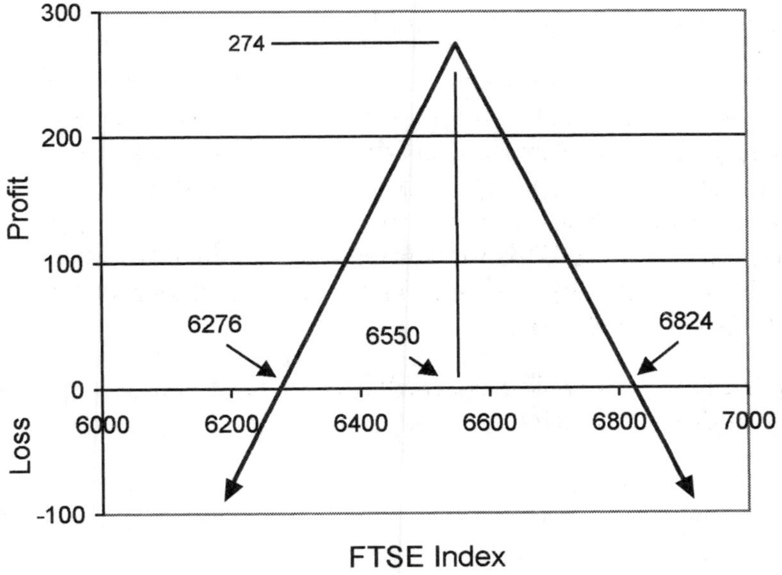

(b) Short Straddle

Figure A.4 Straddle Pay-Off Diagrams

Strangle

The strangle is a variation of the straddle, but now the call and the put options have the same expiry date, but different strike prices.

Long Strangle

Suppose once again that market conditions are such that we expect a sharp move to occur, but are unsure which direction the move will take. We decide to set up a strangle which will show a good profit if the index moves more than, say, 400 points in either direction.

Suppose the FTSE index is at 6550 points, then we buy an out-of-the-money call option with strike price of 6650 points for 95 points, and simultaneously buy an out-of-the-money put option with strike price of 6450 points for 87 points. The cost of buying the strangle is 182 points or 182 x 25 = $4,550 (which is cheaper than buying the straddle), and the pay-off diagram is shown in Figure A.5 (a) opposite. A profit is made at option expiry if the FTSE index has moved up or down more than 182 points from the option strike prices, i.e. is outside the price band from 6268 points to 6832 points. If the FTSE index at settlement is 400 points lower at 6150 points, then the profit is 6268 – 6150 = 118 points or 118 x 25 = $2,950.

If the market just moves sideways, we stand to lose the total cost of the purchase.

Short Strangle

Suppose we expect the market to drift sideways for a while. Once again, we can capitalise on a listless market through selling a short strangle.

Using the values as for the long (bought) strangle, with the FTSE index at 6550 points, we write an out-of-the-money call option with 6650 strike price for 95 points, and simultaneously write an out-of-the-money put option with strike price of 6450 points for 87 points. The total premium from selling the strangle is 182 points or $4,550. The pay-off diagram is the reverse of the long strangle and is shown in Figure A.5 (b) opposite. A profit is made at option expiry if the FTSE index is within the band from 6268 points to 6832 points.

A loss is made if the FTSE index at settlement is outside this band and the further the index moves, the greater is the loss.

The strategy is called a strangle, because the index is strangled between the two option strike prices.

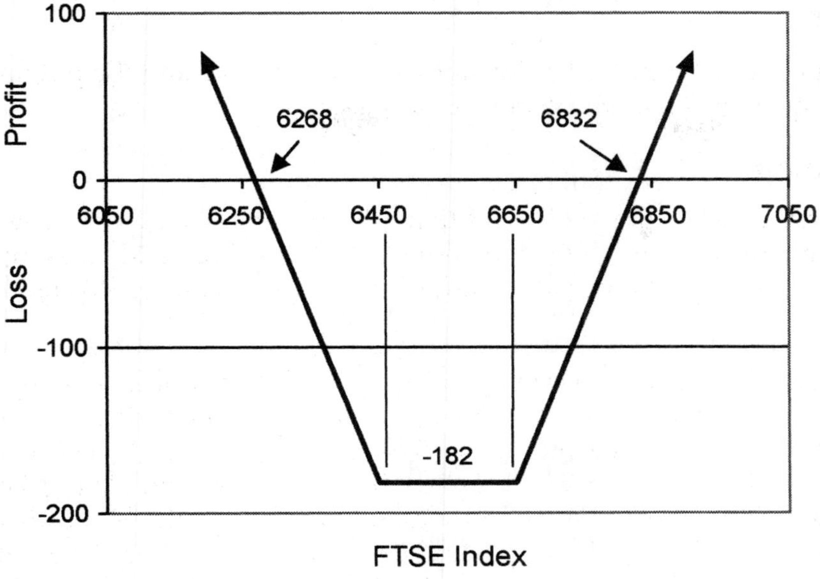

(a) Long Strangle

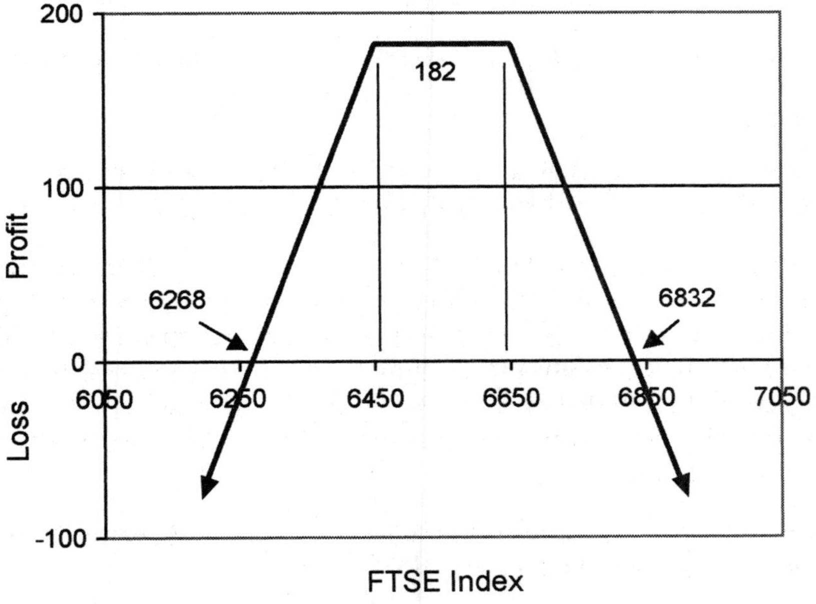

(b) Short Strangle

Figure A.5 Strangle Pay-Off Diagrams

SPREADS

A spread is created by simultaneously buying an option and writing an option with different strike prices, and possibly different expiry dates. The principle behind spreads is that one option will make a profit while the other makes a loss, and the difference between them is the net profit or net loss for the trade.

Spreads are a popular strategy because they deliver a known maximum profit on a winning trade or, conversely, limit the loss to a known maximum loss on a losing trade. Both the maximum profit and maximum loss can be calculated when the spread is opened. Further, as the spread loss is limited, a losing trade is not subjected to margin calls.

Options can be used in a variety of combinations to produce a spread, so we discuss the four basic strategies of call bull spread, put bull spread, call bear spread and put bear spread. The pay-off diagrams are shown in Figures A.6 and A.7 on pages 178 and 182 respectively. Each pay-off diagram has a common horizontal axis spanning 6050 points to 6850 points, thereby allowing visual comparisons between the performance of each strategy.

Bull Spreads

A bull spread strategy is used when we anticipate a rise in the market.

Call Bull Spread

Once again, suppose the FTSE index is trading at 6550 points, and we anticipate a rise of maybe 200 points in the next few weeks.

To open a call bull spread we purchase a call option which is just out-of-the-money, and simultaneously write a call option which is further out-of-the money. Suppose we buy the option with strike price 6650 points for 95 points, and write the option with strike price 6700 points for 77 points for a net debit of 18 points. The data for drawing the call bull spread pay-off diagram is given in Table A.1 opposite.

The pay-off diagram is shown in Figure A.6 (a) on page 178, where we see that the maximum profit occurs if the FTSE index settlement price is above the upper strike price, while the maximum loss occurs when the settlement price is below the lower strike price.

Table A.1 Data for Call Bull Spread Pay-Off Diagram

FTSE Index (Points)	Bought Option (Points)	Sold Option (Points)	Net Profit (Points)
6550	-95	77	-18
6600	-95	77	-18
6650	-95	77	-18
6668	-77	77	0
6700	-45	77	32
6745	0	32	32
6777	32	0	32
6800	55	-23	32

Further:

Maximum profit = difference between strike prices – net cost of spread

= (6700 – 6650) – (95 – 77)

= 32 points or 32 x 25 = $800

Maximum loss = net cost of spread

= 18 points or 18 x 25 = $450

Note that this call bull spread involves buying a 6650 strike call option and writing a 6700 call option that is out-of-the-money. Referring to the pay-off diagram in Figure A.6 (a) overleaf, the maximum profit of 32 points is achieved provided the FTSE index rises above 6700 points. As the written call option has a strike price of 6700, this option will be in-the-money when the maximum profit is attainable. We noted previously that in-the-money options are usually exercised by their holders during the last week before expiry. Thus, prior to the last week of option expiry, if the FTSE rises above 6700 points we close out the spread through selling the 6650 bought call and buying back the 6700 written call. This transaction crystallises the profit, but incurs two more lots of brokerage.

If the FTSE index falls after we open the spread, the maximum loss is incurred if the FTSE index at settlement is below 6600 points, whereby both options expire worthless. This maximum loss is the initial cost of opening the spread.

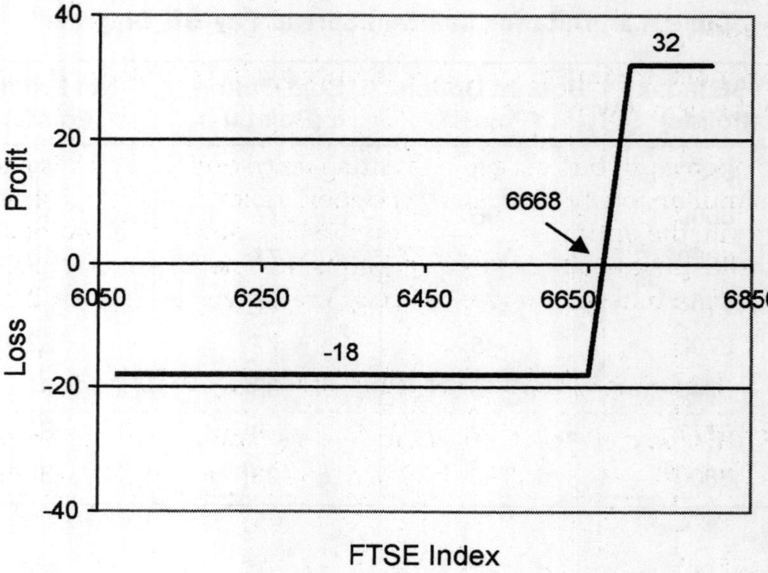

(a) Call Options

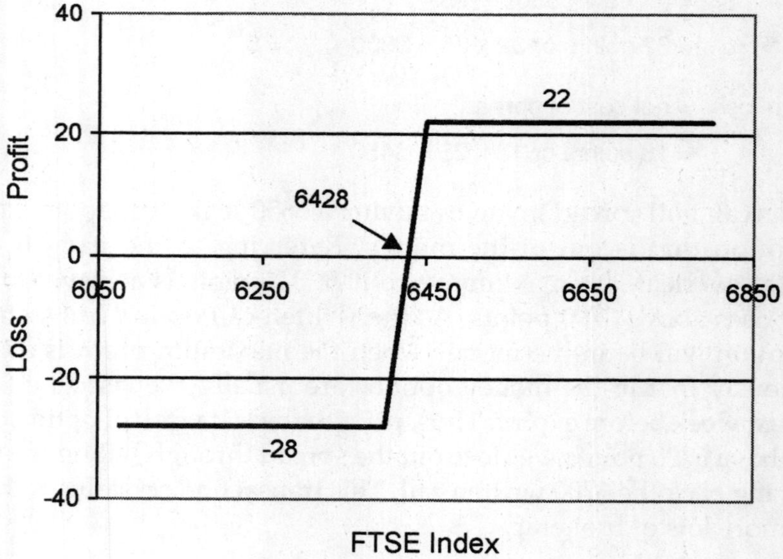

(b) Put Options

Figure A.6 Bull Spread Pay-Off Diagrams

Put Bull Spread

With the FTSE index trading at 6550 points, once again we anticipate a rise of maybe 200 points in the next few weeks.

We choose to open a put bull spread by writing a put option which is just out-of-the-money, and simultaneously buying a put option which is further out-of-the-money. Suppose we write the option with strike price 6450 points for 87 points, and buy the option with strike price 6400 points for 65 points for a net credit of 22 points. The data for drawing the put bull spread pay-off diagram is given in Table A.2 below.

Table A.2 Data for Put Bull Spread Pay-Off Diagram

FTSE Index (Points)	Bought Option (Points)	Sold Option (Points)	Net Profit (Points)
6300	35	-63	-28
6335	0	-28	-28
6350	-15	-13	-28
6363	-28	0	-28
6400	-65	37	-28
6428	-65	65	0
6450	-65	87	22
6500	-65	87	22
6550	-65	87	22

The pay-off diagram is shown in Figure A.6 (b) on page 178, where we see that the maximum profit occurs if the FTSE index settlement price is above the upper strike price, while the maximum loss occurs when the settlement price is below the lower strike price.

Further:

Maximum profit = net credit in opening spread
= 87 – 65
= 22 points or $550

Maximum loss = difference between strike prices – net credit in opening spread
= (6450 – 6400) – 22
= 28 points or $700

In this case, if the FTSE index at settlement is above 6450 points, both options expire worthless and the maximum profit is achieved.

However, if the FTSE index falls below the written put option strike price of 6450 points, we are at risk of being exercised and must buy the option back. The maximum loss of 28 points is achieved when the FTSE index falls below 6400 points, and we close out the spread through selling the 6400 bought put and buying back the written 6450 put. Once again, this transaction crystallises the loss, and incurs two more lots of brokerage.

Call Bull Spread vs Put Bull Spread

Although call bull spreads and put bull spreads are both strategies to profit from a rising market, they have different characteristics as illustrated by the numerical examples:

- The call bull spread is a debit transaction in that it is opened at a loss, and makes its maximum profit provided the FTSE index moves above the higher of the call option strike prices (6700 in this example). To crystallise the profit we must reverse the spread. If the market falls we need take no action, as both the bought and written call options expire worthless.
- The put bull spread is a credit transaction, and holds its maximum profit provided the FTSE index settlement is above the higher of the put option strike prices (6450 points in the example). To achieve the profit we need take no action, as both the bought and written put options expire worthless. However, if the market falls we must crystallise the loss by reversing the spread.

The put bull spread is a credit transaction and is generally preferred over the debit call bull spread for this reason.

In practice, the strike prices chosen in the spreads will be carefully chosen to give satisfactory risk/reward ratios, based on the current value and the anticipated movement in the FTSE index. There is no single best combination of strike prices, though a popular choice is to select one strike price 25 to 50 points below the FTSE index, with the other strike price 25 to 50 points above the FTSE index when the spread is opened.

Bear Spreads

A bear spread strategy is used when we anticipate a fall in the market.

Call Bear Spread

Suppose the FTSE index is trading at 6550 points, and we anticipate a fall of maybe 200 points in the next few weeks.

To open a call bear spread we write a call option which is just out-of-the-money, and simultaneously buy a call option which is further out-of-the-money. Suppose we write the option with strike price 6650 points for 95 points, and buy the option with strike price 6700 points for 77 points for a net credit of 18 points. The data for drawing the call bear spread is the same as that given in Table A.1, but with the signs reversed.

The pay-off diagram is shown in Figure A.7 (a) overleaf, where we see that the maximum profit occurs if the FTSE index settlement price is below the lower strike price, while the maximum loss occurs when the settlement price is above the upper strike price.

Further:

Maximum profit = net credit from opening spread
= 95 – 77
= 18 points or $450

Maximum loss = difference between strike prices – maximum profit
= (6700 – 6650) – 18
= 50 – 18
= 32 points or $800

For the call bear spread, if the FTSE index at settlement is below 6650 points, both options expire worthless and the maximum profit is achieved.

However, if the FTSE index rises above the written call option strike price of 6650 points, we are at risk of being exercised and must buy the option back. The maximum loss of 32 points is achieved when the FTSE index rises above 6700 points, and we close out the spread through selling the 6700 bought call and buying back the written 6650 call. This transaction crystallises the loss, and incurs two more lots of brokerage.

Put Bear Spread

With the FTSE index trading at 6550 points, once again we anticipate a fall of maybe 200 points in the next few weeks.

We choose to open a put bear spread by buying a put option which is just out-of-the-money, and simultaneously writing a put option which is deeper out-of-the-money. Suppose we buy the option with strike price of 6450 points for 87 points, and write the option with strike price 6400 points for 65 points, for a net debit of 22 points. The data for drawing the put bear spread is the same as that given in Table A.2, but with the signs reversed.

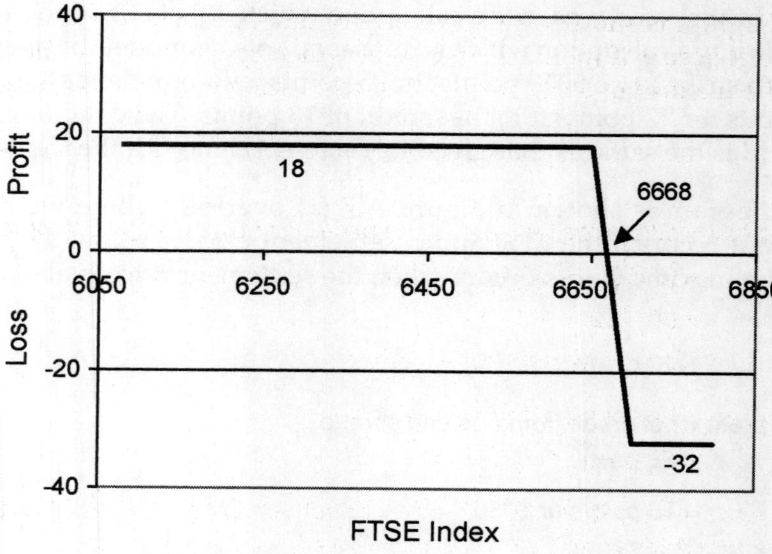

(a) Call Options

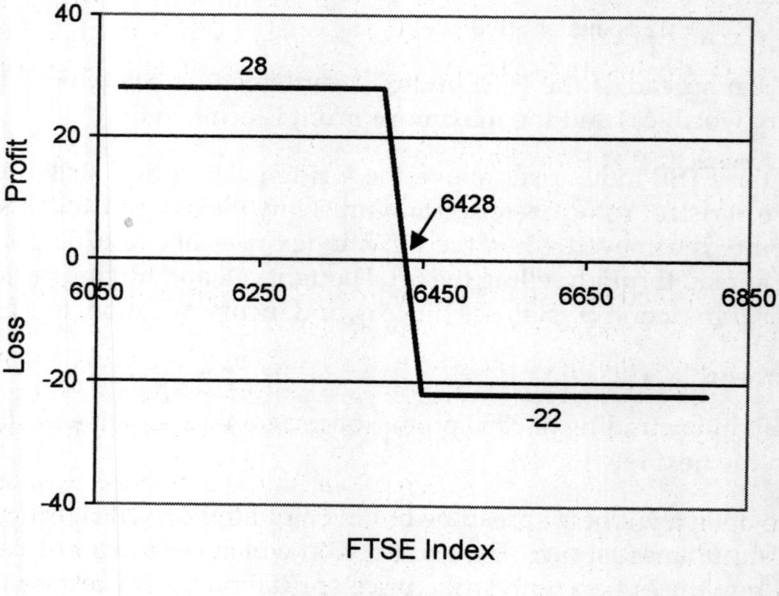

(b) Put Options

Figure A.7 Bear Spread Pay-Off Diagrams

The pay-off diagram is shown in Figure A.7 (b) on page 182, where we see that the maximum profit occurs if the FTSE index settlement price is below the lower strike price, while the maximum loss occurs when the settlement price is above the upper strike price.

Further:

Maximum profit = difference between strike prices – net loss in opening spread
= (6450 – 6400) – (87 – 65)
= 50 – 22
= 28 points or $700

Maximum loss = net loss in opening spread
= 22 points or $550

For the put bear spread, if the FTSE index at settlement is above 6450 points, both options expire worthless and the maximum loss is achieved.

However, if the FTSE index falls below the written put option strike price of 6450 points, we are at risk of being exercised and must buy the option back. The maximum profit of 28 points is achieved when the FTSE index falls below 6400 points, and we close out the spread through selling the 6450 bought put and buying back the written 6400 put. Once again, this transaction crystallises the profit, and incurs two more lots of brokerage.

Call Bear Spread vs Put Bear Spread

Call bear spreads and put bear spreads are both strategies to profit from a falling market, but they have different characteristics:

- The call bear spread is a credit transaction, and holds its maximum profit provided the FTSE index at settlement is below the lower of the call option strike prices (6650 points in the example). To achieve the profit we need take no action, as both the bought and written call options expire worthless. However, if the market rises we must crystallise the loss by reversing the spread.
- The put bear spread is a debit transaction in that it is opened at a loss, and makes its maximum profit provided the FTSE index at settlement moves below the lower of the put option strike prices (6400 points in the example). To crystallise the profit we must reverse the spread. If the market rises we need take no action, as both the bought and written put options expire worthless.

The call bear spread is a credit transaction and is generally preferred over the debit put bear spread for this reason.

Spread Time Considerations

The various spread pay-off diagrams shown in Figures A.6 and A.7 are the profit/loss situations at option expiry. The losses incurred with these strategies are capped and not subject to margin calls, so it is possible to hold the trade should the market move counter to our expectations, yet still make a profit should the market conditions be in our favour at expiry.

Ratio Spread

The *ratio spread* is an extension of the call bull strategy or the put bear strategy. Both these strategies were debit transactions, in that it cost some cash to set them up. The principle of the ratio spread is to convert the debit spread to a credit spread, through buying a close-to-the-money option but writing two further out-of-the-money options.

As an example, suppose the FTSE index is trading at 6550 points, and we anticipate a small rise of say 100 to 200 points. We open a ratio call spread through buying a call option with a 6600-point strike price for 124 points, and simultaneously write two call options with 6650-point strike prices for 95 points, giving a net credit of 66 points. The data for drawing the ratio call spread pay-off diagram is given in Table A.3 below.

Table A.3 Data for Ratio Call Spread Pay-Off Diagram

FTSE Index (Points)	Bought Option (Points)	Sold Option (Points)	x 2	Net Profit (Points)
6550	-124	95	190	66
6600	-124	95	190	66
6650	-74	95	190	116
6700	-24	45	90	66
6750	26	-5	-10	16
6765	41	-20	-40	1
6800	76	-55	-110	-34
6850	126	-105	-210	-84
6900	176	-155	-310	-134

Figure A.8 below shows that the strategy produces a profit provided the FTSE index at settlement is below 6765 points, with the maximum profit occurring at the higher option strike price of 6650 points. If the index rises above 6765 points, then losses occur which can become unlimited. As this ratio spread gives a maximum profit of 116 points at expiry when the index is 6650 points, a prudent strategy would be to close the spread early if a profit above, say, 100 points can be obtained.

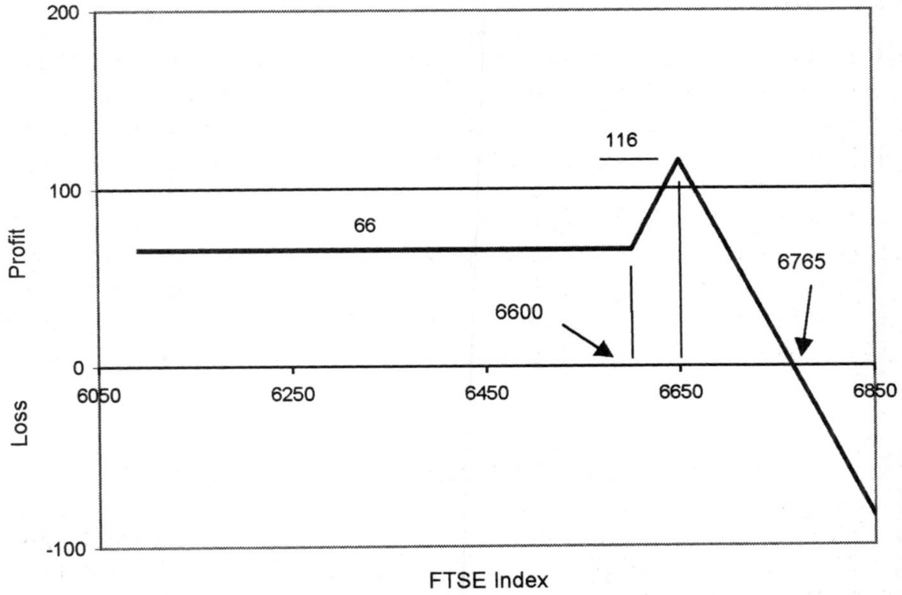

Figure A.8 Ratio Call Bull Spread Pay-Off Diagram

The Free Trade

The *free trade* is a call bull spread, or a put bear spread, where the two options making up the spread are opened a few days apart. The free trade relies upon the first option showing a profit, and then writing the second option further out-of-the-money, thereby offsetting the cost of the first option. The options have different strike prices but the same expiry date.

Rising Market

As an example, suppose the FTSE index is trading at 6550 points and we buy a call option with strike price 6750 points for 65 points. A few days later the index rises, say, 200 points to 6750 points and we write a call option with strike price of 6850 points. As this option is 100 points out-of-the-money it will be worth, say, 90 points. The data for the pay-off diagram is listed in Table A.4 below.

Table A.4 Data for Free Trade Bull Spread Pay-Off Diagram

FTSE Index (Points)	Bought Option (Points)	Sold Option (Points)	Net Profit (Points)
6550	-65	90	25
6600	-65	90	25
6650	-65	90	25
6700	-65	90	25
6750	-65	90	25
6800	-15	90	75
6850	35	90	125
6900	85	40	125
6950	135	-10	125
7000	185	-60	125

Figure A.9 opposite shows that the trade produces a profit irrespective of the value of the FTSE index at settlement. The minimum profit in this case is 25 points or $625, while the maximum profit is this amount plus the difference in strike prices, i.e. 25 + 100 = 125 points or $3,125.

It is important to stress that the free trade only works because the initial bought call option moved up strongly. The second call option locked in some of the profit, and in the event of the index continuing to rise, capped the profit at 125 points. The risk associated with the strategy is that after buying the first call option the market falls, thereby nullifying the strategy. The maximum loss in this case becomes the cost of buying the call option.

Falling Market

The free trade strategy for a falling market is to buy an out-of-the-money put option, and once that shows a worthwhile profit, then write a put option for a higher premium, but with a lower strike value. Both options will have the same expiry date.

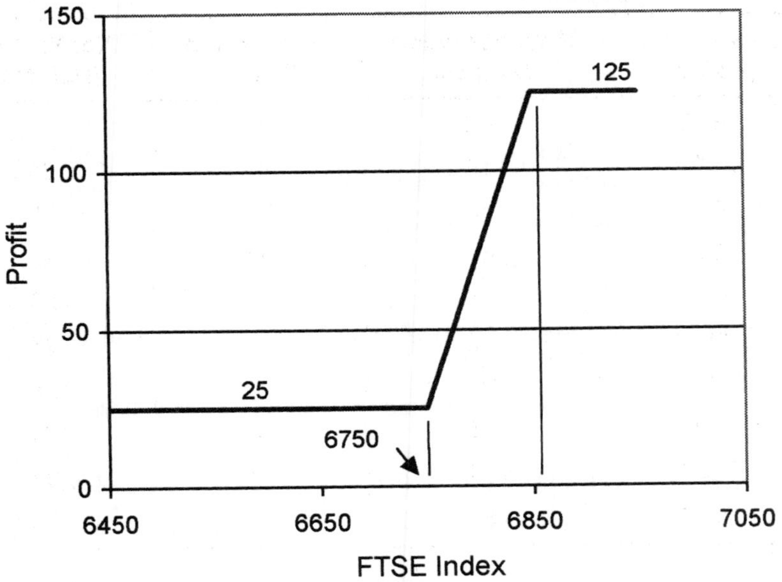

Figure A.9 Free Trade Call Bull Spread Pay-Off Diagram

SUMMARY OF STRATEGIES

To help compare the various strategies discussed above, their pros and cons are listed in Table A.5 overleaf. Each strategy works best for particular market conditions, ranging from sideways trending, to moderately bullish or bearish, to strongly bullish or bearish. Thus the trader needs to have a view on the direction of the market, and may use some form of technical analysis for this purpose, as discussed in earlier chapters (see also *Technical Analysis for Trading Index Warrants*, along with other titles listed in Chapter 18).

The strategies discussed above are by no means exhaustive, and more complex examples can be found in some of the titles listed in Chapter 18.

Table A.5 Comparisons Between Trading Strategies

Strategy	When Used	Profit	Loss	Margin Calls
Buy call option	Anticipate strong rise	Unlimited if market rises	Limited to cost of option	No
Write call option	Anticipate fall or sideways trend	Limited to sale of option	Unlimited if market rises	Yes
Buy put option	Anticipate strong fall	Unlimited if market falls	Limited to cost of option	No
Write put option	Anticipate rise or sideways trend	Limited to sale of option	Unlimited if market falls	Yes
Long straddle	Anticipate strong rise or strong fall	Unlimited if market outside price band	Limited to cost of options	No
Short straddle	Anticipate sideways trend	Limited to sale price of options	Unlimited if market outside price band	Yes
Long strangle	Anticipate strong rise or strong fall	Unlimited if market outside price band	Limited to cost of options	No
Short strangle	Anticipate sideways trend	Limited to sale price of options	Unlimited if market outside price band	Yes
Call bull spread	Anticipate strong rise	Limited	Limited to cost of setting up spread	No
Put bull spread	Anticipate rise	Limited to credit in setting up spread	Limited	No
Call bear spread	Anticipate fall	Limited to credit in setting up spread	Limited	No
Put bear spread	Anticipate strong fall	Limited	Limited to cost of setting up spread	No
Ratio call bull spread	Anticipate limited rise	Limited	Unlimited	Yes
Ratio put bear spread	Anticipate limited rise	Limited	Unlimited	Yes

CONCLUSION

This Appendix has looked at some of the popular trading strategies incorporating options. All the examples are based on options on the London FTSE 100 index, taking option prices on a particular day, thereby allowing numerical profit/loss comparisons between the strategies. As each strategy works best for a particular market move, it is necessary for the trader to have a view on the market, and then chose an appropriate strategy.

There are many trading strategies available using options. It is the nature of the markets to be unpredictable, and overall trading strategies have to take this into account with appropriate risk control. Successful traders expect to make both profits and losses, but rely on their successful trades to outweigh the losses.

GLOSSARY

ADX
Average Directional Movement indicator which shows the strength of a stock's trends.

Algorithm
Set of mathematical calculations for a specific purpose.

Annual percentage return
Option time premium expressed as a percentage of the share price.

ASX
Australian Stock Exchange.

At-the-money option
Option for which the strike price is the same as the underlying share price.

Back-test
Feed historic stock data through a technical indicator to determine the indicator performance.

Bear spread
Option strategy using two different option series to profit from a falling market.

Blue chip stock
Major stock which is actively traded.

Bollinger bands
Technical indicator which shows when a stock has made a strong move and is due for a correction.

Breakout
Stock price moves out of a trading range or pattern.

Brokers
Brokers mentioned in the text are:

Discount brokers	TD Waterhouse Investor Services—*Ph*: 1300 360 359
Stop-loss brokers	Hogan and Partners—*Ph*: (08) 9321 2366

BSOPM
Black-Scholes Option Pricing Model, covered in Chapter 4.

Bull spread
Option strategy using two different option series to profit from a rising market.

Call option
The right to buy a parcel of shares at a fixed price within a set time.

Capital Plus warrant
Five-year contract to purchase a basket of shares, but with a guaranteed minimum redemption value.

Covered option writing
Owning shares and writing (selling) call options against them.

Defensive strategy
Method of getting out of a losing trade with manageable loss.

Delta
Ratio of option price move to share price move. Alternatively, the probability that the option will be at-the-money at expiry.

Deposit
Cash or securities held by broker to cover cost of trading options or warrants.

Derivative
Financial product derived from something else, and having greater leverage than the product it is derived from.

DMI
Directional Movement Indicator which shows a stock's sideways trends and breakouts.

Draw-down
The amount the share price moves in the wrong direction after a trade is opened.

EMA
Exponential Moving Average, a method of smoothing data which gives more weight to the most recent data.

Endowment warrant
Ten-year contract to purchase a stock using the dividend stream from that stock.

Equity warrant
One-year to two-year put or call option on a stock, sponsored by a merchant bank or finance house.

Exchange Traded Options (ETOs)
Exchange Traded Options are called "options" in this book.

Ex-dividend
Stock after the dividend entitlement has been paid.

Exercise of options
Converting options to shares.

Exercise price
See *Strike price*.

Expiry month
Month when an option expires.

Filter
Use of a second indicator of some form to confirm the direction of a trend.

Free trade
Option strategy where two options are opened at different times to lock in a profit.

Gann lines
Lines drawn at fixed angles from major price peaks and troughs, which become support and resistance lines.

Index warrant
Put or call warrant available on the All Ordinaries Index.

Instalment warrant
Two-year contract to purchase shares in two instalments.

In-the-money option
Call option for which the strike price is below the share price, or put option for which the strike price is above the share price.

Intrinsic value
Share price minus call option strike price, or put option strike price minus share price. Negative intrinsic value is set to zero.

Leading indicator
Indicator which gives a signal warning of an impending change in stock trend.

Leverage
Using a derivative to obtain a higher percentage return than that available from the underlying stock.

MACD
Moving Average Convergence Divergence technical indicator used to determine stock trends.

Margin call
Cash paid by broker to the OCH when the price of written options moves against us.

Momentum indicator
Indicator which shows when a trend is running out of steam. See also *Rate of Change Indicator*.

Money management
Matching potential trading profits and losses to the size of our trading kitty.

Naked option writing
Writing (selling) options without owning the underlying shares.

OCH
Options Clearing House which registers all option trades and maintains an orderly options market.

Option stocks
Blue chip stocks on which exchange traded options are available.

Oscillators (momentum oscillators)
Technical indicators which show when a stock is overbought/oversold and due for a change in trend.

Out-of-the-money option
Call option for which the strike price is above the share price, or put option for which the strike price is below the share price.

Parcel size
Minimum number of options or warrants that can be traded.

Pullback
The amount the share price reverses after a fresh price move.

Put option
The right to sell a parcel of shares at a fixed price within a set time.

Rate Of Change (ROC) indicator
Indicator which shows when a trend is running out of steam.

Registered Traders (RTs)
Professional traders whose role is to maintain buy and sell option quotes on a particular stock.

Risk-free interest rate
Interest rate available from a bank or finance house.

Risk-return
Balancing the possible risk (loss) against the possible return (profit) in a trade.

Roll down
In a falling market, to cancel a put option and open another with a lower strike price.

Roll out
To cancel one option and open another with a longer time to expiry.

Roll up
In a rising market, to cancel a call option and open another with a higher strike price.

RSI
Relative Strength Indicator which shows when a stock is overbought/oversold and signals a change in trend.

SEATS
Stock Exchange Automated Trading System.

SMA indicator
Single Moving Average indicator used to determine stock trends.

Spreads
Strategy of holding bought and written options at the same time, resulting in limited losses and limited profits.

Stochastic indicator
Indicator which shows when a stock is overbought/oversold and signals a change in trend.

Stop-loss order
Order to quit a trade if the price falls (or rises) to a particular value.

Straddle
Option strategy involving a put option and a call option having the same strike price and expiry date.

Strangle
Option strategy involving a put option and a call option having different strike prices but the same expiry date.

Strike price (or exercise price)
Price at which options are converted into shares.

Technical analysis
Use of technical indicators and charts to determine past and future share price behaviour.

Technical indicator
A set of mathematical calculations on share price or volume data, resulting in some form of graphical display, that gives information on the stock trends.

Time premium
Option price minus intrinsic value.

Time to expiry
Number of days, weeks or months before the option or warrant expires.

Trading strategy
Trading rules incorporating both trading system and money management procedures.

Trading system
Selection of technical indicators and charting techniques used to determine the start and end of stock trends.

Transparent
Ability for all brokers (and clients) to see the buying and selling quotes and volumes in a stock or warrant.

Trend-following indicator
Indicator which gives a signal after the stock trend has changed.

Volatility
Share price activity that is reflected in the option price.

Wizards (market wizards)
Champion traders popularised by Schwager's book *Market Wizards*.

INDEX